Forms of Modernist Fiction

J. Hillis Miller 1928–2021

In memoriam

Forms of Modernist Fiction

Reading the Novel from
James Joyce to Tom McCarthy

DEREK ATTRIDGE

EDINBURGH
University Press

Edinburgh University Press is one of the leading university presses in the UK. We publish academic books and journals in our selected subject areas across the humanities and social sciences, combining cutting-edge scholarship with high editorial and production values to produce academic works of lasting importance. For more information visit our website: edinburghuniversitypress.com

Edinburgh University Press Ltd
The Tun – Holyrood Road
12(2f) Jackson's Entry
Edinburgh EH8 8PJ

Typeset in 10/13 ITC Giovanni Std by
IDSUK (DataConnection) Ltd

A CIP record for this book is available from the British Library

ISBN 978 1 3995 1245 9 (hardback)
ISBN 978 1 3995 1247 3 (webready PDF)
ISBN 978 1 3995 1248 0 (epub)

CONTENTS

ACKNOWLEDGEMENTS

The research for this book was made possible by fellowships at three institutions: the Stellenbosch Institute for Advanced Study, the Bogliasco Foundation, and the Freiburg Institute for Advanced Studies. I am grateful to the staff of these institutions for their invaluable assistance and to my fellow fellows for their conversation and encouragement. Many of the chapters had their first incarnation as talks; my thanks to the organisers and audiences for these opportunities to try out ideas. Among the many individuals to whom I owe a particular debt are David Attwell, Doug Battersby, Claire Chambers, Michiel Heyns, Neil Murphy, Henry Staten, Asja Szafraniec, Etienne van Heerden, and Ingrid Winterbach. To my family: thank you for your support, as always, and my apologies for not taking retirement to mean the end of writing books.

Earlier versions of some of the material in this book have appeared as follows, and is reproduced by permission of the publishers:

Introduction: Some paragraphs from 'Criticism Today: Form, Critique, and the Experience of Literature', in *The Work of Reading: Literary Criticism in the Twenty-First Century*, eds Anirudh Sridhar, Mir Ali Husseini, and Derek Attridge, Palgrave, 2021, 1–19.

Chapter 1: Parts of '"Eveline" at Home: Reflections on Language and Context' (with Anne Fogarty), in *Collaborative 'Dubliners': Joyce in Dialogue*, ed. Vicki Mahaffey, Syracuse University Press, 2012, pp. 89–107, and some paragraphs from 'Joyce: The Modernist Novel's Revolution in Matter and Manner', in *The Cambridge History of the English Novel*, eds Robert Caserio and Clement Hawes, Cambridge University Press, 2012, pp. 581–95.

Chapter 2: Revised version of 'Joyce and the Making of Modernism: The Question of Technique', in *Rethinking Modernism*, ed. Marianne Thormählen, Palgrave, 2003, pp. 149–59.

Chapter 3: Revised version of 'Joyce's Noises', *Sound Effects*, special issue of *Oral Tradition*, eds Chris Jones and Neil Rhodes, 24.2 (2009).

Chapter 4: Revised and expanded version of 'Pararealism in "Circe"', in *Joycean Unions: Post-Millennial Essays from East to West*, eds R. Brandon Kershner and Tekla Mecsnóber, European Joyce Studies, Rodopi, 2013, pp. 119–26.

Chapter 5: Revised version of 'From *Finnegans Wake* to *The Skriker*: Morphing Language in James Joyce and Caryl Churchill', *Papers on Joyce* (Spain) 7/8 (2001–2), 45–53.

Chapter 6: Revised version of 'Taking Beckett at His Word: The Event of *The Unnamable*', *Journal of Beckett Studies* 26 (2017), 10–23.

Chapter 7: Part of 'Autonomy, the Singular Literary Work, and the Multilingualism of Hermans' *Nooit meer slapen*', *Journal of Dutch Literature* 6 (2015), 17–32.

Chapter 8: Revised version of part of 'Contemporary Afrikaans Fiction and English Translation: Singularity and the Question of Minor Languages', in *Singularity and Transnational Poetics*, ed. Birgit M. Kaiser, Routledge, 2014, pp. 61–78.

Chapter 9: Parts of '"No Escape from Home": History, Affect and Art in Zoë Wicomb's Translocal Coincidences', in *Zoë Wicomb & the Translocal: Writing Scotland & South Africa*, eds Kai Easton and Derek Attridge, Routledge, 2017, pp. 49–63, and 'Zoë Wicomb's Home Truths: Place, Genealogy, and Identity in *David's Story*', *Journal of Postcolonial Writing* 41.2 (2005), 156–65.

Chapter 10: Parts of 'Inorganic Form from James Joyce to Eleanor Catton', in *Joycean Possibilities: A Margot Norris Legacy*, eds Joseph Valente and Vicki Mahaffey, Anthem, 2022, 87–103.

Chapter 11: Parts of 'Secrecy and Community in Ergodic Texts: Derrida, Ali Smith, and the Experience of Form', in *Secrecy and Community in 21st-Century Fiction*, eds María-Jesús López Sánchez-Vizcaíno and Pilar Villar-Agaíz, Bloomsbury, 2020, 23–35, and '*Ars moriendi*: The Experience of Van Niekerk and Van Zyl's *Memorandum*', *Tydskrif vir Nederlands en Afrikaans*. 26 (2019), 103–23. https://www.suiderafrikaanseverenigingvirneerlandistiek.org/_files/ugd/1ca66c_acca397ce81c4d62aa96de6dd8b0ff69.pdf.

Chapter 12: Revised version of 'Modernism, Formal Innovation, and Affect in the Contemporary Irish Novel', in *Affect and Literature*, ed. Alex Houen, Cambridge University Press, 2020, 249–66.

Chapter 14: Revised and expanded version of 'Tom McCarthy's Debt to Modernism: Close Encounters of a Pleasurable Kind', in *Modernism and Close Reading*, ed. David James, Oxford University Press, 2020, 191–207.

The Experience of Form: Joyce and After

Attending to Form

If one were to risk an adjective to describe the dominant mode of literary studies in the English-speaking world at the start of the current millennium it might be 'empirico-historical': the wave of high theory had passed, the principle of canonical expansion had been accepted, and questions of literary evaluation had been put on the back burner. Trend-conscious graduate students in all periods were exploring archives, examining historical contexts, and excavating little-read authors. No doubt classroom teaching still included a fair amount of formal analysis, attention to the major works of the canon, and discussion of what makes a successful literary work, but these concerns were thin on the ground beyond the undergraduate curriculum. However, there were signs that the great ship of academic literary discourse was beginning, slowly, to change course: 2000 was the year in which Isobel Armstrong's *The Radical Aesthetic* was published, as was the special issue of *Modern Language Quarterly* titled 'Reading for Form', edited by Susan Wolfson and Marshall Brown. There followed a steady stream of critical works reclaiming, in one guise or other, the formal study of literary texts,[1] so much so that *PMLA*'s section on 'The Changing Profession' in 2007 featured an article by Marjorie Levinson asking the question 'What is New Formalism?'

The stream has by no means dried up, and has joined with another branch that could be said to have begun in 2003 with Eve Sedgwick's book *Touching Feeling* – more specifically with her chapter 'Paranoid Reading and Reparative Reading' – and to have received a further boost the following

---

[1] See my year-by-year summary in Chapter 1 of *Moving Words*, 'A Return to Form?'

year with the publication of Bruno Latour's essay 'Why Has Critique Run Out of Steam?'[2] This approach, which also helped to open the way for fresh attention to form, queried the tendency of critics to treat literary works with suspicion as symptomatic of societal and ideological ills, emphasising instead the affirmative dimension of literary reading. As the editors of the 2017 volume *Critique and Postcritique* state, 'There is little doubt that debates about the merits of critique are very much in the air and that the intellectual or political payoff of interrogating, demystifying, and defamiliarizing is no longer quite so evident'.[3] This affirmative mode of reading was often carried out in conjunction with a new appreciation of the importance of *affect* – the rapid dissemination of this word, in place of the unscientific-sounding 'feeling', being itself an indicator of the success of the new trend. Other voices in the debate proposed a shift of metaphors in literary analysis from depth to surface, or called for 'just' reading, or argued for the value of 'minimal interpretation'.[4] At the same time, the point of adding to the ever-increasing mound of empirical information about the contexts of past literature began to become less clear; to quote Michael North, 'As Henry James and Jacques Derrida have both noted, context is potentially infinite, and thus the work of providing historical context for literary works can go on forever, until it begins to seem merely repetitive' ('History's Prehistory', 38).

On the one hand, then, we have seen a growing awareness that important questions of literary form had been ignored in the rush to history, and, on the other, an increasing scepticism about the widespread assumption that literary works were to be read against the grain and in the service of ideological unmasking. These twin shifts are evident, in different combinations, in a number of recent books that have garnered considerable attention. In 2015, Caroline Levine's *Forms* proposed a fresh look at the role of form while Rita Felski's *The Limits of Critique* followed Sedgwick and Latour in advocating the replacement of suspicious by affirmative reading. Two years later Tom Eyers, in *Speculative Formalism*, offered a different account of the role of literary form and Joseph North, adopting I. A. Richards as his hero, raised the banner of close reading in *Literary Criticism: A Political History*. Both Eyers and North see their task in part as escaping from the strait-jacket of history: as Eyers puts it, '[H]istory, instead of being a question to be answered, has

---

[2] The first incarnation of Sedgwick's influential essay was as the introduction to a special issue of *Studies in the Novel*, 'Queerer than Fiction'; it was expanded as the introduction to her edited collection *Novel Gazing*.

[3] Anker and Felski, *Critique and Postcritique*, 1.

[4] See Best and Marcus, 'Surface Reading'; Marcus, 'Just Reading' in *Between Women* (73–108); Attridge and Staten, *The Craft of Poetry*.

threatened to become a catch-all *explanans* to be passively assumed, bringing with it an obfuscation of what makes literature, literature' (7); or in North's words, the 'central logic that has dictated so much of the last three decades of literary study' is 'the rejection of the project of criticism – aesthetic education for something resembling, in aspiration if not in fact, a general audience – and the embrace of the project of scholarship – the production of cultural and historical knowledge for an audience of specialists' (114).

Now it should go without saying that a great deal of the literary criticism that appeared during the decades prior to 2000 did in fact take formal matters into consideration, and that not everyone in literary studies was engaged in empirical investigation or ideology critique. (As an initial definition of form let us say that the term refers to those aspects of the literary work that are not in the business of directly conveying meaning or content.)[5] Many literary critics, for instance, took their bearings from continental philosophers who placed a high value on the contribution literature can make to thought and ethical understanding (and I include myself in this category). Literary form remained central to stylistic studies influenced by linguistic theory (another category of which I am happy to acknowledge membership) and to Anglo-American analytic aesthetics. While the new attention to issues that I and many others have been interested in for a long time is to be welcomed, these reconsiderations of the role of form have been only partially successful. Most of them attempt to stay true to the principle of social relevance at the heart of critique by attempting to build a bridge of some sort between formal questions and the needs of the world in which we live, but there is a danger that this admirable desire may get in the way of accurate reporting on the way literary form actually works for the reader.[6]

Experience, singularity, and craft

Form, then, became something of an embarrassment in literary studies in the latter part of the twentieth century: what mattered most was content and context – the material conditions under which works were produced, their references to external reality, and their impact upon the world. Content was understood as both the people, places and events depicted

---

[5] I return to the question of what is meant by 'form' in Chapter 1.

[6] To avoid prolixity, I use 'reader' in this book to mean 'reader, listener, or reciter'. And it should be obvious that the focus of my attention is on works of literature that possess the potential to provide the reader with an experience of unusual intensity that is also in some way pleasurable, rather than the more general category of 'imaginative writing'.

by the writer and the prejudices and intolerances revealed by the astute critic. In grant applications and promotion decisions the archive was king; discussion of narrative methods or metrical schemes was relegated to the classroom. Formalism was the dread name of a naïve focus on the text itself, an irresponsible turning away from the serious business of accumulating facts or changing society.[7]

As I've suggested, formal issues have become more and more acceptable in literary research and criticism since the turn of the century, but traces of that embarrassment around the study of form remain. In particular, there's an unspoken – and sometimes spoken – assumption that formal features exist only to enhance or complicate, or perhaps occasionally to conflict with, the work's content; the critic's job in discussing form is to show how it contributes to the work's representation of outer reality. By this means, form can be rescued from its inward gaze and valued for its impact on the wider world. It's not surprising that David James, introducing a collection on the subject of close reading and modernism, feels the need to make the following statement in his introduction: 'Scholars and teachers of modernism have long known that there's little point (pedagogically or interpretively) in trying to speak of the "aesthetic properties" of modernist literature in isolation from their social and political consequentiality'.[8]

The problem with many claims for the social and political consequentiality of literature is that little is said about how such effectiveness *happens*; sometimes it seems to be enough just for a work to challenge the status quo for it to have broader consequences. But any such impact can only occur if the work in question has an effect upon readers – hence my continuing stress on readers' experiences of literary works, and on the importance of the changes that may be wrought by those experiences. Only if the work takes the reader into unfamiliar zones of thought or feeling, or both, can it bring about an alteration in understanding and outlook, affording new ways of apprehending the self and the world; and the formal operations of

---

[7] This sketch is, of course, a crude oversimplification; but it contains, I believe, sufficient truth to be a useful index of the dominant mode of academic literary study in this period. A similar situation prevailed, *mutatis mutandis*, in musicology and art history.

[8] James, 'Introduction', 12. The scare quotes around 'aesthetic properties' are a particularly telling sign of the embarrassment I'm referring to. (In this book I choose not to use the term 'aesthetic' when discussing the formal properties of literary works: my focus is on what is distinctive about art, not the more general question of formal beauty. I return to the question of beauty later in this introduction.)

literature have an important part to play in bringing about such an engagement with otherness.[9]

Although many of the formal properties of literary works that I'll be considering in this book do have a straightforward relation to the non-verbal world, the pleasures and insights offered by form are numerous and diverse, and I wish also to explore those that are not tied to content in any direct way. But this focus on formal matters should not be understood as the promotion of some notion of the pure 'autonomy' of form, sometimes taken to be an signal feature of modernism.[10] Form, as I understand it, is an aspect of the event that constitutes the literary work as literary, and is thus a salient part of the reader's experience.[11] And every formal device experienced by a reader involves an engagement with human perceptions and values and a broadening of horizons, whether aesthetic, intellectual, ethical, or emotional, and usually more than one of these. But the contribution form makes to the work's capacity to produce pleasure and effect change in the reader is not necessarily tied to its alliance with meaning; formal features have their own way of revealing new possibilities in the perceived world, including such fundamental phenomena as the functions of language, the perception of relations, and the operation of the senses.

While the increasing prominence of aesthetic concerns in the literary criticism of the new millennium has led to a valuable reconsideration of the relation between formal means and extra-textual impact, what is not always borne in mind is that the only way this impact is registered is, as I've suggested, via the experience of readers. 'Experience' is a complex term that figures centrally in several philosophical schools, notably empiricism, which builds on the assumption that knowledge derives from sensory experience,

---

[9] I discuss the relation between formal innovation and political effectiveness in Chapter 14. For full developments of this understanding of literary effectiveness, see Attridge, *The Singularity of Literature* and *The Work of Literature*.

[10] Jameson, for instance, sees the 'ideology of modernism' as 'first and foremost that which posits the autonomy of the aesthetic' (*A Singular Modernity*, 161). As James observes, 'That painstaking formal analysis might amount to an implicit advocacy of the aesthetic autonomy and self-perfecting integrity of modernist experimentation is a suspicion that dies hard' ('Introduction', 3). For an account of the importance of the idea of autonomy to modernist writers and its continuing relevance to literary criticism see Goldstone, *Fictions of Autonomy*. From a predominantly sociological perspective, Goldstone argues that modernist autonomy was always relative, an embracing rather than a rejection of literature's social embeddedness.

[11] The notion of the event is important in a number of theoretical discourses, many of which are discussed in Mukim and Attridge, eds, *Literature and Event*.

phenomenology, which is sometimes labelled the 'philosophy of experience', and existentialism, which emphasises personal decisions. I propose to use it in a fairly workaday sense to refer to what happens, mentally, emotionally, and physically, in the process of literary reading. What I don't want to imply by using the term is that a theory of the literary work as experienced event is primarily an empirical – that is to say, a psychological or neurological – theory directed at what goes on in reader's brain (or, for that matter, a physiological theory directed at what goes on in the rest of the body), even though any conclusions that might be drawn about the reader's experience might be mappable onto these domains.

My approach to the works I discuss is thus always in terms of the reader's experience – in the first place, inevitably, it's my experience that's in the foreground, but I offer my account to be tested by other readers of the same works. In every case, what I'm attempting to capture is the *singularity* of the work as it is experienced, and literary singularity always involves formal as well as semantic constituents. I would go further: it's the operation of form (since, as I've said, form in literature is something that happens) that distinguishes literary effectiveness from all the other ways in which verbal texts can bring about change in their readers. A powerful biography of a political crusader may inspire me to act differently because of its content; a novel on the same topic may be even more powerful because of the writer's handling of narrative, syntax, voice, rhythm, metaphor and all the other elements of the work's formal constitution.

I've elaborated on the concept of singularity elsewhere, and will not dwell on it here, apart from a few general remarks.[12] The work of literature – one that possesses the qualities for which we use the term 'literature' evaluatively rather than simply as a category of writing – is the unique and irreplaceable product of the mental labour of an individual (or more than one individual) occurring at a particular time and in a specific place; on the other hand, it's readable only to the extent that it participates in general codes and conventions shared by the reader. It is thus a singular work, very much itself, but only itself because it is in a (constantly changing) relationship with what it is not. The reader's or critic's response to the work of literature can then be thought of as the equivalent of a countersignature, whose function is to verify, validate, authenticate a previous signature: in countersigning as witness or guarantor I affirm that the signature above

---

[12] See Attridge, 'Singularity', in Frow, ed. *The Oxford Encyclopedia of Literary Theory*; and 'Singularity', in Pryor, ed., *The Cambridge Companion to the Poem*. My understanding of literature in turn owes a great deal to a number of philosophers, most importantly Jacques Derrida.

mine is not a forgery, that it did indeed result from a unique act of writing by the named individual, and that I am willing to take responsibility for the promise it implies. Without countersignatures the signature – which is, of course, nothing but a certain formal arrangement of lines – has no power.

The singularity of the literary work – unlike the singularity of other kinds of text or arrangements of signs – is inseparable from its *inventiveness*: its author's achievement was to produce a new and unforeseen configuration of the available cultural materials, and the experience of reading it involves a version of that singular inventiveness, as a result of the historical continuity between production and reception or, occasionally, the chance operations of history.[13] Thanks to this experienced inventiveness – felt as surprise, a pleasurable encounter with the unexpected – the cognitive, affective, and sometimes somatic power of the work brings about an alteration, slight or momentous, in the reader's known and felt world each time it is fully undergone.[14] (Whether this experience of otherness is fleeting or effects a permanent shift is a significant factor in considering the political efficacy of literary works.)

---

[13] Jameson poses the important but under-investigated question, 'How is it that the aesthetic innovation of yesteryear, long since outmoded by more streamlined artistic technologies, remains new?' (*A Singular Modernity*, 125–26). Appealing to Hegel and Adorno, he points to 'our capacity to feel the innovative mechanism at work within the work of art itself and in the reading process, rather than by way of external consultation of some handbook on the evolution of literary techniques' (128). Felski, too, raises this question without proposing an answer: the recent revival of formal criticism, she notes, 'shows scant interest in the puzzle of how texts resonate across time', and 'we sorely need alternatives to seeing [artworks] as transcendentally timeless on the one hand and imprisoned in their moment of origin on the other' (*The Limits of Critique*, 154). Another critic who acknowledges this problem is Robbins: 'Literature's power to speak across the ages is not absolute (even Arnold admitted that), but it is real. In that sense and to that extent, its transcendence of history is perfectly historical. But this is a paradox that the criticism that followed the 60s has been slow to unpack, a proposition it has been slow to affirm or articulate' (*Criticism and Politics*, 29). Robbins devotes chapter 6 of his book to the question of 'The Historical and the Transhistorical', drawing extensively on Jameson's work.

[14] Peggy Kamuf, arguing that fiction is 'less the name of an entity than the name of an *experience*', cautions against understanding the term here as referring either to the lived experience of a writer or to that of fictional characters; 'Fiction, poetry, would be experience on the condition that one understands: experience of the other' ('"Fiction" and the Experience of the Other', 141–42).

Central to this account of the operation of literature, then, is the reader's experience of the event that constitutes the literary work. Considered apart from the experiences of readers, there are no works of literature, only texts made up of inert signs. When the text is read as literature and not as some other genre (history, autobiography, psychology, moral treatise, and so on) it's experienced as an event, one that takes the reader into hitherto unfamiliar domains of thought and feeling. Each such reading is different, and through these repetitions that are never the same the work gains and prolongs its identity – a process Derrida calls *iterability*. The readings I offer in this book are by no means intended as final words, but rather are invitations to further readings and further countersignatures.

To focus on what is distinctive about the literary use of language, and by implication what is distinctive about the musical, visual or tactile artwork, is to emphasise the operation of singularity, inventiveness, and otherness, and to foreground the particular pleasure produced by the opening up of unanticipated ways of seeing, thinking, and feeling. As I've argued, the operation of form is central to this process. However, there are many artefacts that generate pleasurable responses on the basis of their formal properties without providing this experience; one term often used for this aspect of form is *craft*.[15] Many works of art possess qualities of this kind: when I enjoy the complex rhyming, stanza-linking, and other formal devices in the medieval poem *Pearl*, I'm enjoying the poet's craft in the same way as I might enjoy a superbly fashioned breastplate or a finely wrought chasuble. Part of my affective response is admiration for the creator's skill in handling the materials of the art in question with such deftness and assurance. That the patterning in *Pearl* also functions emblematically does not detract from that enjoyment, which would still be part of my response if the poem were about discord and conflict. Nor should craft be thought of as only a matter of formal patterning; the craft involved in realistic description, for instance, may well be a significant factor in a reader's enjoyment.

Distinguishing between responses to art and to craft – while recognising that the distinction is not clear-cut or fixed, and that what is art to one reader, period, or culture is craft to another – can assist us in fathoming the troublesome term 'beauty', so central to tradition of philosophical

---

[15] The best-known philosophical discussion of the distinction between art and craft is that in Collingwood, *The Principles of Art*, 15–41. In including an account of the importance of craft in the experience of literature I'm indebted to conversations with Henry Staten and to his pathbreaking book, *Techne Theory*. What I'm calling craft – as an element in the reader's experience – is closely related to what Staten, who focuses primarily on the perspective of the creator, calls *techne*.

aesthetics.[16] If we think of beauty as a quality produced by the exercise of craft, as a property works of art have in common with many other artefacts, its role becomes clearer; it's an element in the multifaceted experience of some (though certainly not all) works of art that provides a certain kind of satisfaction. Thus, it might be argued that the intricate sound-patterning of *Pearl* is beautiful in a manner similar to the delicate designs in a ceremonial kimono. Novels are less likely to be called beautiful, although intricacy and formal unity may function as part of their pleasing achievement of a high level of craft.

In the discussions that follow, my main interest will be in the contribution made by formal inventiveness to the power of the work as literature in the fullest sense; 'reading the novel' in my subtitle hints at this focus on innovation. However, the element of craft also has a continuing part to play in my accounts of the reader's experience.[17] Anything that contributes to the reader's pleasure increases the effectiveness of the work; although works lacking in craftsmanship can be powerful, they run the risk of alienating readers from the outset by failing to satisfy the expectation of balance, wholeness, and skilfully deployed detail.

Joyce's Novel Language

A hundred years ago as I write this, the novel gained a new future. The publication of Joyce's *Ulysses* in 1922, although it had been foreshadowed by the serial publication of many of its chapters, was a watershed: henceforth any serious novelist – in English, certainly, but in many other languages as well – had either to find a way to respond to Joyce's literary revolution or to pretend it hadn't happened. This is not to deny that outstanding novels continued, and continue, to be written in the tradition of the great nineteenth-century realist works. Although the contribution these novels make to the history of the genre is largely in terms of content, fully achieved realist writing also manifests a brilliant, if conservative, use of form. However, the most significant developments in that history are those that acknowledge, in some way or other, Joyce's formal achievements.

It's possible, of course, to overstate the single-handedness of this achievement: Joyce, like all great writers, was adept at finding inspiration in the

---

[16] A collection of essays that includes a full engagement with this term in the light of current theoretical and biological research is Levine, ed., *The Question of Aesthetics.* See also Attridge, *The Work of Literature,* 75–79.

[17] I give explicit consideration to the role of craft in responses to the novel in Chapter 10.

culture around him and extracting raw material from his predecessors, and his was not the only challenge to inherited European literary conventions around this time. Six volumes of Dorothy Richardson's *Pilgrimage* had been published by 1922, breaking new ground in the expansion of syntax to represent consciousness, as had the subtly unconventional short stories of Katherine Mansfield's collections *Bliss* and *The Garden Party*. In the world of poetry, Ezra Pound was orchestrating his own revolution, his most prominent beneficiary being T. S. Eliot, whose *Waste Land* also appeared in 1922. In France, four volumes of Proust's *À la recherche du temps perdu* (*In Search of Lost Time*) were available by this date, providing a different impetus to the novel of interiority, and in Germany several of Kafka's radically innovative short stories had appeared, including, in 1915, 'Die Verwandlung' ('The Metamorphosis'). An Italian writer who influenced Joyce when they were friends in Trieste was Italo Svevo (Ettore Schmitz), although Svevo's major contribution to Italian modernism, *La coscienza di Zeno* (*The Conscience of Zeno*), wasn't published until 1923, and owed its fame in part to Joyce's championing of it. The year before the publication of *Ulysses* a startlingly metafictional Italian play had premiered: Luigi Pirandello's *Sei personaggi in cerca d'autore* (*Six Characters in Search of an Author*). Nevertheless, in spite of the many examples of an upheaval in the traditions of European literature, no work can be said to match *Ulysses* for the magnitude of its challenge to those traditions, combining as it did heightened realism with a panoply of techniques that seemed to go in the opposite direction.

To further complicate the simple picture I started with, it's necessary to take into account the later fortunes of *Ulysses* in the worlds of critical commentary and education. At first the *enfant terrible* of European culture, modernism became in the 1950s a firm fixture in the literature classroom and the subject of an avalanche of criticism, its complexity, and frequently its difficulty, providing ample opportunity for the kinds of close analysis then in favour in literary studies. The elevation of modernism to a highly respectable subject received an added boost in the United States, where the CIA and the State Department saw its promotion as a valuable weapon in the cultural sphere of the cold war.[18] Although in the United Kingdom and its former colonies – where the influence of the journal *Scrutiny* and the criticism of F. R. Leavis was strong – Joyce was excluded from the 'Great Tradition' of the English novel, his reputation in North America grew, and by the 1970s *Ulysses* was globally acknowledged as a milestone in the history of prose fiction. (*Finnegans Wake* had to wait another couple of decades before being fully admitted to the pantheon, and then only in a side niche.)

[18] See Barnhisel, *Cold War Modernists*, and Jameson, *A Singular Modernity*, 165–9.

In Ireland, Joyce was transformed from pariah to cash cow for the tourist trade by the 1980s. The considerable presence of *Ulysses* in the conscious-ness of the novelist writing today clearly owes something to this history of reputation-making, and we have to ask whether a different history would have relegated it, and modernism more generally, to a byway or backwater, resulting in a different trajectory for the later twentieth-century novel.[19] It's an unanswerable question, and for my purposes an irrelevant one, since my interest is in the pathways opened up by modernism as it gained prestige both in the academy and the wider world of writers and readers.[20]

This book is not a study of the influence of *Ulysses*, nor of Joyce, nor of European modernism.[21] It's a series of case studies that seek to investigate some of the ways in which the new possibilities for the novel opened up by Joyce and his modernist contemporaries served as a stimulus for a number of later novelists around the globe, and in so doing to present an argument for the centrality of the reader's experience of form in understanding and

[19] Rebecca Beasley, in *Russomania*, documents an alternative to the French-inspired formal innovations of modernism in the shape of imitations of the realist Russian fiction of the same period, and in so doing provides a glimpse of a counter-history that is as intriguing as it is implausible.

[20] Under the soubriquet 'The New Modernism', recent years have seen a consider-able expansion in the group of writers and works deemed 'modernist'; while this extension of interest into hitherto neglected areas of productivity is welcome, it leaves one searching for another label to designate those works that possess the innovations in form and language hitherto thought characteristic of modernism (as opposed to simply modern). When the temporal limits of the term are simul-taneously relaxed, as they often are, it loses most of its specificity and becomes a general catch-all for twentieth- and twenty-first century writing. For a reasser-tion of the more restricted sense of the term, see Gąsiorek, *A History of Modernist Literature*, and James and Sheshagiri, 'Metamodernism', and for a judicious sur-vey of the debate (including arguments against using the term 'metamodernism'), see Battersby, *Troubling Modernism*, 3–8. My own use of the term reflects the narrower sense.

[21] For a wide-ranging collection of essays on Joyce's influence, see Carpentier, ed., *Joycean Legacies*. As Vichnar notes in his contribution to this collection, 'Joyce's presence has become virtually all-pervasive, yet also at the same time neutral-ized, and sometimes well-nigh invisible.' ('Wars Waged with/against Joyce', 168). Vichnar finds only superficial echoes of Joyce's writing in the novels of Jonathan Coe, Martin Amis, and Will Self (Self's *Umbrella* trilogy is not taken into account) but a full and productive engagement with Joyce in the work of Iain Sinclair. Laura Marcus devotes a large part of a characteristically astute essay on 'The Legacies of Modernism' to the influence of Joyce. The index alone of Castle, ed., *A History of the Modernist Novel*, testifies to the centrality of Joyce's work in this history.

appreciating the achievement of these writers.[22] Joyce bequeathed to his successors not only a number of techniques that could be adopted and adapted, but, perhaps more importantly, the example of a writer who was prepared to challenge some of the basic assumptions on which all fiction up to his time had rested (with a few notable exceptions – most of them important to Joyce).[23] As B. S. Johnson, one of the most innovative of twentieth-century British writers, put it, 'It is not a question of influence, of writing like Joyce: it is a matter of accepting that for practical purposes where Joyce left off is a starting point'.[24] In consequence, I don't deal with works such as Chris McCabe's *Dedalus* (2018), an ingenious continuation of *Ulysses* that follows Stephen Dedalus and Leopold Bloom for a further day, recapitulating Joyce's episodes and imitating his styles while weaving into the text references to computing and to the author's own life.

The first four chapters of this book examine some of the aspects of Joyce's formal achievement that proved fruitful for later writers. The first chapter examines aspects of Joyce's development of a 'modernist' style by commenting on one of the stories of *Dubliners* and discussing the language associated with Stephen Dedalus in *A Portrait of the Artist as a Young Man*. This is followed by a chapter that compares the fate of *Ulysses* with another ambitious novel of the early 1920s and asks how important Joyce's formal innovations are for an understanding of his impact on later readers and writers. This chapter introduces the notion of 'inorganic form', which I take to be a crucial feature of *Ulysses* and a feature I explore further in later chapters on contemporary writers; see especially Chapters 10 and 14. Chapters 3 and 4 deal with examples of Joyce's innovative exploitation of linguistic possibilities in *Ulysses*: his play with what I've termed 'nonlexical onomatopoeia' and 'pararealism'.

Joyce's earlier works don't feature in the later chapters to the same degree as *Ulysses*. However, any collection of short stories linked by place is likely to call up memories of *Dubliners* and any autobiographical novel portraying the path from the innocence of childhood to the defiance of young manhood may well be seen as following the mode of *A Portrait of the Artist*

---

[22] I haven't attempted to engage with the extensive inheritance of modernism in North America, which deserves a book of its own.

[23] Joyce could hardly have overlooked the challenges to conventional fictional form mounted by two Irish precursors, Jonathan Swift and Laurence Sterne, for instance.

[24] B. S. Johnson, 'Experimental British Fiction', unpublished transcript; cited by Jordan, 'Late Modernism and the Avant-Garde', 145. Johnson also commented that 'No one can write the same after *Ulysses*. *Ulysses* changed everything' (Burns and Sugnet, eds, *The Imagination on Trial*, 93).

as a Young Man, especially if the language employed is designed to mirror the developing child's perceptions and verbal skills.[25] *Finnegans Wake*, on the other hand, has never acquired this kind of centrality: although a few writers have endeavoured to follow in its footsteps, not to have done so is never understood as a deliberate stepping away from Joyce's work in the way that an avoidance of the inheritance of *Ulysses* inevitably is. Chapter 5 considers one example of a work that develops the techniques of the *Wake* in a fruitful direction, though it involves straying into the domain of playwriting.

Although the history of Western art reveals a constant drive on the part of artists in all genres to advance their artform and thus offer new possibilities to their successors, the unpicking of longstanding conventions – and their exposure *as* conventions – became, with modernism, more central to the artist's endeavours. Among the facets of Joyce's modernist revolution that have proved seminal for later writers, and will feature in the pages to come, are his reassessment of the relation between content and form, his exploration of the space of the page, his rejection of temporal and spatial limits, his play with the components of the English language, his transgression of the boundaries between languages, his deployment of the techniques of realism to present the unreal, and his defiance of syntactic rules in the representation of consciousness. Also important for novelists who deploy innovative techniques is Joyce's demonstration that to play with the norms of language and genre is not necessarily to inhibit affective responses. My concern is not with Joyce's introduction into the novel of items of hitherto excluded content (perhaps the most significant cause of alarm in early reviews of *Ulysses* and the reason for its banning) – although this too opened up new terrain for later writers – but with his formal innovations and the fresh perspectives they made possible.[26] There will be an implicit, and occasionally explicit, attention to the question of literary value throughout, both in the selection of works to be examined and in my comments on their verbal qualities.

[25] I discuss the importance of Joyce's development of this technique in '"Suck was a queer word": Language, Sex, and the Remainder, in *A Portrait of the Artist as a Young Man*', Chapter 6 of *Joyce Effects*. See also Chapter 1 below.

[26] Among the many testimonies to the importance to later writers of Joyce's innovative fiction as a liberatory example is Angela Carter's comment in 1982 that he made her free – 'Free not to do as he did, but free to treat the Word not as if it were holy but in the knowledge that it is always profane' (*Shaking a Leg*, 539). She adds that 'his work has still not yet begun to bear its true fruit'. A different book could have been written about the importance of Joyce for late twentieth-century French thinkers, including Derrida, whose radical reinterpretation of the philosophical tradition owes a great deal to his study of the Irish author (see Mitchell and Slote, eds, *Derrida and Joyce*).

Irish Fiction: After Joyce

For obvious reasons, the gauntlet thrown down by Joyce to later writers is felt with especial force by the Irish writer.[27] Both *Dubliners* and *A Portrait of the Artist as a Young Man* have remained productive exemplars in Ireland. *Dubliners* has an extensive progeny among Irish short story writers who have continued to cultivate the 'scrupulous meanness' of Joyce's economical vignettes of Dublin lower-middle-class life. Stories by John McGahern, Colm Tóibín, and William Trevor, for example, focus on small shifts in the mental and emotional landscapes of not particularly unusual Irishmen and women, described in frugal prose. (Joyce denied having read Chekhov's short stories, which constitute another influential antecedent in this mode.) The very different method of *A Portrait of the Artist* can be sensed behind stories of childhood and adolescence which make use of stylistic deviation to suggest the language of early life, such as Roddy Doyle's *Paddy Clarke Ha Ha Ha*, Patrick McCabe's *The Butcher Boy*, Hugo Hamilton's *The Speckled People*, and Emma Donoghue's *Room* – though in using the first person, these novels are less pathbreaking than Joyce's third-person narrative. (However, Joyce's use of the second person on the first page of the novel, as if explaining to an adult – 'When you wet the bed first it is warm then it gets cold' – is probably the origin of many later uses of the second person by child narrators, like McCabe's 'You could see plenty from the inside but no one could see you' (1) or Doyle's 'You had to do it at night when they were all gone home, except the watchmen' (5).

But it is, of course, *Ulysses* that presents the greatest challenge to the Irish prose writer. (*Finnegans Wake* is easier to ignore.) Samuel Beckett, as has often been noted (first of all by Beckett himself), began by imitating Joyce's Ulyssean extravagances of style in the posthumously published *Dream of Fair to Middling Women* (written in 1932) and the short stories, partly excavated from that manuscript, of *More Pricks than Kicks*, which appeared in 1933. He

---

[27] Later Irish responses to modernism are discussed in Reynolds, ed., *Modernist Afterlives in Irish Literature and Culture*. The contemporary Irish novel is, oddly, missing from this collection's chapters, which range over a number of art forms. In his 'Afterword: The Poetics of Perpetuation', David James focuses on Banville's *The Sea*, which, for all its stylistic brilliance, is not a novel associated with modernist innovation. Patrick Bixby, in 'In the Wake of Joyce', confines his attention to Beckett and O'Brien. The Irish writers who feature in Carpentier's collection *Joycean Legacies* – Kate O'Brien, J. G. Farrell, Patrick McCabe, and Frank McCourt – are also not the most formally inventive. In spite of its title, Neil Corcoran's book *After Yeats and Joyce: Reading Modern Irish Literature* is less an influence study than a survey of Irish writers in this period.

then set out to escape that influence by shedding excesses and moving from the still quite Joycean *Murphy* (1938) to a series of stylistic and narrative explorations that departed further and further from Joyce's tracks, turning to French partly as an aid in that process. In Chapter 6 I discuss the experience of reading the most challenging of the three novels that followed *Murphy*: *The Unnamable* (1953).

Flann O'Brien, although deeply indebted to Joyce, felt constantly inhibited by his predecessor's achievements; his best-known comment, or at least one that is repeatedly attributed to him, is characteristic: 'I declare to God if I hear that name Joyce one more time I will surely froth at the gob.' And he attempted a fictional put-down in *The Dalkey Archive* (1965), featuring Joyce as a devout Catholic denying authorship of his major works and serving in a bar. But there is no doubt that Joyce's example gave him the licence to play freely with the conventions of the novel, notably in *At Swim-Two-Birds* (1939). Between O'Brien and the twentieth century, the most important self-consciously Joycean writer in Ireland was Aidan Higgins, whose *magnum opus*, *Balcony of Europe*, appeared in 1972, with a revised, and shortened, version in 2010. In this work Higgins, like Joyce, drew extensively on his own experiences, but transformed them into a richly allusive weave of fictional narrative in which plot is secondary to verbal elaboration. Dorothy Nelson's two published novels, *In Night's City* (1982) and *Tar and Feathers* (1987), use a variety of styles to depict the often tortured inner lives of the members of dysfunctional Irish families, taking Joyce's technique of interior monologue into some very dark places.

The Ulyssean inheritance continues to invigorate Irish writing: Jamie O'Neill's *At Swim, Two Boys* (2001) signals its debt to O'Brien in its title, making it a kind of grandchild of Joyce, whose technique of interior monologue is successfully reproduced in parts of the novel, and Mary Costello's *The River Capture* (2019) features a hero obsessed by Leopold Bloom, ending with a lengthy imitation of the 'Ithaca' episode. Less obviously influenced by *Ulysses* but more inventive in their development of a distinctive formal design are Sara Baume's novels *Spill Simmer Falter Wither* (2015), formally structured according to the seasons (the names of which are given a Wakean makeover in the title), *A Line Made by Walking* (2017), organised by means of encountered and photographed dead animals and studded with references to works of art (beginning with the title), and *Seven Steeples* (2022), exploiting the spatial dimension of printed text. Claire-Louise Bennett's *Pond* (2015) and *Checkout 19* (2021) are characterised by an unremitting interiority that takes its inspiration from Joyce's (and Woolf's) exploration of the impact of quotidian detail on the mind. Patrick McCabe breaks up the long interior monologue of *Poguemahone* (2022) into short lines. Chapter 12 concerns the innovative work of three contemporary Irish novelists who acknowledge, and have found original ways to extend, the Joycean heritage, Eimear McBride, Kevin Barry, and Mike McCormack. All three develop techniques for the representation of the individual consciousness – the example of the 'Penelope' episode of *Ulysses* looms large – and raise the question: do modernist deformations of the conventions of language and narrative interfere with the evocation of emotion?

Perhaps the most eloquent of those who have testified to the inescapability of Joyce in his native country is John Banville. Here is one of Banville's pronouncements on the subject, speaking on behalf of Irish writers:

> The figure of Joyce towers behind us, a great looming Easter Island effigy of the Father. In the old days it was considered fitting that the children should honour the parent, and I could, indeed, spend the next fifteen or twenty minutes paying tribute to that stone Nobodaddy at my shoulder. But when I think of Joyce I am split in two. To one side there falls the reader, kneeling speechless in filial admiration, and love; to the other side, however, the writer stands, gnawing his knuckles, not a son, but a survivor. ('Survivors of Joyce', 73–4)

Banville knows he is going over the top here, but his hyperbole is only an inflated image of what is undoubtedly a real concern for the Irish novelist. Banville's own writing might have featured in this study for its impeccably moulded style and its occasional forays into a more unorthodox narrative, notably in *Ghosts* (1993), but for the most part his strengths lie in more traditional novelistic forms. Several Irish writers have, like Banville, cultivated a stylistic verve and sophistication that perhaps owes something to the Joycean exemplar; among the names that come to mind in connection with this fastidious and foregrounded attention to style are Elizabeth Bowen, Joseph O'Connor, and Sebastian Barry.[28] Joyce, it seems, is constantly being rediscovered in Ireland.

Innovative form in a global context

The works of Joyce and Beckett belong, of course, as much to the history of the European novel as to that of the Irish novel, both in terms of their residence and the influence of their writing (and in Beckett's case, in the languages in which he wrote). In 1920s Paris, Joyce participated in a ferment of artistic creativity that included both French and foreign writers; among

---

[28] One could, of course, name many other contemporary Irish writers who use language with exceptional skill; most of them would not, however, be thought of as following the example of *Ulysses*.

the most innovative of these were the Americans Gertrude Stein and Djuna Barnes. When we turn to the 1930s, we find Beckett pursuing his own highly original path in Paris, while Joyce was fashioning 'Work in Progress', to become, at the end of the decade, *Finnegans Wake*. In England the 1930s saw the publication of Virginia Woolf's most radical novel, *The Waves* (1931), and further volumes of Richardson's *Pilgrimage*; less radical, but clearly influenced by the earlier achievements of modernist writers, were a series of novels by Jean Rhys. Mary Butts continued to promote nature mysticism in stylistically distinctive novels, while Wyndham Lewis combined modernist technique with scathing satire in *The Apes of God* (1930).

However, it wasn't until the 1960s that there was a flowering of innovative writing in England that could be said to take off from Joycean (or Woolfian) modernism: notable figures include B. S. Johnson, Ann Quin, Doris Lessing, and a writer who continued publishing formally innovative work until the end of the century (and whose writing owed as much to the French *nouveau roman* as to Joyce), Christine Brooke-Rose.[29] The 1960s were also a decade of note in South African fiction: a group of writers in Afrikaans, drawing inspiration from France in particular, introduced into the conservative Afrikaner culture a strain of innovative writing that scandalised the guardians of the culture.[30]

The term 'late modernism' is most frequently used for these immediate successors of 'high modernism', though it has also been applied to more recent authors.[31] Proceeding very sketchily, it's possible to demarcate a

---

[29] This writing, and some of the other works discussed in this book, are sometimes called 'experimental', but I hesitate to use this word, with its associations of the laboratory and the frequent implication that such works fail in some way. B. S. Johnson would have agreed: '"Experimental" is the dirtiest of words, invariably a synonym for "unsuccessful"', he writes ('Holes, Syllabics', 396). See Attridge, 'What Do We Mean by Experimental Art?' For a full discussion of the influence of the *nouveau roman* on British writers see Guy, *The 'Nouveau Roman'*.

[30] See Chapter 8 for a brief discussion of the 'Sestigers'.

[31] For Tyrus Miller, the late modernists include Beckett, Wyndham Lewis, and Djuna Barnes; see his *Late Modernism*. Shane Weller, in 'Beckett as Late Modernist', agrees on the inclusion of Beckett, but adds Paul Celan, Nelly Sachs, and W. G. Sebald. The novelists included in Doug Battersby's *Troubling Late Modernism* are Vladimir Nabokov, Beckett, Toni Morrison, John Banville, J. M. Coetzee, and Eimear McBride. Julia Jordan, focusing on 'experimental' British writers from the 1950s to the early 1970s, applies the label to a large group that includes Brooke-Rose, Johnson, Quin, Alan Burns, Zulfikar Ghose, Alexander Trocchi, and Denis Williams, characterising them as preoccupied with indeterminacy and accident as a result of their 'lateness' vis-à-vis modernism proper (*Late Modernism*). Tom McCarthy is included in her study as a 'late, late modernist'.

subsequent group of writers who rose to prominence in the late 1960s and
the 1970s on the basis of novels and short stories that exploited pastiche
and parody, indulged in metafiction, drew on popular art forms, preferred
playful description, extravagant plots and colourful characters, and favoured
an exuberance of style. 'Postmodern' is not a particularly insightful label for
these writers – it makes more sense in the world of architecture – but it has
stuck.[32] (That many of these features are characteristic of Joyce's later work
is another indication of the breadth of the formal developments in which
he had a pre-emptive hand.)

The writers to be examined in this book may possess some of these characteristics, but their methods and ambitions, and the experience of reading
them, are clearly different, as I hope the following chapters will show. I
am content to refer to them as modernist writers, acknowledging that the
adjective remains a problematic one.[33] Enough ink has been spilled over
the question of the relation between the modernism of the 1920s and the
correct label for those writers who continue to keep faith with modernist
methods and ideals.[34] One proposal, initiated by David Foster Wallace, is

[32] Although he doesn't identify his chosen novelists and novels as 'postmodern',
Ben Masters's description in *Novel Style* of English writers of 'excess' from the
1960s to the present suggests that they could well be subsumed under that category: they are said to exhibit 'a tendency towards poetic language (their sentences
are animated by alliteration, assonance, simile, and metaphor), a facility for
eccentric rhythms and phrases, and a preference for the polysyllabic and hypo-
tactical' (8). His chosen examples, none of whom are discussed in this book,
are Anthony Burgess, Martin Amis, Angela Carter, Zadie Smith, Nicola Barker
and David Mitchell. The rollcall of American novelists labelled 'postmodern' is
a familiar one, including Robert Coover, Thomas Pynchon, Donald Barthelme,
and John Barth.

[33] David James argues for a continuation of modernism up to the present in
Modernist Futures, though his chosen writers – Milan Kundera, Philip Roth,
Michael Ondaatje, J. M. Coetzee, Ian McEwan, and Toni Morrison – are, with the
exception of Coetzee, less formally inventive than the contemporary novelists
discussed in this book. Steven Connor, in 'Modernism after Postmodernism',
makes the strange claim that the 'new modernism' is 'almost entirely an enterprise
of academic interpretation', and proceeds to discuss critical approaches rather
than the literary works of the twenty-first century (821).

[34] Some of the section headings in Rudrum and Stavris, eds, *Supplanting the Postmodern*, offer variations: 'Hypermodernism', 'Automodernism', 'Altermodern-
ism', and 'Digimodernism' as well as the more familiar 'Metamodernism'. For a
defence of this last term, see James and Sheshagiri, 'Metamodernism'. 'Notes on
Metamodernism' was a webzine that ran from 2009 to 2016, employing the term

that postmodernism was displaced by 'The New Sincerity', which could be seen as resuscitating the seriousness of modernism. As Dorothy Hale puts it:

> The always-ironic attitude, the implied position of superiority in constant critique, the complicity in commodification that attends pastiche, the end-lessness of deconstructive play – these postmodernist stances of the 1970s and 1980s have given way to a new regard for an old cultural claim: that literature offers its readers a serious, perhaps even uniquely powerful engage-ment with ethical values. (*The Novel and the New Ethics*, 2).

Fredric Jameson argues that late modernism is a version of modernism that arises when 'the modern has been theorized and conceptually named and identified in terms of the autonomy of the aesthetic' (*A Singular Modernity*, 197); however, it's to be doubted whether many contemporary writers who work in the aftermath of the formal revolutions of modernism are guided by notions of autonomy. More convincing is Jameson's point that the 'classical modernists' worked in the dark, without an identifiable public or clear social role, unlike the late modernists, who have their forebears as models (198–200). One could also argue that the novelists writing in the wake of postmodernism had its extravagances to react against.

The novelists I have chosen to focus on after Joyce, most of whom are still writing, come from several different national backgrounds: Ireland, South Africa, New Zealand, the Netherlands, Scotland, and England.[35] Many more countries will be touched on in passing. My main focus is on writing in English, but my own background has led to a particular inter-est in South African literature, and this book includes engagements with works in Afrikaans and Dutch. However, this is not an exercise in 'world literature', a problematic concept at the best of times, but examples of the renovation of the novel tradition that reflect the global spread of modernist innovation as it touches one reader today.

The transnational character of much recent writing has attracted wide-spread attention, one example being the Scottish–South African novelist and short story writer Zoë Wicomb.[36] Chapter 9 examines the crossing of

to cover a wide range of cultural phenomena; three of its editors also put together an essay collection: van den Akker, Gibbons, and Vermeulen, eds., *Metamodern-ism*. Van den Akker and Vermeulen describe metamodernism as 'a structure of feeling that emerged in the 2000s and has become the dominant cultural logic of Western capitalist societies' (4).

[35] For an account of Joyce's influence in Canada, Australia, and New Zealand, see Lang, 'Modern Fiction/Alternative Modernisms', 193–6.

[36] See Easton and Attridge, eds, *Zoë Wicomb & the Translocal*.

time and place in Wicomb's fiction, with a particular focus on her most formally challenging work, *David's Story*. Chapter 10 continues the discussion of 'inorganic form' broached in the first chapter, revisiting *Ulysses* and exploring *The Luminaries* (2013) by the New Zealander Eleanor Catton, with some examination of other recent examples. The subject of Chapter 11 is what has been called 'ergodic' fiction, in which the linear progression characteristic of narrative prose is interrupted by such features as footnotes or illustrations, as exemplified in the 'Nightlessons' chapter of *Finnegans Wake*; the examples discussed are Scottish writer Ali Smith's *How to Be Both* (2014) and the South African writer Marlene van Niekerk's *Memorandum* (2006). As I've mentioned, Chapter 12 examines the work of three Irish writers. The question of form and politics is addressed in Chapter 13 in the context of postcolonial fiction, with particular attention to the Pakistani-British writer Kamila Shamsie. Finally, we move to England, and a writer who has made no secret of his high estimation of Joyce and his view that very few writers have responded to the Joycean challenge: Tom McCarthy, whose fiction defies many of the persistent expectations associated with the novel yet still achieves moments of affective power.

Another topic that will come into view in these chapters is translation, a topic that, in conjunction with the topic of untranslatability, has recently been the subject of much discussion in the critical arena; already implicit in much postcolonial theory, it has been given added emphasis by the debates around the idea of world literature.[37] Joyce, as so often, was ahead of the game: by incorporating dozens of languages in *Finnegans Wake* he ensured that no single reader could master his text without help, and demonstrated some of the creative potential of working across linguistic systems. With the same gesture, he rendered his work untranslatable – though it's helpful to gloss this term in the way Barbara Cassin does: as 'what never stops being (not) translated'.[38] The linguistic innovations of post-Joycean fiction pose particular challenges to the translator and highlight the conflicting demands of translation. The discussion of Beckett's *The Unnamable* in Chapter 6 notes some of the implications of his self-translation, while Chapter 7 examines the problem of a Dutch text that includes its own play with languages, W. F. Hermans's *Nooit meer slapen* (*Beyond Sleep*). In Chapter 8 an analysis

---

[37] See, for example, Apter, *Against World Literature*.

[38] 'Ce qu'on ne cesse pas de (ne pas) traduire'; see Cassin, ed., *Vocabulaire euro-péen des philosophies*, (un)translated as *Dictionary of Untranslatables: A Philosophical Lexicon*. Cassin has used versions of this phrase on a number of occasions. For an astute study of the multilingual character of *Finnegan Wake*, see Alexandrova, *Joyce, Multilingualism, and the Ethics of Reading*.

of a passage from Etienne van Heerden's novel *30 nagte in Amsterdam* (*30 Nights in Amsterdam*) exposes the verbal inventiveness of both the original and the translation by Michiel Heyns and leads to a discussion of the question of untranslatability.

Reading and Readings

The most resourceful of recent discussions of twentieth- and twenty-first century modernism – such as Alys Moody's *The Art of Hunger* and the final chapters of Peter Boxall's *The Prosthetic Imagination* – rely on highly original acts of reading but refrain from an analysis of the reading process itself. Noting a similar omission, Paul Armstrong terms the 'lived experience of reading' as the 'elephant in the room' in literary criticism, remarking that

> [e]ven when critics or theorists do not explicitly address the experience of reading, they are trying to shape it by the pragmatic implications of the arguments they make. . . . The current (and by now long-standing) dilemma of how to do justice to the aesthetic dimension without reverting to formalism can only be effectively engaged if the eventfulness of reading, the site of the aesthetic experience (however defined), becomes discussable—the locus where form and history, literary value and cultural contexts, artistic aims and political interests interact. ('In Defense of Reading', 89)

Every chapter of this book is concerned with reading: with my reading, and other possible readings, of a literary work or works and, explicitly or implicitly, with what it means to read a text as literature. (In these chapters, I follow the convention of using 'the reader' and 'we' when, as will be obvious, I am usually recording my own responses in the hope that my reader shares them. If this claim provokes disagreement at certain points, this difference of view will itself be of interest; criticism thrives on such clashes.) Chapter 4, for instance, focuses on the question of reading works that employ what I call 'pararealism' and Chapter 6 on the experience of reading Beckett's *The Unnamable*. In Chapters 7 and 8, I examine the challenges to the reader (and the translator) presented, respectively, by works that use more than one language and by works of formal intricacy, and in Chapters 10 and 11 I consider two formal properties with implications for reading possessed by a number of contemporary novels: novels in which form functions inorganically and novels that disrupt the linearity of the reader's engagement. Chapter 12 examines the generation of an affective response by novels that use modernist formal techniques while part of the argument of Chapter 13 is that only by attending to the event of reading can the political significance of literary works be understood. The subject of Chapter 14 is a novelist who throws down a gauntlet to readers, especially those nourished on the realist novel. The other chapters all have the reader in mind in their exploration of the works they discuss.[39]

In tracing the rewards and challenges offered to the reader in modernist works from Joyce to the present this study could have taken any number of different paths. An alternative approach might take Virginia Woolf, Katherine Mansfield, and Dorothy Richardson as founding figures; another might examine American fiction in the wake of William Faulkner's achievement. Further topics in English fiction could include the work of Johnson, whose struggles in the 1960s and early 1970s to win a readership for novels that spurned the comforts of the realist tradition represent a key moment in the history of English modernism,[40] and that of J. G. Ballard, who honed his own oblique relation to realism in a long series of novels from that period until the early twenty-first century. Much more could be written about two of the Irish figures mentioned above: O'Brien and Higgins. Also worthy of study is Scottish modernism, which had a distinguished beginning in the novels of Lewis Grassic Gibbon and Nan Shepherd, and a striking continuation in Alasdair Gray, most remarkably in *Lanark* (1981). Bessie Head in Botswana, Ivan Vladislavić in South Africa, Ayi Kwei Armah in Ghana, and Yvonne Vera in Zimbabwe – to pick rather arbitrarily a few African writers – could have furnished material for further chapters.[41]

Contemporary writers who have found ways to inventively recreate the language and forms of the novel and who could easily have featured in these pages include Anna Burns (in *Milkman*), Will Self (in the trilogy *Umbrella*, *Shark*, and *Phone*), and Jon McGregor (in *Reservoir 13*). One could pursue the question of pararealism raised in relation to Joyce's 'Circe' episode through many articulations of magic(al) realism, novels by Salman Rushdie, Jeanette Winterson, and Angela Carter among them. The style of the 'Penelope' episode has numerous descendants not discussed here, including Ann Quin's novels, James Kelman's Glaswegian fictions, and

---

[39] The 1960s and 1970s saw the flowering of reader-response criticism, but this trend was then largely eclipsed by other theoretical approaches and by the turn to empiricism touched on earlier in this chapter. For a collection of representative essays, see Tompkins, ed., *Reader-response Criticism*. The question of reading is discussed in the context of current cultural and political concerns in Sridhar, Hosseini, and Attridge, eds, *The Work of Reading*.

[40] See Coe, *Like a Fiery Elephant*.

[41] For a survey of South African writing using innovative forms, see Green, 'The Experimental Line'.

Lucy Ellmann's *Ducks, Newburyport*.[42] And there are many more, even without going beyond the English language (or versions of it). The few I have selected will have to stand for the larger number whose output testifies to the lasting validity and value of the opportunities opened up by Joyce and other modernist writers in discovering new verbal resources and generic possibilities, and thus engaging in fresh ways with the words and worlds in which readers think, speak, and feel.

[42] I have discussed Ellmann's remarkable novel in 'Joycean Form, Emotion, and Contemporary Modernism'.

CHAPTER 1

Modernist Style in the Making: *Dubliners* and *A Portrait of the Artist as a Young Man*

Dubliners: On the Way to Modernist style

On September 10, 1904, readers of the *Irish Homestead* turning to the weekly story found a short work titled 'Eveline', published under the name 'Stephen Daedalus' and beginning as follows:

> She sat at the window watching the evening invade the avenue. Her head was leaned against the window-curtain and in her nostrils was the odour of dusty cretonne. She was tired. (192)

This opening shows Joyce, even at the start of his career, at his characteristic best, achieving immense richness with the utmost economy of means. While the technique here is that of finely honed realism rather than anything we could call modernism, the attention to the verbal surface already suggests a writer who has an unusual capacity to make the most of the words of the English language. (Eugene Jolas was later to report Joyce's boast, 'I can do anything with language.'[1]) The second sentence, in particular, seems to me to epitomise his extraordinary skill. Eveline does not lean her head, but her head is leaned; she does not actively smell, but an odour is present in her nostrils. The syntax conveys a draining away of agency, her body parts functioning like independent, mechanical objects as her thoughts pursue a track they have pursued many times before.

Above all, it's 'the odour of dusty cretonne' that has the distinctive Joycean signature on it. *Cretonne* is striking in its specificity: it names an

---

[1] Excerpted in Deming, *James Joyce: The Critical Heritage*, vol. 1, 384; originally published in the *Partisan Review* 8, ii (March–April 1941): 82–93.

eminently practical fabric (the *OED* calls it 'stout') that nevertheless suggests an awareness of fashion, indicative of Eveline's experience at 'the stores'. The word isn't recorded as an English import until 1887, and its evident Frenchness gives it a slightly exotic air. The adjective *dusty*, too, is redolent of a housekeeper's pride, already hinting at a weariness with the daily grind of maintaining cleanliness, while providing the reader, whose consciousness of the sense of smell is already alert thanks to the slightly surprising word *nostrils*, with a vivid sensory image. Whereas the first sentence clearly gives us the words of an observing narrator, and we seem to remain with this narrator for a word like *odour*, the phrase *dusty cretonne* begins to reflect Eveline's thought processes, which will soon take over the narrative.

The play of sound in this second sentence is less marked than in the previous sentence, in which the name of the story and its heroine is echoed in the phrasing – *Eveline, evening, invade, avenue*; but the controlled play of vowels and consonants continues, in, for instance, the chiming of *curtains* and *cretonne* and the redeployment of most of the sounds of *nostrils* in *dusty cretonne*. The last brief sentence – ambiguous as between a narrator's observation and the character's thoughts – is almost unnecessary after this sentence, though nothing explicit has been said about Eveline's tiredness. Its brevity enacts its meaning.

Joyce wrote this paragraph (and the whole story, in something very close to the version he later published in *Dubliners*) in the summer of 1904 at the age of 22; it was his second contribution to the *Irish Homestead*, the first having been 'The Sisters' in July of that year.[2] The only change made to the paragraph for publication in *Dubliners* was the substitution of 'window curtains' for 'window-curtain'.[3] The attainment of this peak of stylistic subtlety and assurance at such an early point in a writing career has few parallels.

The following short paragraph in the final section of the story, on the other hand, is a rare lapse, as Joyce strives too hard to bring home the drama of his climax:

No! No! No! It was impossible. Her hands clutched the iron in frenzy. Amid the seas she sent a cry of anguish.

[2] See Gabler, Introduction to *Dubliners*, 2–3.
[3] Perhaps Joyce would have been well advised to delete 'window' altogether from the second sentence, as he had already used the word in the first sentence and there is no doubt as to the location. He always liked repetition, however, using it for a number of different purposes.

The repeated *no*'s, the slightly excessive *frenzy*, and – especially – the over-heated diction of the last sentence fail to register the particularity of the event, giving us instead the diction of a thousand popular fictions. *Amid* is falsely poetic, and although the phrase *the seas* is not as vague as the paragraph taken on its own might suggest, since we have already read, in a far more powerful sentence, at once metaphoric and somatic, that 'All the seas of the world tumbled about her heart', they remain damagingly unspecific. The *cry of anguish* is a cliché that prevents us from hearing imaginatively the sound a woman in Eveline's situation might have made. I am quoting from Gabler's text, based on the 1910 late proofs; the version printed in the 1914 first edition of *Dubliners* and most editions since then have an exclamation mark after 'anguish' that only makes matters worse.

'Every night as I gazed up at the window I said softly to myself the word *paralysis*.' Commentary on *Dubliners* has exploited to the full the hint given by this sentence in the collection's first paragraph and reinforced by Joyce's well-known letter to Grant Richards in 1906, in which he stated that he 'chose Dublin for the scene because that city seemed . . . the centre of paralysis' (*Letters* II, 134). In 'Eveline' he wrote a story which doesn't use the word *paralysis* but is, in a sense, all about physical immobility, almost as if to set himself the challenge of treating his theme with literal fidelity. For 135 lines (in Gabler's edition) the eponymous character barely moves other than to look around the room; then at line 136 we encounter a short paragraph beginning 'She stood up in a sudden impulse of terror'. After a gap in time signalled by a break on the page, the following paragraph also begins with the words 'She stood . . .'. Eveline does not move from this position until the end of the story – and her not moving at that juncture is, of course, its climax.

Up to now, home has been Eveline's centre of gravity, keeping her anchored through the trials of a mother's insanity and death, a father's increasing drunkenness and violence, the demands of parenting two younger children. (Her sailor lover, by contrast, has taken the world as his domain, leaving Ireland as a deck boy to sail to Canada, traversing the globe by ship, and choosing to settle in Argentina – if we are to believe his own account of his past, that is.) Her immobility in the first part of the story is emblematic of the more general stasis of her life, held in one place by a sense of duty as much as by any positive attachment.

It takes a spasm of terror – induced by memories of her mother's mad behaviour – to end Evelyn's immobility (which has gone on longer than it ought, as 'her time was running out'). But Joyce omits all the actions which follow this sudden movement, until we find her once again stationary, and being called by Frank to go with him on board the ship. The terror she experiences this time, however, has the opposite effect: rather than prompting sudden movement, it roots her to the spot, clutching the railing. Between the impossibility of a home that represents unhappiness and physical danger and the impossibility of a leap into the unknown, Eveline has nowhere to go.

How does Joyce make a story out of these twin immobilities? What urges the reader onward, if there is virtually no action to respond to? Elsewhere I have tried to analyse the process whereby Joyce's handling of literary style in 'Eveline', with its minute fluctuations and resonances, draws the reader in and on.[4] The bulk of the story is presented as free indirect discourse, or, more accurately free indirect thought, Eveline's meditations being presented to us in the third person and past tense.[5] In a practice typical of the stories of *Dubliners* from this point on, however, Joyce surprises us by moving occasionally into different stylistic modes. We have already noted how the first paragraph, although predominantly the narrator's voice, has hints of Eveline's thoughts. The second paragraph continues with what appears to be an objective account of what Eveline sees and hears, but again we are made aware that these sights and sounds are being perceived by a particular character:

> Few people passed. The man out of the last house passed on his way home; she heard his footsteps clacking along the concrete pavement and afterwards crunching on the cinder path before the new red houses.

After a sentence which could be a neutral observation but could equally be one made by Eveline, remarking to herself the paucity of passers-by, the phrase 'man out of the last house' gives us recognisable Irish diction identifying an individual in terms that relate specifically to her. The repetition of 'passed' may seem a stylistic awkwardness, or it may be taken to represent the repetitiveness of Eveline's thoughts. But *clacking* is surely a Joycean narrator's word, unusual and vivid, registering not so much Eveline's mental processes as her unverbalised perception, and contrasting with the different sound of *crunching*. *The new red houses*, however, could well be Eveline's own phrasing, as bare in its expression as the objects being described.

---

[4] See Attridge, 'Reading Joyce', 4–8.
[5] It's not interior monologue, as Jackson and McGinley, in their annotated edition of *Dubliners*, claim (34), but a quite different technique that retains the tense and syntactic completeness of the narrative context.

Central to many of the *Dubliners* stories is the question of *home*: how is it constituted, what is its value, what demands does it make?[6] The homes we see are almost all unsatisfactory. The boy narrator in the first three stories is uneasy at home, and finds excitement in leaving it. The boarding house in the story of that name is a travesty of a home; Little Chandler and Farrington in 'A Little Cloud' and 'Counterparts' return to their homes but not to domestic happiness; Maria in 'Clay' moves between two establishments neither of which offers the true comforts of home. Mr Duffy's home in 'A Painful Case' lacks homeliness, and the Kernan residence in 'Grace' holds an erring husband and a long-suffering wife. Only 'The Dead' celebrates the generosity, tolerance, and hospitality a home can give – and then not without a number of ambiguities.[7]

The word *home* occurs ten times in the story. (Interestingly, the first occurrence is in the passage quoted earlier describing the sound of 'the man out of the last house' as he passes 'on his way home': another subterranean suggestion in this sentence is that Eveline feels that her house offers a homelier environment than the new houses with their bright red brick and their cinder paths.) Eveline's meditation is largely an exploration of the meaning and the force (mental, emotional, bodily) of home: her thought that she is about to 'leave home' prompts her to focus on the word with an internal exclamation, 'Home!' This is followed by a survey of the room she is sitting in while she examines the significance of home to her. Familiarity is one of its key components, and it's this she first feels the attraction of – yet she is soon pointing out to herself that strangeness is also present, in the photograph of the unknown priest. As she goes on to 'weigh each side of the question', the sheer drudgery of her existence is set against the 'shelter and food' that home implies.

Like many of the homes in *Dubliners* this one is a place of alcoholism and violence; the young woman's desire to leave is in part out of sheer fear:

> Even now, though she was over nineteen, she sometimes felt herself in
> danger of her father's violence. She knew it was that that had given her the

---

[6] For an illuminating essay on the importance of 'home' in *Dubliners*, with particular attention to its significance in post-famine Ireland, see Gibbons, '"Have You No Homes to Go to?"'. Law valuably traces some of the complexities of the notion in *Ulysses* in 'Joyce's "Delicate Siamese" Equation'.

[7] There is no need to elaborate on the importance of home in *A Portrait of the Artist* (in which *home* is one of the three words that, to Stephen, sound different on the Dean of Studies's tongue) or *Ulysses* (where it's not only Plumtree's Potted Meat that makes every home complete); and *Finnegans Wake* revolves around a family often glimpsed in a domestic setting.

palpitations. When they were growing up he had never gone for her, like he used to go for Harry and Ernest, because she was a girl; but latterly he had begun to threaten her and say what he would do to her only for her dead mother's sake.[8]

The sequence of thoughts begins with the suggestion that her age is some protection from her father's physical attacks – *even now* and *sometimes* signal that in the past these fears had been more persistent than they are at present. Yet the thought quickly reverses itself, so that it's the very fact of her being grown up that has rendered her a potential victim, no longer protected by her sex. And later she recalls happier times with her father – though their very uncommonness is a silent counter-argument. But it's the memory of her mother's descent into madness and the fear that the same fate awaits her that brings about the end of her reflections.

Home as a magnetic force represents not only the familiar, food and shelter, and the pleasures of family relations (however rare); it also represents obligations.[9] Although the responsibility of keeping house for her father is described in predominantly negative terms, it's clearly a major factor in her deliberations. Added to this is the somewhat mysterious fact that she is caring for two young children. And, to cap it all, there is her promise to her dying mother 'to keep the home together as long as she could' – again the word *home*, here perhaps more forcefully than anywhere else.

It's highly significant, then, that Frank, her sailor lover, has 'a home waiting for her' in Buenos Aires.[10] *Home* here is vague but attractive – one of the many hints that Eveline has been gullible in her acceptance of Frank's tales, perhaps, though it's easy to see why she has fallen for them. She herself thinks of 'her new home'. There is no sign at the end that her paralysis is due to her mistrust of Frank; it's rather the result of the complexity of her own relation to her home. What she prays for as she clutches the railing is not that God should help her decide what is best for her, what home with Frank

---

[8] Joyce changed 'were it not for her dead mother's sake' (in the *Irish Homestead* version) to the Hiberno-English locution 'only for her dead mother's sake'.

[9] The text printed in the *Irish Homestead* (the magazine title may have been a prompt to Joyce) has Eveline wondering not only whether it is wise to leave home, but whether it would be 'honourable' – in revising, perhaps Joyce felt he shouldn't raise the question of duty too early in the story.

[10] Norris points out that Hugh Kenner, in an article in the *James Joyce Quarterly* for Fall 1972, misquotes this sentence as 'he had a house waiting for her' (*Suspicious Readings*, 242). This would be a significant alternative, providing greater solidity than the more nebulous but more romantic notion of 'a home'; but Gabler lists no such variant.

will mean in comparison to her home with her father and the two children, but what is her duty. In the balance are her promise to the man who has courted her (not 'the man she loves'; the word she uses is 'like') and her promise to her mother, a promise that serves to heighten the responsibility that a daughter has for her aging father ('Her father was becoming old lately, she noticed') and a surrogate mother for two children.

Eveline makes two decisions in the story, to go with Frank and then not to go. The first, as we have seen, prompts her to stand up; the second prevents her from moving. Neither is a decision in the sense of a thoughtful, considered preference for *a* rather than *b*; both exemplify the conception of decision as described by Derrida, following Kierkegaard: a moment of madness in which rationality is left behind (though it is careful rational calculation that brings one to this point).[11] Eveline assembles powerful reasons for going and equally powerful reasons for staying; then the memory of her mother's madness – specifically, the aural memory of her mother's unintelligible, repetitive utterances – produces not a rational affirmation but a physical act and an emotional charge: 'She stood up on a sudden impulse of terror'. What follows sounds more like rationalisation of a decision now taken than a further stage in the process of weighing pros and cons:

> Escape! She must escape! Frank would save her. He would give her life, perhaps love too. But she wanted to live. Why should she be unhappy? She had a right to happiness. Frank would take her in his arms, fold her in his arms. He would save her.

The repetitions here, which would be clumsy in the narrator's discourse, are the reflex of the character's desperation as she clings to the decision she finds she has made.

The second moment of decision is also more physical than it is mental. Eveline is again immobile, again torn between alternatives. This time the painfulness of the dilemma compels her into prayer, as she wrestles with the question of her double, contradictory duties. But at the final moment, when the bell clangs ('upon her heart' – another Joycean masterstroke of economic phrasing) and Frank urges her to accompany him, Eveline feels that she is drowning, drawn by her lover into 'all the seas of the world', and her paralysis is like that of 'a helpless animal'. Her face registers no emotion whatever. The parallel with the earlier moment of decision is obvious, and we are left

[11] See, for example, Derrida, 'Force of Law', 252–3. The literary exemplification of Derrida's understanding of decision-making is fully explored by Hillis Miller through Henry James's fiction in *Literature as Conduct*.

with the question: has Eveline descended, not gradually like her mother but in one instant of impossible mental and emotional conflict, into madness?

Joyce's reference to the style of *Dubliners* as one of 'scrupulous meanness', though it highlights the difference between this book and its successors, has perhaps had the unfortunate effect of promoting the idea that it is a simple style, direct and uncomplicated in its representation of the lives of its characters. 'Eveline' is one of the plainest of the stories, yet its apparently straightforward sentences reveal, on close inspection, that the source of its power lies in Joyce's choosing of words that do far more than simply refer to an imagined world. In this respect, *Dubliners* marks the beginning of Joycean modernism.[12]

A Portrait of the Artist as a Young Man: Modernist Style Achieved

The first novel James Joyce embarked on could hardly be called modernist. *Stephen Hero*, probably started in Dublin in 1903 when Joyce was twenty-one,[13] was to be a thinly-disguised autobiography, stylistically undistinguished and immensely long; when he abandoned it, in Trieste in 1905, he referred to the 914 pages he had written as 'about half the book'.[14] Its planned sixty-three chapters would have told the story of a Dublin boy growing up in an increasingly impoverished middle-class family, throwing off the shackles of Catholicism and bourgeois convention, and embarking upon the lonely path of the writer determined to expose his society's failings. The title, combining a formula from Ancient Greek tragedy with the name of the young protagonist, suggests the kind of irony Joyce was to exploit later in his career, but it's hard to discern irony in the eleven chapters that survive: the accounts of the inner world of Joyce's alter ego Stephen Daedalus, and of his interactions with his fellow university students, are not mediated by any sense of stylistic shaping and verbal economy, and as a result feel too close to their subject matter to allow for the play of ironic distancing.

When Joyce recommended his semi-autobiographical project in 1907 it was with a very different approach to the task. He had in the meantime completed *Dubliners*, and – as we have seen in the case of 'Eveline' – had developed an art of economy and compression that makes *Stephen Hero* seem positively elephantine. (Curiously, Joyce pursued the two projects

---

[12] An earlier version of this essay was written in collaboration with Anne Fogarty, who provided a complementary study of the social and historical contexts of this story: see Attridge and Fogarty, '"Eveline" at Home'.

[13] See Gabler, 'Introduction', to Joyce, *A Portrait of the Artist*, 1–2. Gabler contests the more usual dating of 1904.

[14] Letter to Grant Richards, March 13, 1906; *Letters*, vol. 2, p. 132.

side-by-side, without any apparent stylistic interference between them.) The new, much shorter, novel, which he called *A Portrait of the Artist as a Young Man*, was probably completed early in 1914; the title alone indicates the complexity Joyce had introduced into his version of the *Künstlerroman*. Is the 'artist' to be understood as the creator of the artwork so entitled, as would be the case in the world of painting from which the phrase is borrowed? Or does it have a more generic (and thus more ironic) reference? How deprecating (or self-deprecating) is the emphasis on youthfulness? We can already see, merely responding to the title page, that Joyce was exploring ways of loading words with shades of meaning that exceed their communicative function, and that in doing so he was willing to make greater demands on the novel-reader than had hitherto been the norm.

When Joyce began to rewrite *Stephen Hero* as *A Portrait*, among the recently published novels were Conrad's *Lord Jim* (1900), Kipling's *Kim* (1901), Mann's *Buddenbrooks* (1901), and James's *Ambassadors* (1903). While all of these works reflect important innovations in matter or manner, none could be thought of as formally revolutionary. By the time Joyce had finished his novel, evidence for changes in the world of fiction included the appearance of Stein's *Three Lives* (1908), Lawrence's *Sons and Lovers* (1913), and Proust's *Un amour de Swann* (*Swann's Way*) (1913). (The same years had witnessed Pound's *Personae* (1909), Picasso's *Demoiselles d'Avignon* (1907), and Stravinsky's and Nijinsky's *Rite of Spring* (1913).) We don't know the order in which Joyce wrote and revised the five chapters of *A Portrait*, and so we can't say when his most innovative pages were composed, but we can say that the first instalment that appeared in *The Egoist* on Joyce's thirty-second birthday, February 2, 1914, marks a turning-point in English fiction.

The opening of the novel, in contrast to the shock of unfamiliarity engendered by the first sight of Picasso's *Demoiselles* or the initial bars of Stravinsky's *Rite* (or, three years later, the beginning of Eliot's 'Prufrock'), invite the reader into an entirely familiar world, the world of childhood impressions and, as the vehicle for those impressions, the language of childhood:

> Once upon a time and a very good time it was there was a moocow coming down along the road and this moocow that was coming down along the road met a nicens little boy named baby tuckoo . . .
> His father told him that story: his father looked at him though a glass: he had a hairy face.
> He was baby tuckoo. The moocow came down the road where Betty Byrne lived: she sold lemon platt. (25)[15]

[15] See the Introduction for some comments on the importance of this opening for later writers.

Compare this with a representative passage from the last chapter of the novel, when Stephen is about twenty and reflecting on the woman he is, perhaps, in love with:

> A sense of her innocence moved him almost to pity her, an innocence he had never understood till he had come to the knowledge of it through sin, an innocence which she too had not understood while she was innocent or before the strange humiliation of her nature had first come upon her. Then first her soul had begun to live as his soul had when he had first sinned: and a tender compassion filled his heart as he remembered her frail pallor and her eyes, humbled and saddened by the dark shame of womanhood. (250)

The style now manifests the sophistication, or pseudo-sophistication, of the young man, presenting the onset of menstruation as an event to be imagined and described in elegant Paterian periods – and it's the slightly mannered articulation of the sentences that keeps alive the possibility of irony at Stephen's expense.

The adjustment required to understand and enjoy Joyce's radically new technique was subtle but far-reaching, and would be demanded by most of his experiments with fiction from this point on. Put simply, the reader can no longer establish with any security the position of the narrator or implied author vis-à-vis the characters and events described because the language, though carefully crafted, is unmoored from an intentional source. Just as we cannot be sure whether the author in giving us a title is inviting us to take it literally or ironically, so we cannot come to rest firmly on a judgement of the character and actions of the protagonist as his story unfolds. It's not just a question of a complex combination of the admirable and the reprehensible: since Cervantes, the tradition of the novel had shown itself to be a superb tool for such complication of moral judgements. Nor is it a matter of the absence of a narrator: the epistolary novel is only the most obvious narratorless genre in which the implied author can still be sensed adopting a particular stance. (No-one would say that *Pamela* lacks an ethical perspective.) Flaubert had shown over fifty years earlier how powerful and unsettling a narrator who refuses to make judgements could be, and Joyce takes this technique even further. *A Portrait*, although some of it can be read as a relatively traditional, if unusually fastidious, novel of childhood and adolescent development, is at its most radical when the reader's pleasure is derived from the exploitation of linguistic resources unanchored in any narrating consciousness at all. No-one is *informing* us that little Stephen is riveted by his father's story-telling, that he has not yet divorced the world of fiction from the world in which he lives, and that his perception is of discrete fragments rather than unified wholes. In the later passage, we're not being pushed into assessing Stephen's mental world as either sensitive or crass, sympathetic or detached, verbally subtle or vapidly imitative; the onus is on us as readers.

After the extraordinarily economical initial section evoking in a couple of pages some of the significant and lasting influences on Stephen's early childhood – among them story-telling, parental affection, music, political affiliations, religious intolerance, and sexual prohibition – the novel depicts his schooldays by means of an increasingly mature style. Joyce's willingness to thrust his reader into unaccustomed territory is particularly evident in the sermons Stephen hears during a retreat: where another novelist would have provided a taste of the style and a summary of the content, Joyce gives us page after page of Father Arnall's words, most of them devoted to an agonisingly drawn-out depiction of hell. Stephen's new-found religious conviction is not overtly ironised, though in the following chapter his rejection of a priestly vocation and embrace of an artistic one is given equal intensity – and is equally capable of being read ironically. Also a challenge for the novel-reader are the long conversations with fellow university students related in the fifth chapter, and the sudden unexplained shift to a series of diary entries with which the book ends, a foreshadowing of the arbitrary changes of style in the later episodes of *Ulysses*. In the diary entries, the absence of a narrator observing Stephen is obvious, and, unlike Richardson, Joyce gives us no pointers (or too many pointers) to a final judgement on his character.

The experience of reading *Dubliners* is one of relishing the precision of Joyce's words as he evokes the thoughts and feelings of his mostly lower-middle-class city-dwellers, almost all trapped, whether by immaturity, duty, religion, inflexibility of thought, patronisation by others, constraints of gender, political venality, or some other force, internal or external. *A Portrait* also offers the reader a vivid picture of an individual consciousness reacting to, and acting upon, its environment, but offers, too, a rewarding journey through modes of writing in the evocation of that consciousness. *Ulysses* will take to a new level this fusion of realist depiction and the foregrounding of the means whereby it is achieved, and later writers will build on Joyce's demonstration that exploiting the latter need not mean diminishing the former.

CHAPTER 2

Ulysses and the Question of Modernist Form

Two Novels

Let us go back to the year 1922 – perhaps the year that was to change the
course of world literature more decisively than any other in the entire twentieth century[1] – and to the publication of the complete version of a novel
that had appeared in part over the immediately preceding years, a novel
written on a vast scale and remarkable both for its minute reconstruction
of the mundane realities of day-to-day life in an earlier period and for its
depiction of the most intimate psychological currents, especially those that
swirl around the vortex of sexual desire – offering, in this respect at least,
one of the fullest portraits of a marriage ever to have been written. The
author of the novel I have in mind was not, as might be assumed, an Irish
expatriate in Paris but a woman who lived most of her life in Norway and
set her fiction in that country: Sigrid Undset, whose three-volume novel
Kristin Lavransdatter was published between 1920 and 1922.[2] The historical world she recreated was as far from early twentieth-century Dublin as
one could imagine: it was that of fourteenth-century Norway, seen primarily through the eyes of a girl, and then woman, of strong passions and
equally strong moral sentiments. Although this work gained international
esteem between the wars – Undset received the Nobel Prize in 1928 – and
remains both highly regarded and immensely popular in the Scandinavian

---

[1] Two books have been devoted to the literary and artistic production of this year,
North's *Reading 1922* and Rabaté's edited collection, *1922*, and it has frequently
been cited as a watershed year; see, for example, Levin, 'What Was Modernism?'
(618–19), and Sultan, *Eliot, Joyce and Company* (129).

[2] Sigrid Undset, *Kristin Lavransdatter I: The Wreath*; *Kristin Lavransdatter II: The Wife*;
Kristin Lavransdatter III: The Cross.

countries, it has had nothing like the world-wide success of the other work which my first sentence could equally well have been describing.

Why these very different fates for *Ulysses* and for *Kristin Lavransdatter*, appearing in full as they did in the same year (the year, incidentally, that both authors turned forty)? The simplest explanation would be just that one is a better work than the other, but any such judgement of quality presupposes a cultural basis for the criteria being applied, and it's that basis for judgement in which I'm interested. Readers who don't know Undset's novel will have to take my word for it that it's not in any obvious way a markedly inferior aesthetic production – it's huge in extent (its three volumes total well over a thousand pages in the Penguin translation), meticulously detailed, strongly yet intricately plotted, and, as many readers have testified, powerfully moving in its depiction of human characters and their relations. In its recreation of the quotidian realities of fourteenth-century existence in the farms and towns of Norway and in its handling of the political and religious events of that century it absorbs and transmutes an entire library of medieval texts.[3] Perhaps its most remarkable feature is its capacity to produce the illusion of complete familiarity with the milieu it describes, so that the sense of historical distance we experience as readers is never *within* the novel, but rather between the novel's assumption of intimate acquaintance with the texture of medieval daily life and our extra-novelistic awareness that this world is in fact quite other than our own. Undset achieves this in part by throwing historical caution to the winds when imagining psychological states, which are immediately recognisable to a contemporary reader; as a result, we have no difficulty in entering the mind through which the fourteenth-century world in all its foreignness is perceived. Although *Ulysses* or, to take another work which makes for a fruitful comparison, Dorothy Richardson's *Pilgrimage*, invite a similar experience of intimacy with the lived consciousness of a period before that in which they were first read, the gap in those novels is a matter of decades, not centuries; and now that almost another hundred years have passed, we barely notice it as we read unless we are literary historians.

Clearly, one reason for the relative obscurity of *Kristin Lavransdatter* on the global scene is that it was written in Norwegian, though the example of Ibsen a couple of decades earlier shows that this need not have been an insuperable barrier to wider attention. Perhaps Undset was simply unlucky in her original translator in the 1920s; instead of William Archer, whose versions of Ibsen made a strong impact on at least one aspiring author in Dublin in the 1890s, she had Charles Archer, whose fondness for *methinks*'s

---

[3] For a brief discussion, see Sherrill Harbison 'Introduction'.

and 'twas's turned her carefully-judged prose into neo-Victorian pseudo-medieval embroidery. The translation also excised some passages – here we find ourselves thinking of Joyce again – deemed to be too sexually explicit for the 1920s readership. It was only at the end of the twentieth century that an adequate English version of the whole three-volume text become available: Tiina Nunnally's new translation appeared between 1997 and 2000. Although my lack of Norwegian means that I can't judge its fidelity to the original, I can say that from the point of view of the English reader it is superbly rendered, and this version deserves to win for it many more admirers. (If Joyce read *Kristin Lavransdatter* – and it has been claimed that he knew Undset's work – he wouldn't have needed Archer's translation, since he had taught himself Norwegian in order to read Ibsen in the original, and, in the years 1926–27, when Undset's fame was approaching its zenith, he sought out, as part of his labours on 'Work in Progress', a series of Norwegian teachers in Paris to help him refresh his acquaintance with the language.)[4]

I think we can safely say, however, that even in a good translation *Kristin Lavransdatter* would never have achieved the cultural centrality of *Ulysses*, and the reasons clearly go beyond matters of geography, original language, and translation. They include the gender of the author, the waning allure of medieval subjects by the 1920s, and the conservative ideology underpinning the novel. (In a trajectory the reverse of Joyce's, Undset underwent conversion to Catholicism two years after the publication of the final volume of *Kristin Lavransdatter*, an event which early readers of the novel would not have found surprising).[5] Another possible factor, and this is the issue on which I want to focus, is Undset's choice of literary form and technique. We non-readers of Norwegian are told that Undset developed a style that is eminently readable yet tinged with a flavour of Old Norse, since she eschewed modern vocabulary that was not derived from Old Norse and utilised features of that language's syntax.[6] Nunnally's English equivalent is straightforward, workmanlike prose, unmistakably modern but with very few explicit markers of the twentieth century, a mode which is in keeping with Gustafson's description of Undset's use of Norwegian: 'Perhaps the first thing that impresses us in *Kristin Lavransdatter* is the apparent

---

[4] See Tysdahl, *Joyce and Ibsen*, 126–27.

[5] In 'Unfashionable *Kristin Lavransdatter*', Reinert acknowledges the novel's conservative, religious temper, and defends it as a great work 'that comes late in a long line of works great in the same way' (69). This is to underestimate the degree to which the novel is of its time, however.

[6] See Harbison, 'Introduction', xx.

effortlessness of the artistic performance, the seeming lack of any conscious narrative devices or tricks, the complete absence of *style* in the narrow literary sense of the word' (*Six Scandinavian Novelists*, 315). It's hard to imagine a description that would be less appropriate for *Ulysses*.

Joyce, however, or rather the cultural reception and construction of Joyce, is my main topic in this chapter. The question I want to pose is this: did Joyce's formal devices in *Ulysses* play a central role in achieving for that work the status it now enjoys as the modernist novel *par excellence*? (I don't think there's any doubt that in all parts of the globe the most frequent answer to the question, 'Name a modernist novel,' would be, for those who weren't merely puzzled by the adjective, Joyce's *Ulysses*.) Conversely, does our (admittedly vexed) understanding of modernism as a distinct and distinctive literary movement emerge to a significant degree from those aspects of *Ulysses* that would be understood as covered by the notion of literary form? To entertain for a moment a scarcely thinkable proposition, had Joyce continued to use the 'scrupulously mean' style of *Dubliners* to elaborate at enormous length a day in the lives of three Dublin characters, would his novel have suffered something like the fate of *Kristin Lavransdatter*?[7] Or is it conceivable that the connotations of the term 'modernism' would have turned out rather differently, its scope perhaps broad enough to have included Undset's work?

Responding to Modernist Form

These are unanswerable questions, of course, and I'm raising them only as a means of speculating about the role played by form in our current conception, or conceptions, of modernism, and the influence which Joyce's work, and *Ulysses* in particular, have had upon that role. But first it's important to achieve some clarity in the use of terms like 'form', 'style', and 'technique'. Of course, any writer uses formal means to achieve their ends, and Undset is no exception. What we mean by modernist technique, presumably, is the use of formal features that, instead of being entirely in the service of communicative effectiveness, draw attention to themselves in some way. For example, we become conscious of, and perhaps are at first puzzled by, the relation of one word or sentence to the next, the absence of the usual

---

[7] Jackson and McGinley, in the Introduction to their annotated edition of *Dubliners*, offer this intriguing titbit: 'Robert McAlmon reported that Joyce wondered in the mid-1920s whether it might not have been better to have developed his writing in the "*Dubliners*" style "rather than going into words too entirely"' (xiv). See the previous chapter for a discussion of the style of *Dubliners*.

markers identifying a speaker or a consciousness, or the intrusion of other languages or non-verbal signs. One reflex of this is the notorious modernist 'difficulty' – which doesn't mean difficulty in the sense of a complex mathematical theorem or abstruse philosophical argument, but difficulty experienced when the relatively passive mode of reading that almost all texts allow has to give way to a more active engagement in the interpretative process. What is more, and I suspect this is of peculiar importance in thinking about modernism, this foregrounding of formal devices often means that we have to be prepared to accept that reading is always a matter of making sense only of *some portion* of the linguistic (or musical or visual) material we are engaging with, and not the whole of it. Putting this another way, modernist form, in what I would argue is its most characteristic mode, destroys the illusion that every significant element in the text we are reading feeds into a continuous thread of meaning that, however rich and complex, is single and whole, and that any failures of comprehension are either minor or merely temporary, to be made good fairly quickly as one reads on. The random, the contingent, the inorganic, the inexplicable, the radically ambiguous: in the full-blooded modernist work these are not dismissible but demand to be acknowledged and dealt with – even if the best way of dealing with them is to let them stand as blanks in comprehension.

There are two rather easy responses to this phenomenon: one is to claim that the modernist work is deliberately chaotic, lacking in craft and without the orderliness and coherence traditionally expected of art; the other is that it's a complex whole of such elaborate interconnectedness that the meaning of individual items remains inaccessible until an intellectual apprehension of the whole scheme is achieved (usually through the laborious consultation of some kind of external critical apparatus). And when the work's historical context is seen as a period of rapid change and loss of certainty, these two responses give rise to two easy ways of relating it to the world: in the first case, it's taken to be reflecting the chaos of the time in its disorder; in the second case, it's taken to be containing or controlling the chaos of the time in its order. All four of these views were forcefully articulated in early responses to *Ulysses*.[8]

Of course, formal technique can't be separated from the other aspects of a text by a simple division. When, in an otherwise straightforwardly presented tale, an ape speaks or a man turns into an insect, we could describe this moment either as a (formal) transgression of conventional narrative codes or as a (thematic) departure from normal subject-matter.

---

[8] The most famous example of the second response is Eliot's essay '*Ulysses*, Order, and Myth'.

The insertion of snatches of popular song in a poem of high intellectual pretensions is an infringement of formal organic unity but also an unexpected choice of content. However, it's perfectly clear that, whereas the major impact of *A Portrait of the Artist as a Young Man* arose from what was regarded as its 'realism' or 'naturalism', in spite of its revolutionary use of mimetic language, *Ulysses* was immediately perceived to be radically unconventional in technique. Even before publication of the whole work, Clive Bell was writing in the *New Republic*: 'Mr. Joyce does deliberately go to work to break up the traditional sentence, throwing overboard sequence, syntax, and, indeed, most of those conventions which men habitually employ for the exchange of precise ideas.'[9]

Bell was soon being echoed by the early reviews of the published book: here are four reactions to Joyce's formal innovations from 1922:

> There are whole chapters of it without any punctuation or other guide to what the writer is really getting at. Two-thirds of it is incoherent . . .'[10]

> His style is in the new fashionable kinematographic vein, very jerky and elliptical . . .'[11]

> Every trick that a keen-witted man could conceivably play with the English language, and some that were inconceivable until Mr. Joyce arrived, is played somewhere in this book.[12]

> All the conventions of organised prose which have grown with our race and out of our racial consciousness which have been reverently handed on by the masters with such improvements as they have been able to make, have been cast aside as so much dross.[13]

The frequent references to 'boredom' and 'dullness' in many of the early reviews (sometimes by reviewers who are otherwise very positive – Edmund

---

[9] 'Plus de Jazz,' *New Republic* xxviii (21 September 1921): 95; Deming, *James Joyce: The Critical Heritage*, vol. 1, 183.

[10] 'The Scandal of *Ulysses*', *Sporting Times*, No. 34 (1 April 1922): 4; Deming, *James Joyce*, vol. 1, 192.

[11] 'A New *Ulysses*', *Evening News*, 8 April 1922, p. 4; Deming, *James Joyce*, vol. 1, 194.

[12] John Middleton Murry, Review, *Nation & Athenaeum*, 22 April 1922, xxxi, 124–5; Deming, *James Joyce*, vol. 1, 196.

[13] Holbrook Jackson, review, *To-Day*, June 1922, ix, 47–9; Deming, *James Joyce*, vol. 1, 199. Jackson's sentence is not exactly a model of 'organised prose'!

Wilson, for instance, refers to the book's 'appalling longueurs'[14]) are primarily responses to Joyce's technical innovations, as well as to the sheer length at which he indulges in some of them.[15] Readers are bored because they can't understand what they are reading, and they can't understand what they're reading because the text doesn't follow the normal conventions of narrative prose. The result is that it seems 'formless'. (This doesn't prevent many reviewers from fulminating against the book's depravity and salaciousness, which apparently comes across sharply enough.)[16]

Now the history of literary form provides many examples of technical innovations that are at first puzzling and hard to deal with, but which soon become new conventions that readers processed without turning a hair. Defoe's real-seeming fictions or Whitman's free-flowing verse didn't cause problems for very long. One of Joyce's most significant and influential technical innovations, the use of present-tense syntactic fragments to create the illusion of spontaneous thought, quickly becomes as easy to read and enjoy as the normal sentences of past tense narrative reporting. Although the following passage has few precedents in literary history, it poses no lasting challenge to the reader schooled in Victorian novelistic practices:

> Another slice of bread and butter: three, four: right. She didn't like her plate full. Right. He turned from the tray, lifted the kettle off the hob and set it sideways on the fire. It sat there, dull and squat, its spout stuck out. Cup of tea soon. Good. Mouth dry.[17]

[14] Review, *New Republic*, xxxi, No. 396 (5 July 1922); Deming, *James Joyce*, vol. 1, 230.

[15] A few examples from 1922: '*Ulysses* is not alone sordidly pornographic, but it is intensely dull' (review, *Sporting Times*, No. 34, 1 April 1922, 4; Deming, *James Joyce*, vol. 1, 194); 'There are the deadliest of Dead Seas in this ocean of prose. You get becalmed by them – bored, drowsed, bewildered' (Holbrook Jackson, review, *To-Day*, June 1922, ix, 47–9; Deming, *James Joyce*, vol. 1, 199); 'A more serious objection to the novel is its pervading difficult dulness' (Arnold Bennett, review, *Outlook*, 29 April 1922, 337–9; Deming, *James Joyce*, vol. 1, 220); 'It requires real endurance to finish *Ulysses*' (Joseph Collins, review, *New York Times Book* Review, 28 May 1922, 6, 17; Deming, *James Joyce*, vol. 1, 223.

[16] One reviewer tries, unconvincingly, to marry these incompatibles: 'Our first impression is that of sheer disgust, our second of irritability because we never know whether a character is speaking or merely thinking, our third of boredom at the continual harping on obscenities (nothing cloys a reader's appetite so quickly as dirt) . . .' (S. P. B. Mais, 'An Irish Revel: And Some Flappers,' *Daily Express*, 25 March 1922, n.p.; Deming, *James Joyce*, vol. 1, 191).

[17] Joyce, *Ulysses*, ed. Gabler, 4.11–14. All references to Joyce's *Ulysses* will be in the standard form of episode and line number(s).

Technique of this kind is deployed in the service of greater naturalism, more delicate responsiveness to the internal world of thoughts and feelings, and in that sense functions as an extension of, rather than a break with, the tradition of the nineteenth-century novel. This is what Wilson, for example, admired and enjoyed when reviewing *Ulysses* in 1922:

> Mr. Joyce manages to give the effect of unedited human minds, drifting aim-lessly along from one triviality to another, confused and diverted by mem-ory, by sensation, and by inhibition. It is, in short, perhaps the most faithful X-ray ever taken of the ordinary human consciousness.

Much of the achievement of Woolf, Lawrence, and Richardson can be under-stood in similar, if not equally extreme, terms. The interior monologue of *Ulysses*, then, stands as a highly successful instance of this refinement of the tradition of psychological realism, not that far removed from the suppos-edly styleless style of Sigrid Undset. This is not modernist technique in the fullest sense of the word.

Form and Content

There are other formal features of *Ulysses* that posed a greater challenge to its first readers and demanded a mode of interpretation very different from that required by Undset and, indeed, most other novelists of the period or of earlier periods. We can turn to Wilson again for an early and influential articulation; this is from his chapter on Joyce in *Axel's Castle*, published in 1931:

> What is the value of all the references to flowers in the Lotus-Eaters chapter, for example? They do not create in the Dublin streets an atmosphere of lotus-eating – we are merely puzzled, if we have not been told to look for them, as to why Joyce has chosen to have Bloom think and see certain things, of which the final explanation is that they are pretexts for mentioning flowers.[18]

There is thus a certain *excess* of technique in Joyce – and it's an excess of technique not designed to thwart meaning, but to multiply meanings. It works as a joke, of course – revealing unsuspected congruities in the

---

[18] Wilson, *Axel's Castle*, 214. Wilson cites the interpolations of 'Cyclops' and the parodies of 'Oxen of the Sun' as further examples.

apparent arbitrarinesses of language in the same manner as the pun[19] – but at the same time it highlights the operations of language and narrative which normally function so smoothly as to be unnoticeable. The references to flowers in the 'Lotus-Eaters' chapter are an addition to everything else that's going on in the chapter in terms of event, thought, and feeling; and the scandal is not just that they have no organic relation to the events and thoughts being narrated in the chapter, but that they even appear at times to *determine* the events and thoughts being narrated, to provide, as Wilson astutely observes, pretexts for the use of flower-related words.[20]

Joyce's early work shows him to be a devotee of organic form. While the poems of *Chamber Music* employ traditional forms, prioritising their contribution to lyrical grace over their other functions, the stories of *Dubliners* eschew obvious formal devices to create the sense of a slice of unmediated life. (Of course, in the service of this aim Joyce makes subtle use of the formal properties of prose – discussed in the previous chapter – and the generic properties of the short story.) It's in *A Portrait of the Artist* that formal innovation becomes a major feature: the opening pages create for the reader a quite different experience from that of the novels written during the previous two centuries.[21] But although form is foregrounded in those pages, it's still operating in an organic relation to meaning: by departing from the norms of the written language to generate the impression of a child's thought processes, Joyce is fusing form and content in a manner that was to prove highly influential on later writers.

The technique of interior monologue, developed so skilfully in *Ulysses*, takes this innovation further. By fragmenting the regular configurations of language, Joyce conveys a vivid sense of his characters' mental world, and had he written the entire work in the 'initial style' of the opening chapters it would have been received, for all its formal innovations, as a major breakthrough in the tradition of the realist novel, a book to set beside the several volumes of Richardson's *Pilgrimage* – with their stream-of consciousness technique – that had appeared by 1922. But of course, Joyce's play with formal devices soon went in a different direction. In introducing headlines into the 'Aeolus' episode of *Ulysses* – quite literally, as the earlier version of the chapter published in the *Little Review* in 1918 was a continuous

---

[19] See my discussion of the pun and the portmanteau in chapter 7 of *Peculiar Language*.

[20] For a further discussion of Joyce's use of what I am calling inorganic form, see Chapter 10.

[21] For a discussion of the revolutionary nature of these pages, see Attridge, *Joyce Effects*, 59–77; see also Chapter 1 above.

narrative in the same style as the previous episodes – Joyce demonstrated that formal devices could operate without contributing to the representation of his characters' mental worlds.

The headlines in 'Aeolus', like all the stylistic innovations that follow in the book, can of course be related to the content of the chapter, which takes place in the office and printing works of a newspaper. But if we think in terms of the reader's experience, it's clear that this connection is something we make at a remove from our direct apprehension of the fictional narrative; that's to say, we register it consciously once we see what is going on, but our awareness of it doesn't feed into our ongoing engagement with the lives of Stephen Dedalus, Leopold Bloom, and the newspapermen. In a similar manner, the play with sound in 'Sirens' can be connected to the musical performances in the Ormond Hotel, the inflated parodic interpolations in 'Cyclops' can be seen as a comment on the exaggerations of the barflies, the parade of English styles in 'Oxen of the Sun' can be matched to the months of gestation, and so on.[22] In every case, the reader, once they have discovered the relationship (or been informed of it in a critical work), can accept it as proof that there is a purposiveness to this formal feature, and go on to enjoy the stylistic adventures – whether the increasingly unlikely headlines, the hilarious parodies poking fun at various kinds of rhetoric, the brilliant pastiches of prose styles that impede rather than enhance the referential capacity of the language, and so on. Form can be said to enrich content, but only via an intellectual operation.[23] It is still meaningful, but its relation to content is no longer organic.

This loosening of the connection between form and content means that there is a degree of arbitrariness in the choice of the particular style for each

[22] One of the few critics to dismiss these links between style and content is Patrick Parrinder, who regards them as belonging to 'the time-honoured category of Irish Bulls' (*James Joyce*, 163).

[23] In a discussion of the functions of poetic rhythm in an earlier work, I distinguished between 'mimetic' and 'emblematic' iconic devices, a distinction that has relevance here: 'Mimetic devices take effect as an immediate part of the reading activity, and need not reach consciousness as a separate semantic mechanism; they contribute to that sense of heightened meaning which we can experience even when we cannot explain it. Emblematic devices, on the other hand, provide relations between the linguistic substance and the larger world only by means of a conscious intellectual act' (*The Rhythms of English Poetry*, 288). An early version of this distinction was proposed by Alexander Baumgarten: in aesthetic judgements, sensible properties can be either 'intuitive' or 'symbolic' (see Guyer, *A History of Modern Aesthetics*, vol. 1, The Eighteenth Century, 326).

chapter.[24] The goings-on in Bella Cohen's brothel *could* have been related in the initial style, or with parodic interpolations, or in a continuous unpunctuated flow; the reader's experience would have been very different in each case, but an argument could have – and no doubt would have – been made for the appropriateness of each. (It's harder to imagine a different style for the child's experiences at the start of *A Portrait* or an alternative to the initial style to capture the fragmented run of thoughts.) And what goes for individual episodes goes for the Homeric structure as a whole. Detecting parallels between events in the narrative and episodes in the *Odyssey* – noting the shape-shifting in 'Proteus' or the seductive arts of the barmaids in 'Sirens,' for example – is an enjoyable aspect of an engagement with the novel, and can lead to reflections on the nature of epic, the figure of the hero, or the vicissitudes of history, but it doesn't emerge immediately from the words on the page. It's easy to forget that the familiar episode titles aren't present in the book, and it's hard to say how many of them might have become part of the standard commentary if Joyce hadn't circulated them to friends. Indeed, if Joyce had called his novel *Hamnet*, there would no doubt exist a mountain of exegesis tracing the parallels with both Shakespeare's family life and his most famous play.

Without Joyce's tabulating of each episode's title, 'technic', organ, etc. in the famous schemata given to Valéry Larbaud and Carlo Linati, then, much of what we take for granted in our commentaries would probably never have emerged. Certain recurrent features of the chapters might still have been detectable, however. A careful reader of the chapter we know as 'Lotus-Eaters', for instance, might notice recurring motifs, some of which are listed by Hugh Kenner: 'the warmth, the directionless walk, the gelded horses munching in their nosebags, the communicants in the church Bloom passes through, the chemist's chloroform and poppysyrup, the lemony smell of the soap, the anticipated warm bath' (*Ulysses*, 22). Without external guidance, such a reader would be unlikely to think of a specific episode in the *Odyssey*, but would certainly sense that the events and objects in the chapter were obeying some rule external to the fictional world. And in introducing this list Kenner puts his finger on the most revolutionary aspect of Joyce's use of formal devices in *Ulysses*, the feature that Wilson had already noted

---

[24] Karen Lawrence puts it more strongly in what remains the best account of this aspect of Ulysses: 'As the narrative norm is abandoned during the course of the book and is replaced by a series of styles, we see the arbitrariness of all styles' (*The Odyssey of Style in 'Ulysses'*, 9). One critic who attempts to justify the styles in organic terms is Charles Peake (*James Joyce: The Citizen and the Artist*).

in 1931: '[T]he episode's Homeric parallel, Lotos-Eaters, appears to take charge of much of its random detail' (22).

It's not, in other words, just a question of formal features operating independently of content and being associated by the conscious interpretative action of the reader; the content is to some extent experienced as being *determined* by the form (although the connection still requires a conscious mental act). Kenner suggests, for instance, that the discovery by Bloom in 'Nausicaa' that his watch has stopped at half past four in the afternoon, and his immediate assumption that this must have been the exact moment of his wife's adultery, is just the sort of coincidence that would happen in the kind of novel whose sentimental style has dominated the first part of the episode. It wouldn't, he argues, have occurred in any other episode of the novel (105). Whether or not we make a connection with the *Odyssey*, we are aware that the things that happen, and the language in which they are related, follow a pattern in excess of the fictional world itself. Not only is this inorganic form, it's writing in which the usual relation between form and content is reversed.[25] Once detected, they form part of the reader's experience, a pleasure derived not from the content the language is bringing into being but from the writer's brilliance in making language conform to a predetermined schema.

We find something similar happening in many of the episodes, notably in passages where the style is otherwise geared to naturalistic representation. To take one example out of hundreds: in 'Sirens', the terms Miss Douce chooses to express her annoyance with the boots – 'If he doesn't conduct himself I'll wring his ear for him a yard long' (11.104–5) – are there not because, or not only because, they are naturalistically appropriate, but because the reader can relate 'conduct' and 'wring' (differently spelled) and 'ear' to the chapter's theme of music. In order to do so, however, they have to stop treating the text as the evocation of a scene and treat it as a series of words selected by an author – or rather, *possibly* selected by an author, since one of the crucial properties of this type of device is that it rapidly becomes

---

[25] Sara Danius, discussing the operation of the senses in *Ulysses*, observes a related tension between form and content in *Ulysses*: 'Two dominant formal tendencies may be observed in Joyce's novel, and they pull in opposite directions. The ideal of the organic form means that the parts make up the whole. Yet – and this incompatibility lies at the heart of *Ulysses* – the parts are not reducible to the whole. To explore how acts of perception are staged, including their implied matrices of perception, is to uncover a powerful stylistic tendency that, on the level of the sentence, pulls toward differentiation and autonomization' (*The Senses of Modernism*, 153).

a machine that continues to operate for its readers irrespective of any authorial intention. The opposition between the willed and the fortuitous breaks
down; not only is it impossible to say where an effect of this kind is deliberate and where it is a chance product of the language, it no longer matters to
our enjoyment of the work.[26] The same is true of all the eyes (often blind
ones) in the 'Cyclops' episode, the various kinds of windiness in 'Aeolus',
the words suggestive of food and eating in 'Lestrygonians', and so on. And
this particular technical device is only a minor version of the ascendancy of
style over content that characterises all the later chapters of the book, with
the partial exception of 'Penelope'.[27]

Other chapters offer similar pleasures. In 'Hades', for instance, Bloom
remembers Molly saying 'I'm dying for it', notes the '[d]ead side of the
street', reflects on the 'dead weight' of the coffin, refers to the 'dead letter
office', and observes that priests are 'dead against' cremation. If it's possible
to explain these verbal allusions as unconscious reflections of the funeral
in progress (and hence, again, obviating any need to refer to Homer), the
same explanation won't do for the many references to the organ Joyce
allotted to the chapter: 'He took it to heart', 'Wear the heart out of a stone',
'Vain in her heart of hearts', 'That touches a man's inmost heart', and so on.
Equally separate from any character's consciousness, and easy to overlook
without external prodding, are the shape-shifting terms in 'Proteus', the
flower-names in 'Lotus-Eaters', and the windy words in 'Aeolus'. The frequent references to music in 'Sirens' would perhaps be more obvious to an
uninstructed reader: it would be hard to remain unaware that the episode
is awash not only with actual examples of musical performance but words
with a musical resonance, even when music is not being referred to: 'Miss
Kennedy . . . *transposed* the teatray' (11.92); 'Miss Douce *chimed* in' (11.147);
'they urged each each to *peal* after *peal*, *ringing in changes*' (11.174–5); 'Must
be a great *tonic*' (11.219–20); and so on.[28] The device is particularly striking
when characters choose to speak, or think, in words that reflect the episode's governing trope, revealing themselves to be innocent victims of an
imperative outside their ken.

---

[26] I have commented on this phenomenon in the reading of *Finnegans Wake*, where
it is exploited much more fully, in *Peculiar Language*, 206–7, and *Joyce Effects*, 121.
[27] There are signs of this technique as early as *Dubliners*: in their edition Jackson and
McGinley provide notes to 'The Dead' that point out the suggestions of death in
apparently innocent terms and phrases such as 'three mortal hours', 'toddling'
(c.f. German *Tod*), 'perished alive' (meaning 'very cold'), and 'the subject . . . was
buried.' See notes 159k, 159m, 159n, and 179h.
[28] Emphases added.

The enjoyment we derive from noticing how the Odyssean correlation or the nominated category in the schema determines the thought and speech of the characters in a given chapter isn't derived from enhanced realism; on the contrary, it's enjoyment of the formal device itself as it colours the narrative content. (At the same time, attending to this aspect of *Ulysses* doesn't involve any diminishment of the astonishing detail of its content.) As I've noted, there is still an element of arbitrariness – 'Hades' could have been studded with words relating to earth or 'Sirens' with references to water[29] – and the exercise of relating form to content, or, rather, content to form, still has to be consciously carried out, perhaps with the help of a critical commentary or Joyce's schema. Though in using this technique Joyce tightens the connection between form and content that, in examples like the headlines of 'Aeolus', he had loosened, it can't be said to be an organic relationship.

In this respect, as in so many others, *Finnegans Wake* takes a formal device used sparingly in *Ulysses* and makes it a general principle. It abounds in formal devices that are not organically related to any fictional content; that a huge number of phrases, names, and titles begin with the letters HCE or ALP, for instance, is not a reflection of the lives or inner experiences of the characters. Perhaps the most famous example is the interweaving of river names through the 'Anna Livia' episode: since the names of rivers very rarely have sonic qualities that suggest water, this feature has nothing to do with the association between the heroine and the Liffey, nor does it contribute to the distinctive quality of the discourse – Dublin gossip between two washerwomen.[30] Though heroic efforts have been made to relate the complicated verbal surface of the *Wake* to a simple fictional narrative, these only serve to demonstrate the excess of the former over the latter. The reader's pleasure in recognising an occurrence of the letters HCE or an allusion to a popular song or a fusion of two or more languages in a single vocable is anything but one of heightened realism.

The Place of *Ulysses*

To many readers, this use of form in excess of the task of enhancing meaning represented what was worst about Joyce's formal innovations; Wilson's

[29] Daniel Ferrer, in 'Echo or Narcissus', demonstrates that it's possible to find some of Joyce's stylistic categories working for chapters other than those designated in the schemata.

[30] The episode's evocation of gossip is superbly brought out by Marcella Riordan in the complete Naxos recording.

objection is mild in comparison to the well-known complaints made by D. H. Lawrence ('too terribly would-be and done-on-purpose, utterly without spontaneity or real life') or Wyndham Lewis ('What stimulates him is *ways of doing things*, and technical processes, and not *things to be done*') or, somewhat later but very influentially, F. R. Leavis ('There is no organic principle determining, informing, and controlling into a vital whole, the elaborate analogical structure, the extraordinary variety of technical devices').[31] More recently, Leo Bersani's critique of *Ulysses* owes not a little to the discomfort produced in a certain kind of reader by the work's foregrounding of formal technique: 'a text to be deciphered but not read', he calls it, objecting that the 'technical machinery . . . obscures our view of what is happening' (*The Culture of Redemption,* 156). Had Joyce not had powerful early defenders in a number of countries – Ezra Pound, T. S. Eliot, and Valéry Larbaud at the start, and soon Gilbert, Wilson, Hermann Broch, Harry Levin, and perhaps I should add Morris Ernst and Judge Woolsey speaking at the obscenity trial – formal innovation might have proved his downfall, and the story of modernism in literature would have been very different.

Those early supporters of *Ulysses* can't be said to have stressed its most innovative formal features, however, and this was no doubt the wisest course for them to have followed. They tended to ignore or make excuses for Joyce's verbal extravagances, or, like Eliot, to lay emphasis on the systematic coherence of the whole. We've seen that Wilson was quite open about his unhappiness – which may in fact have helped rather than hindered his effort to win readers for the book. By emphasising the vividness of psychological detail and the concreteness of the setting it was possible to turn the book into a super-realist novel; by stressing the structural ingenuity of the book as a rewriting of the *Odyssey* one could reassure readers that it was not the chaotic mess it seemed at first. Following the early critics who first laid down these paths, Joyce scholars of the fifties – primarily American – helped to establish *Ulysses* as a coherent, humane fictional masterpiece, whose techniques are fully in the service of a consistent view of the world (though there was some disagreement about the exact nature of that view). They also lodged it in the centre of what was becoming a clearly-defined period of literary history: modernism.

Without the rapid success of *Ulysses* made possible by its early proselytisers, it's doubtful whether Joyce would have written *Finnegans Wake*, and if, under those conditions, he had, it would simply have clinched his reputation as the writer of extravagantly unreadable works of technical interest

---

[31] Lawrence, *Selected Literary Criticism*, 149; Lewis, *Time and Western Man*, 107; Leavis, *The Great Tradition*, 36.

only. (For many readers, of course, it did.) *Ulysses* would have been con-signed to the side-alley of interesting experimentation. In 1948, Leavis was still able to assert that *Ulysses* was a dead end, and many potential readers of the novel in Britain and its colonies must have nodded in agreement (*The Great Tradition*, 36). Modernism would still have made its mark as a rejection of traditional expectations of continuous sense-making – if any-thing, Eliot, Pound, and Gertrude Stein showed even less respect than Joyce for such demands – but it might not have seemed such a triumph of form, such an explosive increase in the possibilities inherent in language and in literary conventions, such a showing-up of the one-dimensionality of tradi-tional methods.

But what is the place of *Ulysses*, and of its excess of formal technique, now, as we reassess modernism from the perspective of the twenty-first century? Accounts of modernism that treat it as the response to an increas-ingly complex, chaotic, and meaningless world – whether that response is taken to be an imitation of external chaos or an attempt to reduce it to order – have come to seem naïve, based as they are on an excessively simple model of literature's relation to historical circumstances. The expe-rience of a loss of sense in the world, of increasing complexity, of infor-mation overload, is one that many generations throughout history have experienced; and the violence with which the modernists provoked and challenged existing habits of thought, moral norms, and conventions of representation suggests a willingness to increase, rather than control or merely reflect, the changes afoot in the culture at large. Critical responses to *Ulysses*, influenced in part by what became labelled as 'theory', have ceased, by and large, to be embarrassed by Joyce's formal feats; his comic revelation of the workings of language, narrative, and the many other ways in which we try to make sense of ourselves and of the world has come to seem central to his achievement, and to at least one brand of modernism. Though many readers still balk at the arbitrariness of the flowers in 'Lotus-Eaters' or the parodic styles of 'Oxen of the Sun', it has become much easier to take pleasure in these verbal games, and to find them working as an ensemble in a project that goes beyond, while it never cancels, the convinc-ing representation of the realm of consciousness and its objects. Many of the literary practices that we rather inadequately label 'postmodernist' have accustomed us to operations of contingency and chance in our texts, and although the realist narrative thrives as much as it has ever done, we have come to understand that convincing representation can quite happily go hand-in-hand with exposure of the means of representation. *Ulysses*, there-fore, becomes even more central to our account of the literary revolution of this period, and contemporary writers are encouraged to explore formal techniques whose function is more than the enhancement of content – a topic to be discussed in Chapter 10.

I will end with a postscript in the form of a personal reflection, which will bring me back to Sigrid Undset's novel. I enjoy and admire both *Ulysses* and *Kristin Lavransdatter*, and I would like to think that, rather than reflecting a hopeless inconsistency in my literary taste, this dual allegiance indicates that the two works have important features in common. Although Undset's novel is often, and not inaccurately, represented as a signal example of anti-modernism, a work which does anything but attempt an exposure of the means of representation or draw the reader's attention to the writer's choices, it seems to me to participate in other ways in modernism's expansion of the possibilities of literary form. It shares with *Ulysses*, and with the work of many other modernists, an immense confidence in the power of literary language to accomplish tasks not hitherto attempted, and part of the pleasure of reading it is experiencing the effects of that confidence *in the writing itself*, the pleasure of self-imposed challenges triumphantly met. The challenges Undset sets herself are, of course, very different from Joyce's, and don't involve overt formal flourishes, but I would argue that they do involve an element of display, of conjuring with words. (Hence the crucial importance of a convincing translation.) My familiarity with *Ulysses* and my relishing of its unapologetic formal devices don't constitute a bar to my enjoyment of *Kristin Lavransdatter*; on the contrary, I believe that my pleasurable engagement with Undset's great novel is actually enhanced by my Joycean predilection for linguistic prestidigitation.

CHAPTER 3

Nonlexical Onomatopoeia: Hearing the Noises of *Ulysses*

Molly Bloom in Bed

Molly Bloom is lying restlessly in bed, her head next to her husband's feet, counting the days until she will next be with her lover, Blazes Boylan: 'Thursday Friday one Saturday two Sunday three O Lord I cant wait till Monday' (*Ulysses* 18.594–5). The next item we see on the page – one can hardly call it a word – is a bizarre string of letters: 'frseeeeeeeefronnnng' (18.596). All in lower case, it begins the fourth of the so-called 'sentences' of the final episode of *Ulysses*. Its challenge to our reading of the episode is multiple: it is unpronounceable, at least according to the norms of the English language; it is meaningless; and it is hardly conceivable as part of Molly's thought processes in the way that everything in the chapter up to this point has been. Joyce does not leave us mystified for long, however: the verbalised thoughts that follow this strange irruption explain what it is doing here: '. . . train somewhere whistling the strength those engines have in them like big giants . . .' (18.596–7).[1] Distant train whistles may more usually evoke associations of travel, separation, nostalgia, or longing, but Molly's response is clearly coloured by her active desire for the man she has just called, with obvious relish, a 'savage brute' (18.594). This supposition is strengthened by the sudden change of tack in Molly's ruminations as her thought continues: '. . . like big giants and the water rolling all over and out of them all sides like the end of Loves old sweeeetsonnnng . . .' (18.596–8).

What kind of experience does a moment like this offer to the reader? Are we to take this series of letters as representing the actual sound of a train

---

[1] Smurthwaite takes the string of letters to represent Molly's own vocalisation of the train whistle, but it's not clear why she would imitate (to herself) the sound she has just heard ('Verbal or Visual?', 80.)

whistle – perhaps on two notes, higher then lower – as it penetrates the bedroom of 7 Eccles Street? (The train is too distant, I think, for the double tone to be a product of the Doppler effect.) Would it be legitimate for an audio version of the book to substitute for the reader's voice at this point a recording of the real sound? Surely not: although one could argue that the succession of *e*'s and the subsequent *o* do mimic the higher and lower notes of the whistle, and that the prolonged nasal of the second syllable imitates a change in timbre in the second note, Joyce's choice of letters can hardly be said to aim at exact representation. The spelling is connected in some way with Molly's own perception of the sound. Is this how she would write it down if she felt the need to do so?[2] The same question is raised by another peculiar string of letters when she recalls 'rousing that dog in the hotel' (by which she probably means 'arousing', as this recollection occurs while she is mentally reliving her masturbation of Lieutenant Mulvey when a teenager on Gibraltar): 'rrrsssst awokwokawok' (18.812–13).[3]

Given the obvious association between the imagined steam locomotive and Boylan's thrusting masculinity, we may well misread 'like the end of . . .'; then, as so often in 'Penelope', we have to correct our interpretation, as we realise that the comparison Molly is making is between the sound of the train whistle and 'Love's Old Sweet Song', one of the numbers she'll be performing during the forthcoming concert tour with Boylan – and has probably been singing to him during their tryst earlier in the day. (Molly herself, of course, is in no doubt about what is like what in the comparison; it's only the reader who may find a grosser meaning in 'end'. The result of Joyce's removal of punctuation in this episode is not, as is often claimed, a more accurate rendition of mental processes, but a game of constant readerly guessing and reassessment which has little to do with Molly's mental processes.) The 'onnnng' of the train whistle, it turns out, is there less as an attempt at mimesis than as an indication of the already forming connection with the 'onnnng' of the song. (That the word of the song in question is

[2] As I've argued elsewhere, there are many suggestions in the episode that the apparent flow of uncontrolled thoughts is constantly mediated by the constraints and characteristics of writing. See Attridge, *Peculiar Language*, chapter 8, especially 97–105. See also Stewart, *Reading Voices*, chapter 6, '"An Earsighted View": Joyce's "Modality of the Audible"', and Smurthwaite, 'Verbal or Visual?'.

[3] Rice assumes that Molly is recalling Mulvey's 'animal response' to her ministrations ('His Master's Voice', 154), but the onomatopoeic sequence follows on directly from the reference to the dog. That there might be disagreement about the sound represented is an index of the indeterminacy of the sequence. Molly's own language in talking to a dog, as recalled by Bloom, is more conventional: 'O, the big doggybowwowsywowsy!' (8.847).

'song' is, of course, another Joycean joke.) The implied downward change in pitch in the move from *e* to *o* is what links this sound in Molly's aural imagination to the singing of 'sweet song'.

The strength of the association between sound and song is made clear when the train whistle penetrates Molly's thoughts a second time. She is recalling some of her youthful experiences with the opposite sex when her reminiscences are interrupted by the same sequence of letters – now with even more *e*'s (no less than twenty) and an upper-case *F* at the start (perhaps the train is closer?):

> Frseeeeeeeeeeeeeeeeeeeeefrong that train again weeping tone once in the dear deaead days beyondre call close my eyes breath my lips forward kiss sad look eyes open piano ere oer the world the mists began I hate that istsbeg comes loves sweet soooooooooooong (18.874–7)

Again, her thoughts move straight from train-whistle to song, with 'weeping tone' providing a bridge.

The third and last time Molly hears the train, she once again associates it with 'Love's Old Sweet Song', though this time there is a third sound blended with it. Molly has just said to herself: 'I feel some wind in me better go easy not wake him up' (18.903), and she seems to be successful in this endeavour not to disturb Leopold's sleep: 'yes hold them like that a bit on my side piano quietly sweeeee theres that train far away pianissimo eeeee one more tsong' (18.907–8). Here Joyce gives us an extraordinary triple sonic pun: 'sweeee' and 'eeeee' are at once the train in the distance, much quieter now; the farts, released as softly as Molly can manage; and the final words of the song (with the 't' of 'sweet' postponed in order to maximise the musical potential of the vowel, so that it becomes the first sound in 'tsong'[4]). The words 'piano' and 'pianissimo' apply to all three. Anal references have, in fact, been building up in the passage even before Molly articulates her desire to break wind – perhaps as the subliminal effect on her thoughts of an internal gaseous accumulation, or perhaps just another of Joyce's games with the reader – and the connection between singing and farting has already been established. For instance, Molly's choice of words to describe her singing of 'Love's Old Sweet Song' after the previous train whistle – 'Ill let that out full' (18.878) – already seems suggestive; she then describes her rival singers as 'sparrowfarts' who 'know as much as my backside' (18.879–80). And the song she decides to sing as an encore is – wait for it – 'Winds that blow from the south' (18.899).

---

[4] Stewart discusses this postponed 't' perceptively, noting that editions prior to Gabler's 1984 text normalised the words (*Reading Voices*, 237).

Ulysses, like *Finnegans Wake* after it, takes great delight in fusing high and low, the polite and the taboo, the revered and the looked down upon. Language, that mark of civilisation, proves to be a medium well suited to blurring the distinctions on which civilisation is supposed to rest. Train-whistle, fart, concert song: these very different sounds, each with a different set of cultural associations, are hardly compatible with one another; yet Joyce manages to unite them, and to do so without any sense of hierarchy or conflict. At the same time, the representational indeterminacy of the sounds of *language*, its *in*adequacy as a mode of direct imitation, is signalled: these very different sounds are, in the end, represented by nothing more than a row of *e*'s.[5]

Nonlexical Onomatopoeia

In *Peculiar Language* I made a distinction between two types of onomato-poeia, which I called 'lexical' and 'nonlexical' – not a watertight distinction, to be sure, but one that I believe serves a useful purpose (136, 148). In lexical onomatopoeia, the more common variety, the words of the language are deployed in such a way as to suggest a more than usually strong link between the sounds of speech and the non-speech sounds, or other physical features of the world, being represented. In nonlexical onomatopoeia, the rarer form that is the subject of this chapter, the letters and sounds of the language are used for a similar purpose, but without the formation of words. Writers have been traditionally free to exploit the fact that in a language with a phonetic alphabet individual letters can represent sounds without conveying meanings, and the usual strict limits placed on neologisms do not apply when no actual lexical items are involved. (One of the best-known examples in literary history is perhaps the earliest: Aristophanes' frogs going βρεκεκεκὲξ κοὰξ κοάξ ('Brekekekex koax koax'). The group of letters representing the first train-whistle in 'Penelope' is thus a clear example of nonlexical onomatopoeia. 'Sweeee', on the other hand, lies somewhere between the two types, although its use of the lexical potential of the language is unusual in that it's not the meaning of the word that's relevant (unless one wants to make an argument about the sweetness of Molly's singing) but the fact of its being sung.

The other significant fart in *Ulysses* – Bloom's burgundy-induced release at the end of 'Sirens' (an event of which Molly's fart in 'Penelope' is a kind

---

[5] Elsewhere, a row of *e*'s can indicate the dragging of a stick on the ground (1.629), a creaking door (7.50; 11.965), and a turning doorhandle (15.2694). See also Attridge *Peculiar Language*, 144, on these *e*'s.

of unwitting echo or partner) – shows how the simple picture of unmediated imitation one might be tempted to apply to nonlexical onomatopoeia can be complicated. In *Peculiar Language* I identified eight factors that produce such complication, the first four being limits to the directness of the link between linguistic and represented sound, and the second four being limits to its precision.[6] They may be summarised as follows:

1. All onomatopoeia relies on the reader's knowledge of the system of language in which the text is written; in the case of nonlexical onomatopoeia, the knowledge required is of the phonological system of the spoken language and the graphological system of the written language. (In *Finnegans Wake*, Joyce would enrich the possibilities of nonlexical onomatopoeia by bringing several languages into play simultaneously.) Even though the sequence 'frs' at the beginning of the train-whistle contradicts the phonological norms of English, unpronounceability is as much part of the system as pronounceability; and if Joyce wants us to struggle to produce some sort of noise based on our knowledge of the sounds indicated by each letter, he also wants us to be aware of the limits of this kind of representation.

2. Very few sequences of letters are without any lexical associations at all. We've seen that the '-ong' of the train-whistle is linked to the '-ong' of 'song', for example – though it's noticeable that Joyce avoids the usual phonemic clusters linked in English with whistling and related sounds, notably the combination signalled by the letters 'wh' in words such as 'whisper', 'wheeze', 'whoosh', and 'whine'. Like unpronounceability, the avoidance of conventional associations depends on the reader's knowledge of the language's systematic properties.

3. There are conventions attached to the notion of onomatopoeia itself: for instance, that repeated letters indicate prolonged sound. A particular convention operating in the train-whistle – or perhaps it's an extrapolation from other conventions – is that 'nnnng' is an extended 'ng' sound, rather than an extended 'n' sound followed by 'ng' (though there is nothing, finally, to prevent this

[6] See Attridge, *Peculiar Language*, 138–47. All these points are offered in complication of the frequently heard view articulated by Duncan in 'The Modality of the Audible': 'Joyce frequently used onomatopoeic or imitative devices to suggest a wide variety of sounds. . . . Through these imitations Joyce presented the unceasing flux of sound as directly and immediately as possible' (291).

way of pronouncing it). If we read 'deaead' as 'd – e – d', with an extended central monophthong (rather than some complicated diphthong or triphthong) we are aware as we do so that the letter-by-letter spelling suggests something else. Nonlexical onomatopoeia is as much a matter of interpretation as any other use of signs or system of notation.

4. Although we tend to think in terms of sound imitating sound, nonlexical onomatopoeia often has a visual component as well. The string of *e*'s we have been discussing hits the eye as anomalous even before we've attempted to read it, and the idea of prolongation is already present to us. It's perhaps also relevant that the beginnings of the two tones are signalled by letters that poke up above the sequence, and the end by one that drops below it.

5. Interpretation of nonlexical onomatopoeia is highly context-dependent. As I've already noted, the example I began with conveys very little by itself. Given on its own to a group unfamiliar with *Ulysses*, I don't imagine many people would identify it as a train-whistle. The sense we may have of the vividness of an onomatopoeic representation is seldom a result of the precision of its imitation independently of meaning, whether provided by the words themselves (in lexical onomatopoeia) or by the immediate context (in nonlexical onomatopoeia).

6. Appreciation of any type of onomatopoeia also presupposes familiarity with the sound itself. Someone who has not heard, directly or in a recording or simulation, the whistle of a train is not going to bring it into being it on the basis of Joyce's string of letters.

7. The existence of these two preconditions – an identifying context and prior familiarity with the sound – is still not enough to produce exact imitation. The sounds of language are not, after all, widely found outside language. Had Joyce given us Molly's response to the train whistle without the string of letters, we would not have had any difficulty in imagining the sound she hears – but of course the interweaving of train-whistle and song, and later fart, would have been impossible.

8. Finally, the tendency in reading nonlexical onomatopoeia is to produce in the voice an imitation of the sound, rather than a literal reading (literal in the most literal sense) of what is on the page. Its avoidance of recognised lexical items, therefore, acts for many readers as an instruction: 'Make a sound like a train whistle'. Recordings of Molly's monologue invariably do the same,

often with impressive histrionic inventiveness. The danger of this way of treating nonlexical onomatopoeia is that some of Joyce's subtleties in choosing and arranging letters may be lost in a bravura performance.

Nonlexical onomatopoeia, then, might appear to operate as a puncturing of the mediated, conventional surface of the language by something close to the actual occurrence of an extralinguistic sound, but all the factors I've listed combine to make this a rare event. Joyce, far from trying to escape from the complications that prevent direct imitation of sounds in language, exploited them brilliantly, just as he exploited most of the conventions governing the genre of the novel.

Joyce's Noises

Joyce was slow to develop an interest in the possibilities of nonlexical onomatopoeia. There is only one example in the pared-down style of *Dubliners*. (Joe Dillon's '"Ya! yaka, yaka, yaka!"' in 'An Encounter' is simply a war-cry (176)). In 'Ivy Day in the Committee Room' Mr Henchy puts two bottles of stout on the hob, saying 'Did you ever see this little trick?' (291). A few minutes later, one of the corks flies out, and Joyce represents the sound by '*Pok!*,' with uppercase P, italics, and exclamation mark all working to magnify the dramatic effect – yet at the same time, he makes the drama seem absurd by qualifying the sound with the adjective 'apologetic' (a belittling in keeping with the whole story, of course). As an instance of onomatopoeia, this is pretty conventional; Joyce has no interest in playing with the processes of sonic imitation. That this minor sound, and the trick it clinches, should be given such salience in this gathering serves merely to underline the bankruptcy of Dublin party politics at this historical juncture.

 A Portrait of the Artist as a Young Man also makes very limited use of nonlexical onomatopoeia, but there is a new consciousness of some of the complications involved in its employment. Curiously, the most obvious example in the book is a close relative of the uncorking sound in 'Ivy Day', as if Joyce was revisiting this moment with a fuller sense of the device's potential. On the playing fields of Clongowes Wood College, young Stephen hears the sound of balls hitting cricket bats: 'They said: pick, pack, pock, puck: like drops of water in a fountain slowly falling in the brimming bowl' (34). As in the case of Molly's perception of the train-whistle, we get not so much the sound of the cricket bats as the *heard* sound, already transformed in its reception. For Stephen, the bats speak, and it's perhaps *his* visualisation of the words they utter that produces the sequence of recognisable English words 'pick', 'pack', 'pock', and 'puck'. (As we've seen, the stout bottles, by contrast, say *Pok*, the spelling of which immediately signals that we are dealing with the representation of a sound, not a word.) It might be possible to make some claims for the meanings evoked by each apparent word in this series, although there is such an array of unrelated associations that no strong semantic implication emerges, and it seems justifiable to class this as an example of nonlexical onomatopoeia, in which the work is done by the plosives at the beginning and end of each item and the modification in the vowels across the series, rather than the meanings attached to all these strings of letters in an English dictionary.

Familiarity with the sound Stephen hears is undoubtedly helpful here: American readers may have a weaker impression of imitative accuracy in representing the sounds of a cricket match than many readers in Britain or the former British colonies. Stephen's own interest in the sounds he hears and in the words used to represent these sounds – elsewhere he comments on what he takes to be the onomatopoeic quality of 'suck' and 'kiss'[7] – leads him to relate the cricket-bat noises to water drops. It's a somewhat puzzling association: is Stephen thinking of the slight differences made to the sound by the effect of wind or unevenness in the size of the drops? Joyce will later develop this technique of sequencing vowels to represent falling liquid; in the 'Sirens' episode of *Ulysses*, for instance, Bloom recalls the sound of Molly peeing in a chamber pot, with highly self-conscious onomatopoeic play: 'Diddleiddle addleaddle ooddleooddle' (11.984).

It's in *Ulysses* that Joyce gives full rein to his onomatopoeic impulses. The novel is studded with textbook examples of lexical onomatopoeia, and it may seem that these would be the places where his creativity is most evident. After all, the resources of nonlexical onomatopoeia are extremely limited compared to its lexical counterpart, which can draw on all the riches of meaning and emotion embodied in the language. Even though, as I've suggested, lexical associations are often operative in nonlexical onomatopoeia, these can never be anything like as powerful as those of actual words. However, where Joyce is interested in noise – in sounds that suggest neither music nor language – nonlexical onomatopoeia has a distinct advantage. Combinations of letters, and hence of sounds, forbidden by the norms of the language become available to the writer, and new possibilities for mimesis, and for the problematisation of mimesis, offer themselves.

The main characters in *Ulysses* all have an interest in onomatopoeia. In Molly's case, as we've seen, it remains unclear how much of the onomatopoeic exorbitance triggered by the train-whistle can be ascribed to her; but

[7] See Attridge, *Joyce Effects*, chapter 5.

it's certainly the case that her experience as a singer has given her a sensitivity to the sounds of words, and that she relates external sounds to the words of the songs she performs. Stephen, the aspiring poet, also has a professional interest in the sounds of words, an interest made especially vivid in the 'Proteus' episode. He provides a verbal equivalent for his footsteps on Sandymount strand reminiscent of the cricket bats heard by his younger self in *A Portrait*, in this case shifting from lexical to nonlexical onomatopoeia: 'Crush, crack, crick, crick' (3.19).[8] His memory of the post office door shut in his face in Paris prompts a cartoon sequence involving noisy violence: 'Shoot him to bloody bits with a bang shotgun, bits man spattered walls all brass buttons. Bits all khrrrrklak in place clack back' (3.187–90). And the process of composition – the short gothic stanza that begins to form itself in Stephen's mind in this chapter – is depicted by Joyce as having much to do with sounds and their suggestiveness, and rather less to do with the subtleties of sense and syntax. Joyce uses a mixture of lexical and nonlexical onomatopoeia to convey the creative process:

> His lips lipped and mouthed fleshless lips of air: mouth to her moomb. Oomb, allwombing tomb. His mouth moulded issuing breath, unspeeched: ooeeehah: roar of cataractic planets, globed, blazing, roaring wayawayaway-awayaway. (3.401–4)

This sequence doesn't necessarily constitute a recommendation of Stephen's method of poetic creation – the poem that results, which we finally get to read in the 'Aeolus' episode (7.522–5), turns out to be a weak imitation of Douglas Hyde. There can be no doubting Stephen's pleasure in the production of suggestive sound by mouth and breath, however, and it's a pleasure that's not difficult to share. Later, he hears in the incoming tide a 'fourworded wavespeech: seesoo, hrss, rsseeiss, ooos' (3.456–7).[9] Here

---

[8] The *OED* (Third Edition) doesn't recognise 'crick' as an onomatopoeic word, though it does acknowledge the verb 'to crick' as 'to make a thin, sharp sound, *esp.* (of a cricket or other insect) to make a sharp chirping sound' and lists 'crick-crack' as an interjection 'representing a repeated sharp sound'.

[9] Stewart is alert to the lexical hints in this sequence of letters: 'The opening disyllable, if more than sheer onomatopoeia, is an echo of the seesaw motion it locally enacts, a rhythm to which the last syllable offers a chiastic response ("soo" into "ooos") – even as it phonetically calls up its phonemic variant in "ooze". With the incremental iteration "rss rsseeiss", there is not only the hint again of "sea's" but the cadenced overlap of the sea's "*rece* ding", without ever "*ceas* ing" its motion. This is the speech before language waiting in the "signatures" of the phenomenal world' (*Reading Voices*, 253).

Stephen's extravagant attempt to represent different qualities of sound by means of nonlexical onomatopoeia (avoiding traditional water-words) is only a partial success: the reader can imagine a repeated four-fold sequence of watery noises but can hardly read it directly off this sequence of letters. This, I would suggest, is part of the point.

Leopold Bloom, too, is interested in the noises made by nonhuman entities: in the newspaper printing works he listens to the presses:

> Sllt. The nethermost deck of the first machine jogged forward its flyboard with sllt the first batch of quirefolded papers. Sllt. Almost human the way it sllt to call attention. Doing its level best to speak. That door too sllt creaking, asking to be shut. Everything speaks in its own way. Sllt. (*U* 7.174–7)

And in 'Sirens' he meditates on the distinction between sound as music and as noise:

> Sea, wind, leaves, thunder, waters, cows lowing, the cattlemarket, cocks, hens don't crow, snakes hissss. There's music everywhere. Ruttledge's door: ee creaking. No, that's noise. (*U* 11.963–5)

Both these passages refer back to a sentence near the beginning of 'Aeolus': 'The door of Ruttledge's office whispered: ee: cree' (7.50). What we probably took there to be the narrator's nonlexical onomatopoeia turns out to have been Bloom's, who, in both these latter passages, completes the word implied earlier, 'cree' becoming 'creaking'. (Once again, the boundary between lexical and nonlexical is tested.)

But there are far more examples of nonlexical onomatopoeia in *Ulysses* than can be explained by the characters' explicit interest in the device. Among the other noises represented by this means are the following:
Pebbles dislodged by a rat:

> Rtststr! A rattle of pebbles. . . . An obese grey rat toddled along the side of the crypt, moving the pebbles (6.970–4)

Dental floss twanged on teeth:

> He took a reel of dental floss from his waistcoat pocket and, breaking off a piece, twanged it smartly between two and two of his resonant unwashed teeth.
> —Bingbang, bangbang (7.371–4)

A yawn:

> Davy Byrne smiledyawnednodded all in one:
>   —Iiiiichaaaaaaach! (8.969–70)

A rap with a doorknocker:

> One rapped on a door, one tapped with a knock, did he knock Paul de Kock with a loud proud knocker with a cock carracarracarra cock. Cockcock. (11.986–8)

A fire brigade answering a call:

> Pflaap! Pflaap! Blaze on. There she goes. Brigade! . . . Pflaaaap! (14.1569–71)

And several types of bell –
A mass bell:

> And at the same instant perhaps a priest round the corner is elevating it. Dringdring! And two streets off another locking it into a pyx. Dringadring! (3.120–2);

A handbell:

> The lacquey lifted his handbell and shook it:
>   —Barang! (10.649–50);

Bicycle bells:

> THE BELLS

> Haltyaltyaltyall (15.180–1);

Animal cries may demand this type of onomatopoeia, the most famous one being Bloom's cat's escalating cry: 'Mkgnao! . . . Mrkgnao! . . . Mrkrgnao!' (4.16, 25, 32). We also hear a different sound from this cat: 'Gurrhr! she cried, running to lap' (4.38). There is a noisy hen in the 'Cyclops' episode:

> Ga Ga Gara. Klook Klook Klook. Black Liz is our hen. She lays eggs for us. When she lays her egg she is so glad. Gara. Klook Klook Klook. Then comes

good uncle Leo. He puts his hand under black Liz and takes her fresh egg. Ga ga ga ga Gara. Klook Klook Klook. (12. 846–9; see also 15.3710)

In 'Circe' the gulls cry is rendered as 'Kaw kave kankury kake' (15.686) and the horse's neigh as 'Hohohohohohoh! Hohohohome!' (15.4878–9).

The use of playtext format in 'Circe' allows even objects to speak (as the cricket bats had in *A Portrait*), and they sometimes employ nonlexical forms to do so: examples include the already-mentioned bicycle bells (15.181); a trouserbutton: 'Bip!' (15.3441); and a pianola: 'Baraabum!' (15.4107). Especially colourful are the flying kisses:

THE KISSES

(*warbling*) Leo! (*twittering*) Icky licky micky sticky for Leo! (*cooing*) Coo coocoo! Yummyyum, Womwom! (*warbling*) Big comebig! Pirouette! Leopopold! (*twittering*) Leeolee! (*warbling*) O Leo! (15.1272–4)

Human characters also produce nonlexical utterances in the book, though in these cases they can be understood to be playing Joycean games themselves, and I shall not discuss them here.[10] Davy Byrne's yawn is an exception, as an involuntary human sound on a par with the book's farts.[11]

It's true that some of these examples can, like Molly's train-whistle, Stephen's wavesounds, and Bloom's creaking door, be understood as reflecting a mental response to a sound rather than the sound itself. It might be Stephen who converts the imagined sound of a massbell to 'Dringdring! . . . Dringadring', and we can't be sure whether the 'Rtststr!' of the rat's movement among the pebbles comes to us via Bloom's perception or not. (What is curious in the second example is that the particular animal producing the noise, which is unknown to Bloom when he first hears it, is alluded to in the string of letters themselves.) In most cases, however, the noise punctuates the progression of the text without any indication that its conversion into the letters of the English alphabet is the responsibility of a character. The 'sllt' of the printing press might seem to be Bloom's representation at first, but as it interrupts his thoughts at

---

[10] For an insightful account of some of the implications of these human sounds in *Ulysses* (as well as non-human sounds), see Connor, '"Jigajiga"'.

[11] Another sound which might be involuntary is that which is made when Bella Cohen's *sowcunt barks*': 'Fbhracht!' (15.3489–90). As Connor points out, this is an anomaly in 'Circe', as it's the only place where an object or organ is not presented as a character with its own speech prefix ('"Jigajiga"', 136).

unpredictable intervals it gives the strong impression of coming from outside his mental world.

Joyce follows no consistent rules in constructing his nonlexical interruptions, not even self-determined rules. Sometimes the letters he uses suggest the sound they are meant to convey quite directly: 'barang', for instance, is an apt equivalent for the sound of a handbell rung with a double strike: two syllables with the same vowel to represent the two sounds at the same pitch, beginning with a voiced plosive and ending with a nasal as the sound dies away. (It also, of course, suggests the conventional onomatopoeia 'bang' and contains the word 'rang'.) 'Bip', to take another example, is probably as good a representation of a snapping button as more familiar sound-words (such as the word 'snap' itself).

At times Joyce is happy to use a conventional onomatopoeia, such as 'thump' for the printing machines (7.101), 'tink' for the diner's bell in the Ormond hotel (11.286), and the frequently repeated 'jingle' for the sound of Boylan's jaunting-car (11.212) – though the last of these is subject to a number of Joycean variations, including 'jinglejaunty' (11.290), 'jing' (11.457), 'jiggedy jingle' (11.579), and 'jingly' (11.606). Other examples use conventional words as a basis on which to build: the traditional 'miaow' of the cat (which Bloom himself uses in addressing his cat (4.462)) becomes the unpronounceable 'Mkgnao!' when uttered by the cat itself (4.16), with those even more complicated versions following as the animal – presumably – becomes more insistent. There is enough correspondence with the conventional word to allow for a pronunciation not too far removed from the traditional one, but there is also an invitation to the reader to be more inventive in emulating these feline utterances. Similarly, the 'Klook Klook Klook' of the hen (12.846) allows us to hear 'cluck cluck cluck' but defamiliarises it by means of the upper case K's and the double o's. (Did Joyce know the Australian term 'chook' for a domestic fowl?). The same switch of letter, without an impact on pronunciation but with a distinct shift in associations, occurs when the gulls in 'Circe' utter not 'Caw' with a C but 'Kaw' with a K (15.686).

In many examples, however, convincing imitation of a noise seems to be far from Joyce's purpose. Often, as in the case of the train-whistle that punctuates Molly's ruminations, the reader needs a pointer to the sound being represented. Thus, a stage direction specifies the sound made by the nannygoat before it is given to us: '(*bleats*) Megeggaggegg! Nannannanny!' (15.3370). The supposedly onomatopoeic sequences of letters by themselves hardly suggest the noise of bleating, and the comic absurdity of two very different sequences of letters for the same sound (the second clearly derived from the name of the animal) is part-and-parcel of 'Circe''s mad playfulness.

In most cases, Joyce can assume that we know the sound already and that there is no point in trying to match the sounds of the language to it. Rather, he takes advantage of the traditional licence to invent new collocations of letters when imitating sounds to undertake a creative deformation and reformation of the words of the language. Thus, the gong of the tram (perhaps a sound now more familiar to denizens of San Francisco than of Dublin) moves from a conventional onomatopoeic word to a surprising sequence which isn't sonically accurate but is comically suggestive: 'Bang Bang Bla Bak Blud Bugg Bloo' (15.189). (This is another example of the sequence of varied vowels we have seen before, both in A *Portrait* and in *Ulysses*.) There are echoes here, especially in the penultimate 'word', of the 'British Beatitudes' listed in the previous episode: 'Beer, beef, business, bibles, bulldogs, battleships, buggery and bishops' (14.1459–60), though at its climax the gong appears to interpellate our hero, just as the fearsome sandstrewer bears down on him.[12] To take another example, the horse's neigh has been infected by the last word of the previous speaker – both Bloom and Corny Kelleher end speeches with 'home', and as if in sympathy, or perhaps mockery, the horse twice follows them by emitting its 'Hohohohome!' (15.4879, 4899). Similarly, the gulls' 'kankury kake' (15.686) reminds us that Bloom has earlier fed them Banbury cakes; Major Tweedy's 'Salute!' becomes the retriever's 'Ute ute ute ute ute ute ute ute' (15.4752–4); and the bawd's 'coward's blow' mutates into the same retriever's 'Wow wow wow' (15.4763–6).

In some examples, particularly in 'Circe', the supposed onomatopoeia is very hard to interpret, even though we are given clues to the sound. Would we realise that the retriever was 'barking furiously' with its repeated 'ute's if it weren't given as a stage direction? What kind of bicycle bell goes 'Haltyaltyaltyall' (15.181)? Do quoits on a bed really make a sound anything like 'Jigjag. Jigajiga. Jigjag' (15.1138) – or is what is important the association with the set of sounds already linked to Boylan's assignation with Molly (such as 'Jiggedy jingle jaunty jaunty' (11.579))? The sound emitted by the 'Dummymummy' – 'Bbbbblllllblblblobschb!' – is as obscure as the object emitting it, a 'dummy of Bloom, wrapped in a mummy' (15.3380–81). It's hard to imagine exactly what noise the gasjet in the brothel makes when it needs adjusting or when struck by Stephen's ashplant, as these are rendered 'Pooah! Pfuiiiiiiii!' (15.2280) and 'Pwfungg!' (15.4247). And two examples I find particularly puzzling are the twanging dental floss, which sounds far too loud when rendered as 'Bingbang, bangbang' (7.374), and the

---

[12] Connor hears 'something like "Get back you bloody bugger Bloom"' ('"Jigajiga"', 107).

fire-brigade's repeated 'Pflaap' (14.1569, 1577, 1589), which I can't connect with any imagined horn or other warning sound.[13]

In the light of these examples, three points emerge:

First: the significance of the device we are considering goes beyond the local pleasures they provide, for Joyce uses many of these examples to link distant parts of the book, capitalising on their salience and memorability within the dense texture of the writing. We've already seen how Bloom's fart at the close of 'Sirens' receives a response in Molly's fart near the end of 'Penelope', and how the refrain around the words 'jingle', 'jaunty', and 'jig' not only extends through much of 'Sirens' but is recapitulated in 'Circe'. 'Circe', in fact, recycles a number of the earlier examples of nonlexical onomatopoeia, among them Davy Byrne's yawn (15.1697), the fire brigade from 'Oxen of the Sun' (15.1925), the lacquey's bell (15.3096, 4140), and the clucking of Black Liz (15.3710). The complexly patterned architecture of *Ulysses* is thus built not just out of repetitions of and variations upon words and phrases but out of sonic echoes and refrains.

Second: there are, of course, numerous examples in *Ulysses* of the intermediate category that lies between full lexical onomatopoeia and full nonlexical onomatopoeia: the deformation of words to suggest mimetically the sounds or movements to which they refer. Some of our examples lean in this direction, as we've noted. 'Sirens' in particular relies on such effects for much of its aural effectiveness; to give one example, the piano's 'dark chords' are described as 'lugugugubrious' (11.1005). Often it's an already onomatopoeic word that is developed: for example, this cadenza on the word 'clap': '—Bravo! Clapclap. Good man, Simon. Clappyclapclap. Encore! Clapclipclap clap. Sound as a bell. Bravo, Simon! Clapclopclap' (11.756-8).

And third: there are also occasional uses of a perfectly normal word for what seem to be purely onomatopoeic purposes. One example is the moth that flaps against the lightshade in the brothel, going 'Pretty pretty pretty pretty pretty pretty petticoats' (15.2477). Here Joyce seems to be evacuating these words of sense so we can attend to their sounds.

The Sounds of Modernity

If we step back to consider Joyce's use of nonlexical onomatopoeia in *Ulysses* as a whole, can we make any generalisations about its relation to wider cultural developments? It's tempting to argue that these irruptions of noise into the textual stream are a reflection (or should I say echo?) of the

---

[13] Jim Norton, in his excellent reading of the complete *Ulysses*, speaks the repeated 'Pflaap' in a whisper, which I don't think helps.

new sounds of the early twentieth century – the sounds of mechanisation, of mechanised war, of automation, of recording instruments themselves.[14] And it's true that Joyce was remarkably alert to new developments in communications media, the references to television in *Finnegans Wake* being the most familiar instance. There's one striking passage in *Ulysses* in which Joyce perfectly exemplifies a claim made by theorists of the cultural shifts produced by the invention of sound recording. MacDonald, for instance, notes that with the invention of recording techniques 'the separation of voice and body changed our relationship to death' ('Editorial', 2).[15] Bloom is indulging in one of his extended meditations in the 'Hades' episode:

> Have a gramophone in every grave or keep it in the house. After dinner on a Sunday. Put on poor old greatgrandfather. Kraahraark! Hellohellohello amawfullyglad kraark awfullygladaseeagain hellohello amawf krpthsth. Remind you of the voice like the photograph reminds you of the face. (6.962–7)[16]

Joyce not only recognises the changed relation to death of which MacDonald speaks, but through nonlexical onomatopoeia suggests the technological limitations that can turn pathos into absurdity, mourning into laughter. These limitations are explicitly adverted to when 'Circe' returns to the gramophone: 'Whorusaleminyourhighhohhhh . . . (*the disc rasps gratingly against the needle*)' (15.2211–12).

But despite this alertness to technological change (the gramophone had only been in production for around ten years in 1904), I'm not sure a case can be made that Joyce's exploration of the representation of noise through

---

[14] It's often argued that the sounds of new technologies had an impact on modernist writing; see, for instance, Danius, *The Senses of Modernism*; Frattarola, *Modernist Soundscapes*; and Cuddy-Keane, 'Modernist Soundscapes' and 'Virginia Woolf'. The argument is given a British focus in Mansell, *The Age of Noise*. On the importance of sound in modernism, see Kahn, *Noise, Water, Meat*, and Murphet et al., eds, *Sounding Modernism*. Halliday, in *Sonic Modernity*, discusses the variety of attempts to capture modern sound in various art forms. Rice discusses the possible significance of recording technology for *Ulysses* in 'His Master's Voice'.

[15] Sterne, in *The Audible Past*, devotes a chapter to the subject of sound recording techniques and death.

[16] For Danius, commenting on this passage, 'Joyce's concern is . . . with the ways in which experience is derived, the continuous making and unmaking of immediate experience in a historical situation in which technological devices are capable of storing and reproducing sensations, at the same time articulating new perceptual realms' (*The Senses of Modernism*, 183).

nonlexical onomatopoeia is a product of the new sounds he was hearing as he wrote or that he remembered from his childhood and youth. For one thing, there would have been a significant difference between the urban sounds of 1904 and those of 1922, whether in Dublin or Paris (or Trieste or Zurich). Emily Thompson emphasises the change over this period, noting that

> [w]hen Dr. J. H. Girdner catalogued 'The Plague of City Noises' in 1896, almost all the noises he listed were traditional sounds: horse-drawn vehicles, peddlers, musicians, animals, and bells. 'Nearly every kind of city noise', he reported, 'will find its proper place under one of the above headings'.[17]

By 1925 the sound of the city was very different: an article in the *Saturday Review of Literature* mentions 'the motor, the elevated, the steel drill, the subway, the airplane'.[18] When New Yorkers were polled in 1929 about the noises that they were bothered by, only seven per cent mentioned the sounds listed by Girdner in 1896; the ten most disturbing noises were all products of the 'machine age'. If, then, Joyce was being true to his memories of 1904, it's perhaps not surprising that most of the examples I've cited have no particular twentieth-century association: bells of several kinds (and none of them electric); door, doorhandle, and doorknocker; a number of animals; waves, bed quoits, a button. Even the machinery we hear in operation doesn't appear to be recent in origin: the printing press, the steam locomotive, the tram gong, the fire-engine (whatever it is that 'Pflaap' is taken to represent). Although we're very aware in *Ulysses* of the technological achievements of the nineteenth century as they manifest themselves in Dublin in 1904 – trams, telephones, gas-lighting, that gramophone, and so on – Joyce's noises are drawn from a much wider range of sounds. However, it may well be that the invention of recording itself, in separating sounds from their origins, made it easier for Joyce to indulge in his exuberant aural games.

To sum up: the enjoyment and insight offered by nonlexical onomatopoeia in *Ulysses* are not the product of vivid and precise imitation. Nor has this type of onomatopoeia available to it the intensity of signification produced by *lexical* onomatopoeia – when the reader experiences the words of

---

[17] Thompson, *The Soundscape of Modernity*; see, in particular, Thompson's Introduction, 'Sound, Modernity, and History' (1–12) and the first part of chapter 4, 'Noise and Modern Culture, 1900–1933' (115–20).

[18] Thompson is quoting from the *North American Review* of September 1896, 300, and the *Saturday Review of Literature* 2, 24 October 1925, 1 (*The Soundscape of Modernity*, 117). The following sentence is also drawn from this source.

the language with unusual forcefulness. What we have is another instance of Joyce's exploitation of the resources of inorganic form: he makes the inevitable *failure* of his mimetic sallies a productive resource, revealing the language's own entertaining proclivities and challenging a long tradition of aesthetic practice and theorisation based on the idea of imitation.[19] It could be said that nonlexical onomatopoeia has been marginalised in serious literature (it thrives in the comic book genre, of course) because it takes literature's supposed mimetic function *à la lettre* and in so doing exposes its limits. Instead of letting the world break into the text, nonlexical onomatopoeia, in Joyce's hands at least, reminds us, with comic brilliance, that the text produces a world. Many later writers were empowered by this demonstration.

Although the instances of nonlexical onomatopoeia in *Ulysses* amount to only a minuscule proportion of the text, I would argue that they played a crucial part in Joyce's creative development. For it must have been in these playful challenges to the normally binding rules governing the construction of the words of the language that Joyce glimpsed a new way of writing. If letters could be strung together with comic effect, if words could be manipulated into new shapes and made to flow into one another, would it not be possible to write a whole book on this basis? There are many ways in which *Ulysses* can be seen to have prepared the ground for its successor, but we should not overlook the significance of Joyce's pleasure in the noises he could make with nothing more to play with, and play on, than the twenty-six letters of the alphabet.

---

[19] In 'Joyce's Noises', Maud Ellmann, discussing *Ulysses* and *Finngans Wake*, presents a related argument, noting that 'Joyce draws our attention to the noises of language, the acoustic detritus that cannot be assimilated into meaning or intention' (384) and concluding that he 'fractures speech from speaker, song from singer, by drawing our attention to the noises in the voice, the parasitic interference in the utterance' (389).

CHAPTER 4

Joycean Pararealism: How to read 'Circe'

Pararealism

I can still recall the frisson with which I first read the opening stage direction of 'Circe' around half a century ago. This moment was stranger than all the strange moments I'd encountered so far in the book, and had a peculiar intensity and vividness that I couldn't explain but that gripped me immediately. Thinking about it now, I can identify several sources for its peculiar power. There were the completely unexpected, verbless stage directions announcing the scene ('*The Mabbot street entrance of nighttown . . . Rows of grimy houses . . . Rare lamps with rainbow fans . . .*).[1] There was the enticing notion of nighttown itself, a whole town dedicated to the night and its secret doings, made even stranger by Joyce's hyphenless spelling. There was the odd sense that this was and wasn't a theatre – as if a whole street had become a stage on which mysterious actions would be played out. And there was the garish hyperreality of the descriptive method, as though a perfectly normal scene – an evening street with children buying ice creams near tram-tracks – was being relayed through an alien, and distinctly sinister, consciousness that perceived the tram-tracks as skeletons, signals as red and green will-o'-the-wisps, and ice cream as lumps of coal and copper snow. (This was in the days before Hans Walter Gabler, in his 1982 edition, corrected 'coal' to 'coral'.) Although the chapter has lost some of the sheer bewildering potency it had for me then, I still find the intensity of its descriptions – often in contrast to the comic and even banal speech of the episode – unlike anything I've come across elsewhere in literature. This quality has something to do with the chapter's peculiar relation to realism,

---

[1] *Ulysses* 15.1–4. On the initial parenthesis of 'Circe', see Ferrer, 'Circe, Regret, and Repression', 127–8.

immediately evident in the opening sentence. I propose to call this mode *pararealism*,[2] taking advantage of all the adverbial senses of the prefix *para-* listed by the *OED*, 'to one side, aside, amiss, faulty, irregular, disordered, improper, wrong', as well as the notions, also mentioned in the definition, of perversion and simulation.

In invoking this category, I am seeking to resist any attempt to locate the exorbitant farrago of the episode in a *mind*: my argument is that the full power of Joyce's imaginative creation is felt only when we accord to the objects, events, and speeches as much material reality as we can muster. Part of our readerly activity, certainly, is the excavation from the mass of crazy detail a realistic narrative of relatively mundane events – Bloom's pursuit of Stephen into a brothel, the interactions with the prostitutes, Stephen's damaging of the lampshade, their exit and encounter with British soldiers, and so on – but the greatest rewards offered by the chapter come from a full engagement with the encompassing performances on a stage that knows no limitations of scale or physical possibility. It is able to bring into being these impossible events by escaping the constraints of fictional narrative and exploiting the freedom of the play mode, where anything can happen as a stage direction or give voice to an utterance.

Circean Pararealism: An Example

Let us take as an example the relatively restrained passage in which Bloom's grandfather, Lipoti Virag, makes his appearance, beginning with an exchange between the prostitute Zoe and the medical student Lynch:

ZOE

(*Lynch with his poker lifts boldly a side of her slip. Bare from her garters up her flesh appears under the sapphire a nixie's green. She puffs calmly at her cigarette.*) Can you see the beautyspot of my behind?

LYNCH

I'm not looking.

ZOE

(*makes sheep's eyes*) No? You wouldn't do a less thing. Would you suck a lemon?

(*Squinting in mock shame she glances with sidelong meaning at Bloom, then twists round towards him, pulling her slip free of the poker. Blue fluid again flows over her*

---

[2] Although the term has been used occasionally in print, it has not (yet) been consecrated by the *Oxford English Dictionary*.

flesh. Bloom stands, smiling desirously, twirling his thumbs. Kitty Ricketts licks her middle finger with her spittle and, gazing in the mirror, smooths both eyebrows.)
(15.2287–2304)

How does the reader handle a passage like this? We're aware of two believable speakers, the prostitute Zoe and Stephen's companion Lynch, who exchange highly naturalistic sexual innuendo – all the more naturalistic for our not understanding exactly what's implied. (Who knows precisely what is meant by the expression 'Would you suck a lemon?' conjured up in early 20th century Dublin, or perhaps imported from Yorkshire, Zoe's claimed origin?[3]) At the same time, these speeches are more than throwaway comments: they are presented to us as playtext, which is usually designed to be interpreted again and again by different actors. The words gain a sense of permanence or idealisation which is in tension with their informality.

The stage directions also function quite normally at first. The early part of the passage is entirely compatible with traditional writing for the stage. '(*She puffs calmly at her cigarette*)' could come from a thousand plays before and after 1922, and although '(*makes sheep's eyes*)' is metaphorical, it conveys admirably Zoe's pretence at innocence – which is, of course, her way of mocking Lynch's similar pretence at innocence. Some of these early stage directions, it's true, have a literary flair that goes beyond workmanlike advice to the actor: as in George Bernard Shaw's plays, we are clearly meant to enjoy reading them on the page.[4] There is, for instance, the slightly rearranged word-order of the first sentence of the extract, as Lynch rearranges Zoe's clothing, or the very full description of the moment at which she shifts her attention from Lynch to Bloom.

But something different happens when Zoe's naked flesh is described, an extension of realism that produces an intensity similar to that of the chapter's opening stage direction: '*Bare from her garters up her flesh appears under the sapphire a nixie's green.*' What is presumably a normal effect of light and colour – Zoe's slip has already been described as sapphire, and under

---

[3] Dent comments, 'Perhaps nothing colloquial is involved', and cites earlier examples which are either literal or relate to the refreshment taken by a boxer (*Colloquial Language*, 211). Gifford provides a cross-reference to the use earlier in the chapter of the phrase 'The answer is a lemon' (*'Ulysses' Annotated*, 492). Neither of these is any help in understanding Zoe's remark. The expression of dismissal, 'go suck a lemon', doesn't seem relevant either.

[4] The chapter thus presents a strong contrast with Joyce's only surviving play, *Exiles*, whose stage-directions are precise and practical, in the mode of Ibsen rather than that of Shaw.

the gaslight it's casting a greenish shadow on her body – is portrayed as if it were a lurid transformation of the human form, an effect enhanced by the reference to a nixie, or water sprite. We seem to have moved from the world of the theatre to the world of Technicolor film. When Lynch allows the slip to fall to its former place, the description is again transformative, as the satin (if that's what it is) becomes liquid, and this time without that explanatory and distancing 'appears': '*Blue fluid again flows over her flesh.*' Like the will-'o-the-wisps and snow in the opening stage direction, this is a reader-trap: for a moment we take it literally, and the effect is weirdly beautiful (enhanced by that *bl-fl-fl-fl* sequence). But the literal reading is not a *mistake* that we leave behind; it's a necessary stage on the way to understanding the metaphor – and one we go through each time we read the passage.

This over-vivid stage direction is followed by something more conventional. First we have Bloom, '*smiling desirously*' – a somewhat archaic version of 'desiringly' – and '*twirling his thumbs*', as he affects a nonchalance while in fact giving away his sexual excitement. Then we see Kitty Ricketts grooming herself. The eroticism of her action is heightened by the excessive precision of the description: not '*licks a finger and, gazing in the mirror, smooths her eyebrows*' but '*licks her* **middle** *finger* [in doing so producing a sexually suggestive gesture] **with her spittle** [a completely unnecessary phrase as far as literal description is concerned] *and, gazing in the mirror, smooths* **both** [again unnecessary, but suggesting the deliberateness of the action] *her eyebrows.*'

It's after this that the stage direction moves us even more fully into the world of the parareal – and it does so without the least hint in tone, syntax, or representation on the page that something strange is happening. An important aspect of 'Circe''s play with realism is the fact that the literary foundation on which the episode rests is one of the most traditional and secure in all of *Ulysses*. From start to finish, we know, thanks to clear typographical distinctions (whatever edition we're using) whether we are reading a stage direction, the name of a speaker, or a speech. All the surprises, and all the comedy, lie in the uses to which this conventional apparatus is put – and they are all the more surprising, and funny, because the framework remains completely unaffected by the bizarre goings-on it's being deployed to articulate. The effect is something like the contrast between Buster Keaton's poker face and the extraordinary trouble he is constantly getting himself into. Thus we read the following just as if we were reading further accounts of Zoe's sexual teasing or Bloom's uncomfortable arousal, without even a paragraph break to signal that we're in a different representational mode:

Lipoti Virag, basilicogrammate, chutes rapidly down through the chimneyflue and struts two steps to the left on gawky pink stilts. He is sausaged into several overcoats and wears a brown macintosh under which he holds a roll of parchment. In his left eye flashes the monocle of Cashel Boyle O'Connor Fitzmaurice Tisdall Farrell. On his head is perched an Egyptian pshent. Two quills project over his ears. (15.2304–6).

Here is the kind of challenge to the reader that occurs on every page of 'Circe', a challenge no less marked after the passage of a century since its first appearance. How is the reader to deal with it?

One strategy – the one that new readers are likely to begin by attempting – is to do everything possible to sustain the fiction that the chapter is a realistic account of events in a part of Dublin during the night of June 16, 1904. To achieve this, we have to ignore the continuity of typography and tone that I've just mentioned and assume that from one sentence to the next the text undergoes a radical shift from a realistic descriptive mode to an account of someone's imaginary or hallucinatory visions – presumably Bloom's. As a recuperative strategy, it's a poor one: there's no reason to suppose that Bloom has been imbibing a hallucinogen or that he suffers from an occasionally surfacing psychotic condition. He might, perhaps, find his sexual excitement leading him to think of his grandfather – if we can assume that Virag's fixation on the female anatomy has some basis in the Bloomian psyche – but the visual forms we are presented with can hardly be explained in this way. A weaker (and therefore more useful) form of this approach is that proposed by Hugh Kenner, who describes the logic of Joyce's method as the placing of 'all figures, all analogies, all ruminations on the plane of the visible and audible' ('Circe', 346). However, if the chapter were to truly follow this logic, every detail would have to be traceable back to something one of the characters – in the 'real' world – is doing, thinking, or feeling. This seems unlikely, and puts a huge interpretative burden on the reader instead of allowing them to enjoy the free-wheeling circus of 'Circe' as it plays out before them.

A more successful mode of reading is at first sight the most naïve one: simply to accept what typography and tone tell us, that in just the same way as Zoe pulls her slip free or Kitty Ricketts smooths her eyebrows, Lipoti Virag slides out of the chimney flue. If this is a stage set – in a remarkably well-equipped theatre in which there seems to be no limit to the special effects possible, and one which, as has often been pointed out, has much in common with the cinema – there's no reason to suppose that Kitty Ricketts and Lipoti Virag possess different attributes of solidity and visibility as far as the imaginary audience is concerned. What *is* different is that the controlling mechanism that kept the characters and the actions within the conventional realms of realism is now in abeyance, and the much freer operations of pararealism are at work. So although Virag is described by means of the same sliding between factual and metaphorical that we have already witnessed, it's now less easy to know where the borderline between these two domains lies. When he *'struts two steps to the left on gawky pink stilts'* and in our mind's eye we see him moving awkwardly on bird's legs, or perhaps on actual stilts, do we then shift – as we do with the 'blue fluid' of Zoe's slip – to a different, more normal, plane of reality (if not the reality of realism) and see a stiff-legged old man? When we read at the end of the stage direction that *'Two quills project over his ears'*, do we see him as a secretary bird or as a secretary: are these quills feathers or pens? The image shifts uncertainly between man and bird, and this oscillation is part of its effectiveness.[5] Descriptions of Virag continue to slide between human and animal throughout his stay on the Circean stage.

When the old man speaks, his utterances are represented in the same way as everyone else's: there's nothing on the page to suggest that we're invited to hear a phantasmal or phantasmagoric voice. (The stage direction at this point is, for once, restrained: '(*he coughs thoughtfully, drily*)' (15.2312–13).) And again, rather than imagine it as a voice heard by Bloom alone, thanks to inebriation or exhaustion or a sudden emergence of repressed materials, an appreciation of the episode's pararealistic mode makes it possible to treat it as a voice like all the others. After all, Virag's hilarious verbal pedantry combined with lubricious fascination with female bodies is not something we can imagine Bloom inventing, in any part of his mind: 'Promiscuous nakedness is much in evidence hereabouts, eh? Inadvertently her backview revealed the fact that she is not wearing those rather intimate garments of which you are a particular devotee' (15.2313–16). And it's noteworthy that Bloom himself responds quite calmly to this apparition of his long-dead grandfather; he doesn't seem to find it particularly unusual that Bella Cohen's brothel is visited, via the chimney, by his bizarrely apparelled ancestor, offering only a hesitant qualification after the latter's opening speech: 'Granpapachi. But. . . .' (15.2318).

If the reader accepts that everything that is said to happen *does* happen, that everything presented as speech is actually spoken, do we have to assume

---

[5] There are other challenges we probably have to forgo when first reading the passage, and later explore by means of annotations, dictionaries or (a great aid in reading Joyce) Google. *Basilicogrammate* is a word that turns up in French texts on ancient Egypt, meaning 'royal scribe' – hence the parchment and the quills – while the *pshent* that is perched on his head is the tall peaked bicoloured crown visible in ancient Egyptian images. Even without this information, it's clear that Virag combines modern western attributes – overcoats, a macintosh, a monocle – with something much more exotic (though not, I would suggest, Hungarian).

no distinction can be drawn between the events that would, as Kenner helpfully puts it, be recorded by a cine-camera present on the scene and those that would not? Certainly not: realism and pararealism may shade into one another, but they are not the same thing. It's always a surprise when the former gives way to the latter, as when Virag makes his sudden appearance from the chimneyflue or when Bloom is set upon by a rampant mob. And pararealism thrives on giving visual and vocal reality, albeit distorted and exaggerated, to usually hidden impulses and inclinations. But *for the space of the chapter, within its theatricalised world,* both are equally present to us. Imagine a film version in which the realistic stretches were separated out and shown in black-and-white, while the pararealistic episodes were in colour (or the other way round): this sharp distinction would be a considerable falsification of the episode, insisting on an absolute difference where there is in fact constant slippage and mutual interference. In a film adaptation, Zoe's sapphire slip should be in the same vivid colour as Virag's Egyptian crown. The process of separating out realism and pararealism, and detecting motivation for the events and characters of the latter, is a secondary and always imperfect and incomplete one. The most important transformation effected by Circean magic is that of the reader: into someone who will accept, on the same plane and with the same kind of attention, a prostitute smoothing her eyebrows and a man on pink stilts emerging from the chimneyflue.

The freedom exhibited in 'Circe' is also a matter of linguistic freedom: all the dictates of good style give way before the no-holds-barred verbal exuberance of the text, much of which replays earlier moments and phrasings of the book in the Circean distorting mirror. When the exorbitance of the imagery makes it impossible to visualise what is going on, the verbal fireworks may still be enjoyed. Take the stage direction that follows the dance in the brothel, for instance:

(*Bang fresh barang bang of lacquey's bell, horse, nag, steer, piglings, Conmee on Christass, lame crutch and leg sailor in cockboat armfolded ropepulling hitching stamp hornpipe through and through. Baraabum! On nags hogs bellhorses Gadarene swine Corny in coffin steel shark stone onehandled Nelson two trickies Frauenzimmer plumstained from pram falling bawling. Gum he's a champion. Fuseblue peer from barrel rev. evensong Love on hackney jaunt Blazes blind coddoubled bicyclers Dilly with snowcake no fancy clothes. Then in last switchback lumbering up and down bump mashtub sort of viceroy and reine relish for tublumber bumpshire rose. Baraabum!*) (15.4140–50)

It's hard to keep track of the figures who appear here, including a number of personages encountered in previous episodes – the auction house lacquey,

Father Conmee, the onelegged sailor, Corny Kelleher, the two Dublin vestals, the two women on Sandymount Strand, and several more. (We might note that no single character in the novel has seen all of these figures, so they could not appear in any individual's burst of mental delirium.) But the verbal texture continues to entertain even though the pararealism staggers. The lyrics of 'My Girl's a Yorkshire Girl', which the pianola is playing, weave through the text, ending in the kind of comic rhythmic parallel that will become a feature of *Finnegans Wake*, as '. . . sort of a Yorkshire relish for my little Yorkshire Rose' becomes '. . . *sort of viceroy and reine relish for tublumber bumpshire rose*'. And the energy of the words' onward rush contributes to the sense of a gathering climax as the dance becomes ever more frenzied.

May Goulding's Ghost

One sequence in 'Circe' complicates my claim that the text swings easily between realism and pararealism. It occurs immediately after the stage direction just quoted.

> (*The couples fall aside. Stephen whirls giddily. Room whirls back. Eyes closed he totters. Red rails fly spacewards. Stars all around suns turn roundabout. Bright midges dance on walls. He stops dead.*)

STEPHEN

Ho!

> (*Stephen's mother, emaciated, rises stark through the floor, in leper grey with a wreath of faded orangeblossoms and a torn bridal veil, her face worn and noseless, green with gravemould. Her hair is scant and lank. She fixes her bluecircled hollow eyesockets on Stephen and opens her toothless mouth uttering a silent word. A choir of virgins and confessors sing voicelessly.*)

THE CHOIR

Liliata rutilantium te confessorum . . .
Iubilantium te virginum . . .

(15.4151–65)

There is no textual indication that the entrance of Stephen's mother is any different from Virag's emergence from the chimney or several other unexpected appearances in the episode; the 'Stephen' named here could be as much an inhabitant of the parareal as the one in the earlier stage direction, '*His Eminence Simon Stephen Cardinal Dedalus, Primate of all Ireland, appears in the doorway, dressed in red soutane, sandals and socks'* (15.2654–6). Yet almost all of Stephen's actions and utterances so far in the episode have taken place in the mode of realism, and the reader is very likely to take his 'Ho!' as an actual response to something he has really seen, albeit in his mind's eye – the ghost of his mother. The intensely emotional exchange that follows between them (with additional commentary from a parareal Buck Mulligan *'in particoloured jester's dress of puce and yellow and clown's cap with curling bell'* (4166–7)) is certainly not real, in the sense that no-one else appears to hear it; but when Florry points to Stephen with, 'Look! He's white', our conclusion must be that the parareal has fused with hallucination – not necessarily as described (the choir seems excessive) but in some form at least. And it has real effects: not just Stephen's pallor, but his frantic attack on the chandelier and rapid exit. When Bloom hurries after him, the parareal returns: our hero becomes a fox pursued by a troop of several dozen characters from earlier in the book.

What emerges clearly from this passage is that the parareal events are not random, though they certainly develop a momentum that leads them far from any close association with the events going on in Bella Cohen's house. That Virag should appear when Bloom finds himself in a brothel is not unconnected with the latter's sense of familial morality; that Mulligan should arise from nowhere to mock Stephen for his behaviour towards his mother is entirely appropriate to the scene, though we have no reason to suppose Stephen is thinking of Mulligan at this moment. The connections between realistic and pararealistic events are made by the text, not by the characters; and all we can say about Stephen's actions in the brothel is that they are prompted by a sudden powerful consciousness of the sinfulness of his behaviour towards his mother. The vivid ghost of May Goulding, with her impassioned warning to Stephen of God's wrath (which the machinery of pararealism turns into *'A green crab with malignant red eyes'* (15.4220), exists on the same plane as Lipoti Virag on pink stilts.

After Joycean Pararealism

The extraordinary freedom of the technique of Circean pararealism allowed Joyce to proliferate visual extravaganza and verbal exorbitance with abandon, and laid the foundations for later creative spirits to romp from the believable to the unbelievable, each as vivid as the other, in film as well as in fiction.[6] The effect is not always comic, however; it's worth remembering

---

[6] An undisguised pastiche of 'Circe', with pararealistic touches, occurs in the Trafalgar Square scene of Orwell's *A Clergyman's Daughter*. See Hoberman, 'The Nightmare of History'.

that before Joyce had begun writing *Ulysses* a young writer in Prague was beginning a short story with the memorable sentence, 'When Gregor Samsa woke one morning from troubled dreams he found himself transformed in his bed into a monstrous insect'. The deadpan style with which Kafka reports this horrific experience, as if it were on a par with the discovery of a fleabite, is one of the hallmarks of pararealism. In later chapters we shall encounter versions of it in the writing of Caryl Churchill (where it also appears in stage directions) and Kevin Barry. When, in Coetzee's *Slow Man*, Paul Rayment opens his door to find, as real as any other character in the fiction, the author responsible for his existence, something like pararealism is at work.

Pararealism is ancestor of magic, or magical, realism, another genre in which the impossible happens with the same unremarked character as the possible, and no sharp line could be drawn between the two modes. There could be an argument for enlisting Toni Morrison's *Beloved*, Salman Rushdie's *Midnight's Children*, Zakes Mda's *Ways of Dying*, Etienne van Heerden's *The Long Silence of Mario Salviati*, and André Brink's *Imaginings of Sand* in either category, and perhaps the most accurate description would be that they partake of both. Magic realism involves the creation of an alternative world in which the rules governing the possible are different from those that govern the world we are familiar with, but it's when the interpenetration of the possible and the impossible follows no discernible rule, when literally anything can happen and still be depicted with the tools of conventional realism, that we have moved into the territory of the parareal. Gregor's insect, Stephen's grandfather, Rayment's author appear, impossibly, out of nowhere; but the world they arrive in is our own.

CHAPTER 5

After *Finnegans Wake*: Caryl Churchill's *The Skriker*

In the Wake of the *Wake*

Finnegans Wake, however great an achievement in itself, has acquired the reputation of a literary dead-end, a work without successors. In large part, as I suggested in the Introduction, this reputation is justified, at least when we look at what has been written in the eighty-odd years since its publication. This is not to say that the *Wake* has been without influence: the course of literature in many languages would have been quite different if it had never been written. In 1977 David Hayman and Elliott Anderson collected a number of specimens of, and commentaries on, literary writing that, in their view, bore the imprint of Joyce's last book; their work appeared as a special issue of *Tri-Quarterly* and was later published as a volume titled *In the Wake of the 'Wake'*.[1] Among the authors they selected were Christine Brooke-Rose, Raymond Federman, Gilbert Sorrentino, and John Cage (writing in English), Maurice Roche, Philippe Sollers, and Hélène Cixous (originally writing in French), Arno Schmidt (originally writing in German), and Samuel Beckett (writing in French and English).

Being influenced by a predecessor is not the same as building upon his or her work, however. The writers in Hayman and Anderson's collection may use one or more of the techniques we associate with *Finnegans Wake*, and they may feel emboldened in their literary experimentation by Joyce's example, but I don't think any of them could be said to have profitably exploited or extended the particular stylistic innovations of the *Wake*. One of the remarkable features of Joyce's final style is that its dense linguistic deformations and reformations don't result in a text that works only for the

---

[1] Paul K. Saint-Amour reports positively on the teaching of the *Wake* and texts that could be seen as influenced by it ('Late Joyce').

eye; as thousands of readers have testified, it's a style that calls out for, and responds wonderfully to, vocal performance. A common characteristic of the authors brought together by Hayman and Anderson, however, is their exploitation of the *visual* dimension of the printed page, a spatial exuberance which frequently makes reading aloud difficult and perhaps unnecessary.[2] For example, the work most commonly cited as a successor to *Finnegans Wake*, Arno Schmidt's magnum opus *Zettels Traum* (1970), although it's as obsessively concerned with multilingual punning as Joyce's book, can't be performed as an adventure of the human voice in the way Joyce's can; it's emphatically a work that lives on the page, deriving from the 'Nightlessons' episode of the *Wake* (2.ii) its use of columns and notes but employing type-script, handwriting, erasures, corrections, and variations in spacing in ways that can't be represented aloud. Brooke-Rose and Roche are other examples of writers in the *Tri-Quarterly* collection who play with the visual more than the aural medium (in the former's *Thru* (1975) and the latter's 'Cantata funè-bre' from *Circus* (1972)), and the spatial imperative remains strong in much later anti-conventional fiction such as the large-scale novels *The Tunnel* by William Gass (1995) and *House of Leaves* by Mark Z. Danielewski (2000), novels whose debt is finally much more to *Ulysses* than to *Finnegans Wake*.[3] Authors such as these can be said to be writing in the wake not only of Joyce but also of Pound, Mallarmé, Sterne, and ultimately of the Greek 'figure-poems' ascribed to Simias of Rhodes, a poet of the early third century BC.[4]

An alternative post-Joycean style that eschews visual delights and allows the voice, or imagined voice, to dominate is the use of unpunctuated, run-on language, exemplified in the Hayman and Anderson collection by Sollers and Federman. Here are a few lines from Carl Lovitt's translation of part of Sollers' *Paradis*:

> that's it sunder flounder your death coma grossly inverted placenta cancer
> aureola from where i sit i see them drip drop by drop bazooka siphoned

---

[2] See Chapter 11 for a discussion of what I there term 'ergodic' fiction, in which the visual dimension plays an important part.

[3] With one exception, the novels I discuss in Chapters 10, 11, and 12, Eleanor Catton's *The Luminaries*, Ali Smith's *How to Be Both*, Mike McCormack's *Solar Bones*, and Kevin Barry's *Beatlebone*, rely more on visual than on aural innova-tion. Eimear McBride's *A Girl is a Half-formed Thing*, though it uses a few Wakean verbal distortions, takes syntax as its main target; it is, however, highly suited to the spoken voice, as McBride's own recording reveals.

[4] See Hollander, *Vision and Resonance*, chapter 12, 'The Poem in the Eye' (245–306) for a valuable discussion of this tradition as it developed in poetry. I touch on the tradition of visual poems in *The Experience of Poetry*, 73, 127–8.

typhoon i'm back on the track bascule mask crackled stares from forebears' portraits galleries pupils starred waxed flash foundation of aspiration trumpet pump passing on the quotient tidbit idiot famishing flashflood chromos of men . . . (Hayman and Anderson, *In the Wake of the 'Wake'*, 101)

This is quite unlike the *Wake*, both in its respect for the lexical integrity of the language and in its disrespect for syntax, punctuation, and capitalisation. The model is clearly the 'Penelope' episode of *Ulysses*, but the greater liberties taken with syntax produce a text much less suited to oral performance.

Since the publication of *The Wake of the 'Wake'* in 1977, Joyce's exhilarating freedom with language (and with languages), his blending of popular and high culture, and his comic exorbitance has continued to encourage writers hoping to break new ground in fictional technique. Perhaps the best-known novel that consistently uses a distorted form of the English language is Russell Hoban's *Riddley Walker* (1980), set in the far distant future when scattered communities of humans struggle to make sense of the broken remains of the culture destroyed in a nuclear cataclysm. In his valuable study of the novel's language in relation to quantum physics, Jeffrey Porter observes that '[w]ith the exception of *Finnegans Wake*, no work has gone so far as *Riddley Walker* toward shaping an idea of quantum language' ('"Three quarks for Muster Mark"', 450–1). Hoban's 'postatomic wordplay' (458), he argues, reflects a world that 'has been poisoned by radioactive decay', in which 'words as well as people are no longer what they once were' (456). Here's an example of Walker's characteristic style:

> What with 1 thing and a nother I dint qwite feal like sleaping in my shelter that nite. Lorna had the same fealing so we slyd up on top of the gate house when the lookouts wernt looking. If the skyd ben clear it wudve ben the failing moon littling tords the las ¼ but it wer cloudit over solid. Looking at the candls and the nite fires in the divvy roof and littl glimmers here and there from candls in the shelters. Lissening to the crowd shutting down for the nite. Coffing and farting and belching and peeing 1 place and a nother. (70)

It will be immediately evident that for the most part the strangeness of Riddley's language has nothing in common with Wakean linguistic inventiveness: it's purely a matter of spelling errors, such as a child might make. The use of numbers for words is also an indicator that we are reading a written document, not listening to a speaker. There are, however, sporadic examples of something more creative at work: familiar words are sometimes taken apart and relexicalised, rather like the operation of folk etymology. For example, 'accelerating' becomes 'axel rating', 'trial and error' becomes 'tryl narrer', and 'prime minister' becomes 'pry mincer'. Without mentioning *Finnegans Wake* (or Lewis Carroll), Hoban introduces his Glossary of Riddleyspeak with the comment, 'As much as possible I tried for more than one meaning in the words' (233). One of the examples given is 'revver newit', which combines 'revenue' with the idea of the 'tax engine' being revved up to impose a new tax (234). However, such portmanteaus are only sporadic in *Riddley Walker*, not a continuous feature of the style as they are in the *Wake*.

Brooke-Rose's novel *Amalgamemnon* (1984) uses a richly allusive interior monologue that owes much to Joyce, including occasional puns and portmanteaus; examples include 'from the daytaunt to the daybuckle of the third world war' (19), 'may the beast man wane' (30), 'may the boast man whine' (52), and 'the unclear missiles of affreux dizzy acts' (102). The title itself is, of course, a Joycean portmanteau. For the most part, however, the words appear in their standard form, even though the sentences they form are often far from normal as the fraught narrator pours out Cassandra-like predictions that intermingle the characters of Ancient Greek myth with the contemporary purveyors of technological marvels.

One of the four narrators of Iain Banks's *Feersum Enjin* (1994), Bascule the Teller, uses a style that, like Riddley's, reproduces a way of speaking by means of phonetic spelling, though it takes the use of symbols for words – 'in2' for 'into', '@oll' for 'at all' – even further than Hoban's character. In this passage, Bascule is feeding his pet ant morsels of bread, during a visit to his friend Mr Zolipara:

> Ergates is playin wif her food; sheez moldin thi bredy-bits in2 funny shapes wif her mouf-parts & front legz & not botherin 2 eat it @ oll no moar. Rite now sheez makin a tiny bust ov Mr Zoliparia & I wundir if he can c her doin that or if heez so ded agenst inplants & inproovments in jeneril that he haz ordniry old-tipe Is & cant zoom in on details like I can.
>
> Do u think iss a gude likeniss, Bascule? she asks me.
>
> Mr Zoliparia is lukin thotful & starin in2 space, or in2 thi atmisfear nway; buncha birdz circlin way in thi distinz over a bartizan – maybi heez lookin @ them. (38)

Bascule himself reveals that he is writing this account of his adventures, and he's well aware of the deficiencies in his orthography: 'I got this weerd wirin in mi brane so I cant spel rite, juss ½ 2 do evrythin foneticly' (102). Although at first sight this looks like language as inventively reimagined as the *Wake*'s, it turns out to be relatively straightforward. Just occasionally a potential Joycean play with meaning emerges ('resourceful' becomes 'race-horseful' (35); 'wretch' becomes 'retch' (40); and 'atmosfear' in the extract above could hint at danger), but this happens so rarely that it feels like coincidence. If anything, Banks has done everything he can to avoid Bas-cule's misspellings becoming portmanteaus. (There are a few *Ulysses*-like nonlexical onomatopoeias, though: 'Gididibididibididigididigigigibididigibibibi' (105), 'Skreek! Skrawk! Awrk!' (178), 'Gidibidi-urp!' (208), 'blurbi-lurbilurbil' (243).)

Paul Kingsnorth also uses phonetic representations of spoken language in his 2014 novel *The Wake*, but in this case infiltrated by the Old English originals of modern English words, distorted by the more limited alphabet of Old English (though without making use of the distinctive Old English characters), and further defamiliarised by the absence of upper-case letters and sparse punctuation:

> it was that night i had the first sight of him yes i see it now that night when all was first tacan from me though i did not cnaw then how micel mor wolde be lost. ah for micel time it had been cuman sum thing had been locan for me sum thing had been growan had been callan from the deorcness and when i locs baec now all is clere. (69)

Here there is no wordplay; in spite of the appearance of the text (and the allusion in the work's title), the sentences are relatively uncomplicated, and once the oddities of the archaising spelling become familiar it's not difficult to read. In all these examples, the influence of 'Penelope' is as strong as, or stronger than, that of *Finnegans Wake*: Joyce led the way in using numerals instead of words (suggesting a representation of writing as well as of thought) as in the first and third of these examples, and eschewing upper case letters and punctuation as in the fourth.[5]

One of the extraordinary features of *Finnegans Wake* is its productive combination of an aurally inviting style, in which rhythm and syntactic organisation play an important role, and the characteristic of the work that caused (and still causes) the most immediate, but also probably the most lasting, difficulty for its readers: its systematic use of lexical distortion. Deformation of syntax, dismantling of the traditional plot, fusion of distinct times and places, fragmentation and transformation of characters:

---

[5] On the writtenness of the 'Penelope' episode see Attridge, 'Molly's Flow', chapter 8 of *Joyce Effects*. The written character of Hoban's and Banks's texts is suggested by the many nonstandard spellings that reflect standard pronunciations, such as 'qwite' 'feal' 'sleaping' 'nite'; and 'sheez', 'bredy', 'legz', 'ov'.

these were not entirely new when 'Work in Progress' began to appear, and ways could be found of dealing with them. But to modify the very words themselves, so that they seemed to belong to no known language: this was challenge of a different sort.[6] At the same time, it was this portmanteau technique which provided the special comedy of *Finnegans Wake*, making it, for those readers who took to it, one of the funniest, as well as one of the linguistically richest, books ever written.

It's this combination that has proved resistant to further development. Though many of the writers mentioned above use puns and portmanteaus, the effect they produce is very different from that produced by Wakean language: less immediate, less comic, less sheer exuberant fun. The effort required to get to grips with a page of Brooke-Rose or Sollers can seem too great for the rewards it has to offer, the struggle with the language seldom lifting it off the page. Although many of those who have encountered the *Wake* would say the same about Joyce's baffling book, its language can work very directly on the reader who is not crippled by preconceptions about its difficulty and who takes the trouble to perform the text aloud (or who hears it read by a skilled performer). It's of course possible to go on picking meanings out of a passage of the *Wake* till the cows come home, but it's also possible to get enough of its sense (or rather senses) on a first reading or hearing to produce a certain degree of comprehension and a considerable charge of pleasure. Further study increases both comprehension and pleasure, filling in many of the gaps left on the first encounter; but it's that initial experience of meanings tumbling out in rich profusion, sometimes in coherent sequences, sometimes in baffling disjunction, and always carried forward by the rhythms and intonations of the spoken language, that marks the *Wake*'s uniqueness, and its unique appeal. None of its successors has offered the reader or hearer this experience – with one exception.

The Language of the Skriker

Caryl Churchill's play, *The Skriker*, was first performed in London (to great acclaim) in 1994, and was published in the same year. In 1996 it had a short run at the Public Theater in New York, again to critical praise, where I was lucky enough to see it. There have been numerous performances since then. It's a work that explodes powerfully on stage in the hands of skilled performers, but one that, for a full appreciation, also needs to be read on the page. Thinking of it as a descendant of *Finnegans Wake* may mean

---

[6] See Attridge, *Peculiar Language*, chapter 7, 'Unpacking the Portmanteau; or, Who's Afraid of *Finnegans Wake*?'

overlooking its dramatic intensity, but it does draw attention to its remarkable linguistic creativity. (Joyce's own surviving play, *Exiles*, is linguistically conservative, modelled as it is on Ibsen's drama.)

The play focuses on the relationship between a shape-changing fairy, the Skriker (taken from the folklore of Northern England), and two young women struggling to get along in a harsh late twentieth-century urban setting. Moving between the human world and the underworld, the play shows the fairies who inhabit the latter engaged in a constant struggle to tempt humans into their domain, since it's through the imbibing of human blood that they prolong their lives. But the gradual degradation of the earth's environment by human exploitation is producing problems for both worlds, and the Skriker views her task with frustration and despair.[7] For anyone who knows the opening of the 'Circe' episode of *Ulysses* (see Chapter 4 above), reading the opening of the play on the page is likely to strike a chord:

> *Underworld.*
> **Johnny Squarefoot**, *a giant riding on a piglike man, throwing stones. He goes off.*
> *The* **Skriker**, *a shapeshifter and death portent, ancient and damaged.*

A bizarre world that is and isn't our own – the world of pararealism – is brought before us in the staid tones of italicised stage directions.

However, it's in the Skriker's own language that Churchill crystallises the concerns of the play while at the same time giving her character an unworldly distinctiveness and an eerie power. The verbal performance begins, like *Finnegans Wake*, without concessions: the first speech we get is a long monologue from the Skriker (four-and-a-half pages in the printed text), demanding of the audience that they undergo a rapid learning process in order to make some sense of the strange language. Here are the opening sentences:

> Heard her boast beast a roast beef eater, daughter could spin span spick and spun the lowest form of wheat straw into gold, raw into roar, golden lion and lyonesse under the sea, dungeonesse under the castle for bad mad sad adders and takers away. Never marry a king size well beloved. Chop chip pan

---

[7] A number of critics have commented on Churchill's emphasis on the damaging effects of advanced technology and human disregard of the environment under global capitalism; see, for instance, Diamond, 'Caryl Churchill'; Rabillard, 'On Caryl Churchill's Ecological Drama'; and Vigouroux-Frey, who links *The Skriker* with Churchill's radio play about atmospheric pollution, *Not Not Not Not Not Enough Oxygen* ('Pour des mythologies profanées', 182).

chap finger chirrup chirrup cheer up off with you're making no headway. Weeps seeps deeps her pretty puffy cream cake hole in the heart operation. Sees a little blackjack thingalingo with a long long tale awinding. May day, she cries, may pole axed me to help her. So I spin the sheaves shoves shivers into golden guild and geld and if she can't guessing game and safety match my name then I'll take her no mistake no mister no missed her no mist no miss no me no. (1)

The Skriker, we realise, is telling the story of a girl whose mother's boast that her daughter can spin straw into gold leads to a bargain with a little supernatural creature: he will carry out the magical feat on her behalf but claims the girl herself as his reward – unless she can guess his name. It's best known, perhaps, as the story of Rumpelstiltskin, but in this northern English version the otherworldly figure is called Tom Tit Tot, and is none other than the Skriker in one of her many guises – here she is the 'small little black thing with a long tail' who offers to save the girl from the beheading threatened by her husband the king.[8] The point of the story, of course, is that the girl learns the name and the Skriker fails to get her hands on the girl. It thus provides the first example of the shape-changer's difficulties and desperation:

Then pointing her finger says Tom tit tot! Tomtom tiny tot blue tit tit! Out of her pinkle lippety loppety, out of her mouthtrap, out came my secreted garden flower of my youth and beauty and the beast is six six six o'clock in the morning becomes electric stormy petrel bomb. Shriek! shrink! shuck off to a shack, sick, soak, seek a sleep slope slap of the dark to shelter skelter away, a wail a whirl a world away.[9] (1–2)

A number of academic critics have called the Skriker's peculiar variant of English 'Joycean language', though none has attempted to specify its precise relation to Joyce's variety of styles.[10] Most perceptive among commentators

[8] 'Tom Tit Tot', https://www.sacred-texts.com/neu/eng/eft/eft02.htm.
[9] Churchill uses this unusual style primarily for the Skriker's soliloquys, which punctuate the action; when the fairy is conversing with humans she is given a language that suits her disguise of the moment. In the underworld, however, both the Skriker and the spirits employ the morphing style.
[10] Thus Reinelt calls it 'a Joycean-like [sic] language, part fairy-like, part gibberish' (188), and Remshardt 'a Joycean language', describing it as 'a hodge-podge of resonances, references, and puns; a word-salad and cascade of constantly self-subverting, slippery sentences, as if all human parlance had penetrated the earth's crust in shards and were being manically regurgitated by the Skriker' (121). Aston notes that 'reviewers invariably characterized the Skriker's fragmented, associated speech patterns as "Joycean"' (101).

is Michael Billington, reviewing the revival starring Maxine Peake in 2015, who observes in *The Guardian*: 'At other times the play seems like an experiment with language in which the skriker adopts a densely pun-filled style ('champagne the pain is a sham pain the pain is a sham') that brings to mind Joyce's *Finnegans Wake*. What Churchill has done is to substitute for Joyce's technique of lexical and phrasal *superimposition* a technique of lexical and phrasal *overlapping*, maintaining the *Wake*'s ability to present quite disparate meanings simultaneously (often with comic effect) but achieving this by having one word or phrase ending at the same time as the next one begins, or sometimes cutting off the end of the first word or phrase as it morphs into the second one. Like Joyce, Churchill renders it easier for the listener by making extensive use of familiar phrases. To take one relatively simple example: 'Never marry a king size well beloved' concentrates into seven words the phrases 'Never marry a king', 'king size', 'Sizewell' (the name of a British nuclear reactor – echoing the reference to 'Dungeness' in the previous sentence and drawing our attention at the outset to environmental concerns), and the Biblical (and Hardyesque) 'well beloved'.

A second technique, also common in the *Wake*, is to conjoin words by affinities of sound as well as, or sometimes instead of, sense. Thus, in the first sentence 'boast' leads to 'beast' and then to 'roast', while 'beast' in turn leads to 'beef' (while 'roast beef' and 'beef eater' – or Beefeater – indicate the Englishness of the woman who is boasting about her daughter's skill), creating an interlacing pattern of echoes. The continuation of the sentence also shows both these techniques at work: 'spin' is echoed by 'span', which provokes the remainder of the phrase 'spick and span' (in inverted order) before coming up with a third inflection, 'spun'. 'Spun' is then treated as if it were a Joycean portmanteau, in a self-referential allusion to the familiar saying 'a pun is the lowest form of wit' – except that 'wit' becomes 'wheat', which leads to 'straw', and we are back with the claim being made about the daughter's prowess as a spinner: 'straw into gold'.

The effect is one of language following its own inclinations, no longer under the control of the speaker; only when a sequence of overlapping phrases and puns has played itself out can the Skriker reassert control in a fresh sentence. Thus her mention of the girl's utterance of her 'secret' (itself combined with 'secreted', meaning both hidden and discharged) leads to 'garden' (*The Secret Garden* being a tale of illness and mystery), which leads to 'flower', which leads to the phrase 'flower of my youth' (the Skriker is hundreds of years old); 'youth' is then absorbed into 'youth and beauty', and 'beauty' into 'Beauty and the Beast' (another story of the entrapment of a young girl); the beast's number, 666, follows, the last 'six' setting off the phrase 'six o'clock in the morning', which in turn sets off a rapid overlapping series of phrases: 'Mourning Becomes Electra' (crime and revenge), 'electric storm', 'stormy petrel', 'petrol bomb'. Not all of these seem relevant to the matter at hand, and sense seems to ebb and flow, though as is often the case with *Finnegans Wake* the more you examine a passage the less random its connections become. Certainly, the final word brings us back to the bombshell that the girl's correct guess represents for the Skriker, and leads to the shriek that sets going another series that conveys like a dying echo the fairy's miserable exit from the scene.

Naturally, an audience can't take all this in on first hearing; just as a first-time (or, for that matter, umpteenth-time) reader of the *Wake* is aware of missing a great deal. But the important point is that the fragments that do make immediate sense (which may be different for different auditors), together with a general understanding of what is being said, provide enough semantic satisfaction to be going on with; at the same time, a vivid impression is given of a unique being with a strange, oblique relation to the English language and to British culture. The opening stage direction describes the Skriker as 'ancient and damaged', and the sense of utterances constantly going out of control, as, at the mercy of sound echoes and clichés, they follow the path of least resistance, is one aspect of the damage.

Churchill has succeeded in developing a stylistic technique that builds on Joyce's distinctive linguistic methods in *Finnegans Wake* while at the same time taking them in a new direction, a direction particularly suited to the stage. We can compare two brief passages to highlight both the similarities and the differences between the two works:

> It was of a night, late, lang time agone, in an auldstane eld, when Adam was delvin and his madameen spinning watersilts, when mulk mountynotty man was everybully and the first leal ribberrobber that ever had her ainway everybuddy to his lovesaking eyes and everybilly lived alove with everybiddy else, and Jarl van Hoother had his burnt head high up in his lamphouse, laying cold hands on himself. (*FW* 21.5–11)
>
> We'll be under the bedrock a bye and by. We'll follow you on the dark road at nightingale blowing. No but they're danger thin ice pick in your head long ago away. Blood run cold comfort me with apple pie. Roast cats alive alive oh dear what can the matterhorn piping down the valley wild horses wouldn't drag me. (*The Skriker* 4–5)

Whereas my spellchecker highlights every second or third word in the *Wake* passage, the language Churchill has invented for the Skriker breaks no lexical rules. Where Joyce combines two or more words into one – 'ago', 'gone', and 'alone' becoming 'agone'; 'elm', 'old', and 'age' becoming 'eld' (the third of these only by virtue of the implied phrase 'Old Stone Age'); 'alone' and 'in love' becoming 'alove', and so on – Churchill blends beginnings and ends of phrases and, less frequently, words – 'Oh dear what can the matter [be]', 'Matterhorn', 'hornpipe', 'piping down the valley wild', (an allusion to Blake's *Songs of Innocence*), 'wild horses wouldn't drag me'. Joyce's double or triple meanings are usually signalled by the oddity of the resulting combination, both on the page and in the ear; Churchill's by the unusual context or contexts of a word which in itself is perfectly normal.

Where she does combine different meanings in a single lexical unit, which happens infrequently, she prefers puns to portmanteaus: if two phrases overlap by a word that has a different meaning in each phrase, for instance, as in 'safety match my name' and 'stormy petrel bomb', the hinge-word is usually a straightforward pun. If it's a homophonic pun like *petrel/petrol* it doesn't matter how the word is spelled, since it's the overlapping phrases which create the double meaning. All this means that Churchill's language relies less on its existence on the page than Joyce's; instead of requiring both visual and aural dimensions to produce the multiple meanings, it can convey its overlappings and morphings to the ear alone.

As a playwright, Caryl Churchill aims to write speeches that will lend themselves to vocal articulation and that will make an impact in the theatre. *Finnegans Wake* might seem an unlikely place to turn for a model, were it not for the fact that, as I have stressed, it's most engaging and meaningful when read aloud.[11] Churchill has accomplished what previous writers in the wake of the *Wake* have for the most part failed to achieve: the creation of a distinctive language, richer and funnier (and sometimes more disturbing) than the one we normally encounter, that can be immediately, and profoundly, enjoyed. Joyce, I think, would have approved.

---

[11] The best-known dramatic offspring of *Finnegans Wake* – apart from Mary Manning's stage version of the *Wake* itself, used by Mary Ellen Bute as the basis for her film version – is Wilder's *The Skin of Our Teeth*. Wilder, however, made no attempt to imitate the linguistic peculiarities of Joyce's last book.

CHAPTER 6

The Event of Reading:
Samuel Beckett's *The Unnamable*

Reading Beckett

In the spring of 1989, I was teaching a graduate course on deconstruction, ethics, and literature at Rutgers University, and preparing to fly to California to carry out an interview with Jacques Derrida as part of a new project of collecting, in a single volume, English translations of his most important studies of literary texts. Not long before leaving, I asked the class if anyone had any questions they would like me to put to Derrida – we were studying one of his essays at the time – and I suppose I shouldn't have been surprised that the response was, at first, a rather stunned silence. Then one of the students made a suggestion in line with his own particular interests: 'Can you ask him why he has never written on Beckett?' (The student was Stephen Dilks, now a respected Beckett scholar.) I did ask the question, and Derrida's answer – later published in *Acts of Literature* (60–2) – has been quoted and mulled over many times by scholars and critics writing on Beckett. (I think especially of the probing discussions by Asja Szafraniec in *Beckett, Derrida and the Event of Literature*, Daniel Katz in *Saying I No More*, and Ewa Ziarek in *The Rhetoric of Failure*.) Going back to Derrida's comments in preparing this chapter, I was struck by the degree to which they resonated with my thoughts about *Molloy, Malone Dies*, and *The Unnamable* as we might read them today, no doubt because Derrida's understanding of literature has been highly influential for me. Nevertheless, the implications of his comments have not, I believe, been fully taken on board in Beckett studies (or, for that matter, in literary studies more broadly). Here are a couple of Derrida's remarks in answer to my question: 'How could I write, sign, countersign performatively texts which "respond" to Beckett? How could I avoid the platitude of a supposed academic metalanguage?' and 'The composition, the rhetoric, the construction and the rhythm of his works, even the ones that seems the most "decomposed", that's what "remains" finally the most "interesting", that's the work, that's the signature, this remainder which remains when the thematics is exhausted' (*Acts of Literature*, 60–1).

What does Derrida mean when he claims that, in the case of Beckett's texts, he is unable to 'countersign *performatively*'? If the signature doesn't come into its own as a signature – rather than merely a handwritten name – until it's countersigned, either physically in writing or in the act of recognition and affirmation by a competent reader, we can say that the literary work remains an inert string of words until it is, in some sense, *performed*. At its least developed, a performance of this kind would mean reading with a full engagement with the work's particular constellations of sound and meaning, movement and reference, fictional inventions and historical embeddings – at the same time acknowledging that a countersignature, like any signature, is the unique product of a singular signer at a specific time and place. But in reflecting on my question Derrida was talking about a response in the form of *writing*: like the written countersignature that transforms the scrawled name into a signature, the written commentary finds a singular but readable way of bringing into being – for other readers – the special power of the work to which it responds. Again, it must be borne in mind that, although the singularity of the critical response is not opposed to but imbricated with generality, it emerges from a specific context and lays no claim to universal truths. If I write a text that performs the singularity and inventiveness of a literary work as that singularity and inventiveness happen *for me, now*, my hope is that I will contribute to the richness of the experience others have of that work. And in doing so, I help to keep the work alive for future readers.

This emphasis on the experience of the work for the reader – not, I hasten to add, the reader understood as some sort of pure subjectivity but as a node within a given culture at a given historical moment, what I've termed an idioculture[1] – points to another aspect of the literary that I drew attention to in the Introduction and that I want to bear in mind as I turn to Beckett: the work of literature, understood as literature and not as any of the other kinds of work it may be, from historical document to moral treatise to psychological revelation, is not an object but an *event*. To say this is not to hypostatise some ideal temporal sequence moving from beginning to end, taking place in countable minutes; it draws our attention, rather, to the way the work happens, the sequencing of elements, the build-up and relaxation of tension, the enigmas and their

---

[1] See Attridge, *The Singularity of Literature* and *The Work of Literature, passim.*

resolutions, the withholding and unfolding of information, and so on. I'm in sympathy with what Margot Norris calls, in a study of Joyce's *Ulysses*, 'virgin' reading: withstanding, heuristically, the temptation to read into earlier parts of a work information only provided later, while at the same time acknowledging that what she calls the 'veteran reader' will have this knowledge ready to hand to complicate the virgin reading (*Virgin and Veteran Readings*). To this conception of the work I want to add a preference for *minimal* over *maximal* interpretations – a resistance, in other words, to the generation of allegorical or symbolic readings, to searches for hidden meanings, unconscious ideological biases, or ingenious polysemy. If such complications of meaning are to be adduced, I believe it should only be *after* an attempt has been made to read as literally as possible.[2]

There's not much evidence that Derrida's reluctance to write on Beckett is widely shared. Even his fellow-philosophers have shown little hesitation where Beckett is concerned, and we are the beneficiaries of commentaries by Alain Badiou, György Lukács, Theodor Adorno, Stanley Cavell, Maurice Blanchot, Georges Bataille, Gilles Deleuze, Slavoj Žižek, Simon Critchley, and others. But the explosion of material on Beckett in the last twenty years or so has had little to do with this philosophical interest; as anyone who works in Beckett studies knows, empirical approaches have dominated the field. Important work has been done on Beckett and Ireland, Beckett and medicine, Beckett and science, Beckett's debts to other writers, Beckett's notebooks and manuscripts, Beckett's letters, and Beckett's life, to go no further.[3] Much of this work is of great interest – Beckett was and remains a fascinating individual, and the sources of an extraordinary creative output such as his will always engage and intrigue – and some of it makes a lively contribution to the kind of literary reading I've been describing. (The plays and screenplays raise somewhat different issues: here we are primarily indebted to directors, designers, and actors for sustaining the works as living performances, though they still have much to offer the reader who encounters them on the page.) If we read Beckett for reasons other than literary ones (and I don't mean to belittle these reasons) – for example, to throw light on Parisian intellectual life, to discover features of his personality or habits, to understand how the texts came into being, to trace buried allusions to historical events – we're in a much better position now

---

[2] I owe some of my thinking here to Henry Staten, with whom I had a protracted email conversation on these topics, published as the co-authored study *The Craft of Poetry*.

[3] See the reflections by Paul Sheehan in his Introduction to the special issue of the *Journal of Beckett Studies* on 'Post-Archival Beckett'.

than at the beginning of the millennium, thanks to the outstanding labours of so many scholars. There's a familiar pattern of academic commentary here, especially when the author in question is perceived as difficult: first, a focus on the text and on ways of making it as intelligible as possible (including the application of various theoretical models), then, when this mode runs out of steam, a formidable array of new possibilities is presented by the increasing availability of manuscripts, notebooks, memoirs, letters, and other archival materials. I've witnessed something like this happening in Joyce studies, and I can see it now beginning in Coetzee studies. My question, then, is this: has the world of Beckett studies been, for some time, overlooking – or at least taking for granted – the reason why this particular author has been the subject of such an enormous scholarly effort: the extraordinary experiences of reading, hearing, and watching the work itself?[4] Somewhat to my surprise, I find myself wanting to echo Alain Badiou: it is time, he has said, to take Beckett *at his word*, 'prendre Beckett au pied de sa lettre'.[5] This is what I would like to do in revisiting *The Unnamable*.

Beginning *The Unnamable*

The Unnamable has some claim to be Beckett's most substantial challenge to literary norms – not only those operative in the 1950s when it was published, but equally those that govern our reading today. Not that some of his shorter texts don't operate even further outside those norms, but the length of *The Unnamable* and its position as the culmination of the three novels we customarily call 'the Trilogy' (in spite of its author's disapproval of this term) give it special salience in Beckett's output.[6] While not going quite as far as Žižek, who terms it 'the absolute masterpiece of twentieth century literature',[7] I regard it as one of the most important literary works since the publication of *Ulysses*, and, more to the point, I find it engrossing,

---

[4] The value of a focus on reading Beckett is brilliantly demonstrated by Audrey Wasser in her chapter 'From Figure to Fissure' in *The Work of Difference*. Wasser recommends 'a way of reading . . . that would suspend the question of what Beckett's text says about itself by means of its figures, in favor of an examination of the *way* it has of saying' (109).

[5] Badiou, *Beckett*, 9; *On Beckett*, 40. The inadequacy of Badiou's understanding of Beckett is well brought out by Connor in *Beckett, Modernism and the Material Imagination*, 3–7 (though he is more positive about Badiou in his Preface to the Faber edition of *The Unnamable*).

[6] Begam has suggested that a more useful label would be the Pentalogy, starting with *Murphy* and *Watt* (*Samuel Beckett and the End of Modernity*).

[7] Quoted in Boulter, *Beckett*, 130.

baffling, funny, painful, and heartening. Having thrown off the direct Joy-cean influence of his early work, Beckett has now fully come into his own with a novel that is wholly singular – in the fullest and most philosophical sense of that word.[8] While it's impossible to imagine Beckett reaching this summit of literary achievement without the ladder provided by his intimate acquaintance with Joyce's writing and the example of the older writer's willingness to challenge convention, the arsenal of formal techniques he deploys in *The Unnamable* is wholly his own. That he continued to find new ways of handling the French and English languages, though never on the same scale, testifies to the consistency of his adherence to the modernist injunction to 'make it new'.

In commenting on the experience of reading, I shall bear Derrida's advice in mind: both the danger of falling into the platitudes of academic metalanguage – something to which professional critics all too easily resort when at a loss – and the need to attend to 'the composition, the rhetoric, the construction and the rhythm of his works,' which for Derrida consti-tute the signature that has to be countersigned if one is to do justice to the singularity of Beckett's work. And these features of Beckett's writing are, as Derrida says, what 'remains when the thematics is exhausted' (a foreshad-owing, perhaps, of Deleuze's 1992 discussion of 'exhaustion' in Beckett).[9] Whereas many commentators have struggled to articulate the *content* of *The Unnamable*, Derrida is fascinated by what is left over when we have digested (or perhaps failed to digest) that content. I want to ask, in particular, on the assumption that central to the experience of art is some form of pleasure, what does this work offer for our *enjoyment*?

As is the case with any work of literature, we make a number of choices as we start to read. At what speed do we read, for instance? (We might recall Pascal's *pensée* 69: 'When we read too fast or too slowly, we understand nothing.') It's not that reading *The Unnamable* at the same speed as one might read, say, a Stephen King novel, is useless, but much of the work's power and pleasure would fail to come across – even more than is the case with *Molloy* or *Malone Dies*. I'm going to assume a slow reading, then, not quite reading aloud (although Beckett's prose certainly benefits from vocalisation) but at roughly the speed at which reading aloud would happen, perhaps with silent articulation. Another choice arises from the existence of *L'Innommable*, written before the English version: do we ignore it, or do we attempt to read across the two texts? I wouldn't dream of being

---

[8] See the discussion of singularity in the Introduction.

[9] Deleuze, 'The Exhausted'; first published in 1992 as 'L'épuisé' in an edition of Beckett's short plays for television.

prescriptive here – the reader without French has plenty to be going on with in the English version alone – but since the practice of cross-referring enriches the experience of both, either by emphasising the particularity of each version or by clarifying one version in the light of the other, I will have recourse to occasional dips into the French.[10]

One way to begin with the question of Beckett's singularity in this text is to begin at the beginning.

> Where now? Who now? When now? Unquestioning. I, say I. Unbelieving. Questions, hypotheses, call them that. Keep going, going on, call that going, call that on. Can it be that one day, off it goes on, that one day I simply stayed in, in where, instead of going out, in the old way, out to spend day and night as far away as possible, it wasn't far. (1)

As a practised reader of novels, I bring to the opening of a work a host of interpretative tools and expectations. Some of these belong to the mechanisms of language itself: I assume not just that the words I'm reading when I begin *The Unnamable* are the record of an author's act of composition at some earlier date but also that, appearing as they do in a public document and utilising the deictic *now*, they mime the utterances of a speaker (or possibly a diary writer) on a given occasion. The reading protocols that govern my reception of the words that open a novel lead me to posit not a character as such – there are no quotation marks to suggest this – but some kind of narrator, a purveyor of the story I am about to start who will have a recognisable personality. We're familiar with such openings – 'Call me Ishmael', 'My father's family name being Pirrip', 'There was no possibility of taking a walk that day'; they immediately begin the work of providing a body and location for the imagined speaker, as these famous examples do by providing a name or a moment in time. The opening of *The Unnamable* not only defeats any such expectations, but undermines them, since the voice immediately goes on to deny that the questions just uttered involved the act of questioning, and goes on further to deny any belief in the first-person subject who appeared to have asked them.

At least this seems to be the meaning of these gnomic utterances. If I have the French text to hand, I can consult it; and there I find greater clarity (though I realise that others might prefer the wider range of possibilities that emerge from the English considered on its own.) 'Où maintenant?

---

[10] For a fine account of the two versions of the Trilogy and their complex relationship, see Hill, *Beckett's Fiction*, chapter 3, 'The Trilogy Translated'. Fitch also provides a detailed discussion in *Beckett and Babel*.

Quand maintenant? Qui maintenant? Sans me le demander. Dire je. Sans le penser. Appeler ça des questions, des hypothèses.'[11] The first person pronoun appears earlier than in the English – 'Sans me le demander', 'Without asking it of me' rather than 'Unquestioning'[12] – and the following sentences spell out the speaker's lack of belief in this first person, 'Dire je. Sans le penser': 'Saying I. Without crediting it', or, more literally, 'Without thinking it'.[13] The doubt that has been cast on the 'questions' is then further intensified, as they are given an alternative name, 'hypotheses'; and whether they are questions or hypotheses depends apparently just on what one chooses to term them. French and English agree here: 'call them' / 'Appeler ça', though the ordering of the sentence is different.

As the text proceeds, the uncertainties about the source of the voice multiply. At first I seem to be in the presence of a recognisably solid speaker who wonders if he or she (or it: we could, after all, be hearing the imagined voice of an animal or other non-human being) 'simply stayed in', though even within this sentence the assertion itself is questioned – 'in where' – and soon the whole story is being undermined: 'No matter how it happened. It, say it, not knowing what'. Then the act of recounting is itself questioned: 'I seem to speak, it is not I, about me, it is not about me.'

A few pages later I seize with relief upon what seems to be a description of the speaker who has been producing these self-cancelling words: 'I have always been sitting here, at this selfsame spot, my hands on my knees, gazing before me like a great horn-owl in an aviary' (3).[14] Moreover, '[T]he tears stream down my cheeks from my unblinking eyes'. In the pages that follow I hear more about those fixed eyes, and then receive a further precise description of a body, apparently a human one, sitting in the same posture (14–15). And yet that human body is quickly revealed as a construction of the voice, which has the power to remove the tears in the space of a single sentence: 'I'll dry those streaming sockets too, bung them, there, it's done,

---

[11] The French ordering of the questions – Where? When? Who? – seems a more logical progression than the English.

[12] The meaning of this French phrase is unclear: on its own, the most obvious translation would be 'Without asking me for it', but there is nothing for 'it' to refer to.

[13] The opening is the subject of a lengthy analysis by Fitch in *Beckett and Babel*, comparing the English and French versions, and noting the considerable differences.

[14] Beckett translated the French 'grand-duc', with its aristocratic connotations, not by the literal equivalent 'eagle-owl' – a term that occurs in *Molloy* – but by the more comic and ornithologically inaccurate 'great horn-owl' (though Kenner, in his *Reader's Guide to Samuel Beckett*, perhaps citing from memory, has the correct 'horned owl' (108)).

no more tears, I'm a big talking ball' (16). Soon there is only a voice, and a voice with no certainty of origin: 'It issues from me, it fills me, it clamours against my walls, it is not mine, I can't stop it, I can't prevent it, from tearing me, racking, assailing me. It is not mine, I have none, I have no voice and must speak, that is all I know' (18). Those readerly presumptions with which I started are in tatters. It seems wrong to talk of a narrator (except as something fabricated within the text only to be abandoned) or even a speaker, or to use personal pronouns; and if we use 'the Unnamable' as a moniker we limit the term's possible relevance (the name might also apply to the place, the time, the events)[15] – though there is, it's true, an appropriate paradox in a name that denies itself.

A further fact plays into my experience of this opening: if I begin *The Unnamable* as, previously, a reader of *Molloy* and *Malone Dies*, I start this one – whatever Beckett's own misgivings about their connectedness – with a strong feeling that it follows on from the other two, and later references in the text will only strengthen this feeling, just as some proleptic moments in the earlier works are now fully realised.[16] For such a reader, the 'now' in those opening questions carries the implication 'now that we have moved beyond the end of *Malone Dies*', and raises the problem of going on after apparently exhausting both human life and the resources of fiction. The latter suggestion also encourages a degree of identification between the voice we are hearing and the implied author who has created it, the author responsible for those earlier works, now left with nothing to say and nowhere to say it from.

What is true of the opening of *The Unnamable* remains true throughout: it demands constant mental activity and a high degree of alertness to the language. As Adorno put it at the start of his notes on *The Unnamable*: 'Necessity to read each sentence rigorously from beginning to end' ('Notes on Beckett', 172). Part of the strenuousness arises from the constant effort these sentences make to evacuate from the text those novelistic and linguistic

---

[15] Hill cites Blanchot's contention that the title refers to 'the impersonal process which expropriates the narrator of all identity and which is none other than the fundamental movement of writing and language itself' (*Beckett's Fiction*, 56).

[16] Some critics, like Hill, are hostile to this idea, and of course there is nothing to stop readers from tackling the works in a different order or resisting any sense of continuity (*Beckett's Fiction*, 56–8). Whether they are read as a series or not depends in part on the language in which they are encountered: in French they are primarily known as three separate books published successively by Minuit, in English as a trilogy published as a single volume by Calder and Boyars in the UK, and by Grove Press in the USA in 1959 – though the more recent Faber single editions may begin to change that perception.

assumptions we as readers bring to it. Some assumptions do, of course, survive: for instance, I read the work without ever doubting that the words are all to be imagined as emanating from a single source – not because they form a consistent narrative (far from it), or because there is a stylistic continuity from start to finish (there isn't), but because there is no overt signalling of a change of verbal origin, as there is, for instance, in *Molloy*. And I assume that source is to be imagined as human, or at least having some connection with human being, despite the challenges this notion receives, as the default assumption for the occurrence of natural language and in the absence as the work continues of any strong indication of a speaking animal or object. This is not to say that a discourse without a single origin, human or otherwise, is impossible in literature: some contemporary poetry, such as 'language poetry' or the later work of J. H. Prynne and the 'Cambridge school', is premised on the elimination of any imagined speaker. And *Finnegans Wake*, which Beckett knew intimately, has a plethora of speakers (and writers). *The Unnamable*, however, is not just a staging of language, it's a staging of the continuous act of *producing* language. For convenience, we may refer to the producer of the language as the 'voice', while acknowledging that the term is too suggestive of a human body with vocal organs to be wholly satisfactory.[17] As I read, I assume, too, a single implied addressee, occasionally addressed as 'you' – though the overriding impression is that I am overhearing a self-addressed monologue. The reader clings thankfully to these few remaining generic protocols like Ishmael to his coffin.

A Passage, an Event, an Experience

My discussion of the opening of *the Unnamable* has not strayed far, if at all, from Derrida's 'platitude of a supposed academic metalanguage'; and though attempting to specify what is singular about Beckett's writing, it can hardly be said to be a performative countersignature. There are many ways in which a critic might attempt such a countersignature, from reflecting on the experience of the entire work, bringing it into contact with other works, placing it in a variety of possible contexts, and so on. I'm going to examine a very short passage chosen more or less at random, in the hope that, by tracing the elements that play an important role in my reading of it, I can convey something of my sense of the whole work's singular eventfulness.

[17] One of the most astute discussions of the 'voice' of *The Unnamable* is that by Katz, *Saying I No More*, 114 and chapter 4, *passim*. Like Katz, Steven Connor, in commenting insightfully on *The Unnamable*, refers to the 'voice' and uses the pronoun 'it' (*Samuel Beckett: Repetition, Theory and Text*, 82–98). Katz, however, signals the unsatisfactoriness of the notion of voice by putting the word in quotation marks.

By the time I reach the passage I've chosen, about three-quarters of the way through the book, the rhythms of the voice have become very familiar, though they have modulated from the staccato sentences of the opening through a variety of longer and shorter sentences to extremely long sequences of phrases separated by commas. And I have heard the voice exploring a huge number of hypotheses in answer to those opening questions that were not questions: from the weeping owl-like figure it has come to an awareness of itself as a hairless ball, though this in turn has been interrogated; it has swapped identities with a series of characters, the most enduring of which are named Mahood and Worm; it has indulged in stories of a one-legged individual returning to his family to find them reduced to mush by ptomaine poisoning and of a human trunk buried in a jar outside a restaurant; it has inveighed repeatedly against a group it most often just calls 'they', at times identified with characters from earlier Beckett novels, who in turn appear to serve a 'master'; and so on. But any assertion it has made has, in due course if not immediately, been retracted. It has constantly referred to the necessity of speaking and of a yearning to be done with speaking, a goal which, it seems, can only be achieved, impossibly, through speech. At the point at which my chosen passage begins, the voice has just been imagining the departure of the group (or 'herd of shites', as they have just been called) while it goes mad and screams. The suggestion of screaming then returns it to an earlier series of questions about its doubtful possession of a mouth, prompting the idea that it could grow one, allowing the air to gush in and out. The voice continues:

> But is it not rather too much to ask, to ask so much, of so little, is it really politic? And would it not suffice, without any change in the structure of the thing as it now stands, as it always stood, without a mouth being opened at the place which even pain could never line, would it not suffice to, to what, the thread is lost, no matter, here's another, would not a little stir suffice, some tiny subsidence or upheaval, that would start things off, the whole fabric would be infected, the ball would start a-rolling, the disturbance would spread to every part, locomotion itself would soon appear, trips properly so called, business trips, pleasure trips, research expeditions, sabbatical leaves, jaunts and rambles, honeymoons at home and abroad and long sad solitary tramps in the rain, I indicate the main trends, athletics, tossing in bed, physical jerks, locomotor ataxy, death throes, rigor and rigor mortis, emergal of the bony structure, that should suffice. (101)

The immediate content of this passage is not difficult of access as we read it: most of the short phrases make perfect sense, and there is a logical (if hardly run-of-the-mill) sequence: the idea just formulated of growing a mouth is questioned, and followed by a different suggestion, that of a tiny movement in the smooth surface of the imagined ball which would initiate larger and larger movements, ending in death. We are worlds away from *Finnegans Wake*'s jam-packed prose, each vocable loaded with multiple suggestions. But beyond the individual phrases, the sense of the passage presents challenges. We struggle to imagine a physical source for this voice, as it denies its own possession of a mouth and describes its unlined surface; we puzzle over the series of depicted movements, which seem to have little to do with what we have gleaned of the voice's situation. In this respect, of course, the passage is characteristic of the entire work. Numerous explanations of this perplexing thematic substance have been offered, all of which to some degree reduce the otherness of the text by providing an explanation for its strangeness: the book is about the effortful process of artistic creation; it embodies Beckett's painful struggle to write after *Molloy* and *Malone Dies*; it's concerned with the fervent search for the essence of selfhood; it's an attack on the uplifting rhetoric of post-war Gaullism; it's a manifestation of the inevitable self-undermining of language; it's an exposure of the oppressive power of an anonymous 'they'; it's a heroic demonstration of fidelity to the Truth; it's a manifestation of the posthuman; and so on.[18] Each of these responses offers valuable insights, and the fact that such a large number of alternative interpretations have been proposed is testimony to the richness of Beckett's text.

But what seldom emerges from these accounts is what makes *The Unnamable* an enjoyable literary work, and, in particular, what makes it sporadically very funny.[19] Porter Abbott, writing about *The Unnamable* and *Texts for Nothing*, put it well several decades ago: '[I]t is so easy to forget that

---

[18] Levy, in *Trapped in Thought*, summarises a number of these approaches (100–1). My slightly parodic list includes glances at work by Hannah Copeland on artistic creation; C. J. Ackerley on the circumstances of composition; Ruby Cohn, Paul Foster, and many others the investigation of subjectivity; Andrew Gibson on post-war Gaullism; J. E. Dearlove on linguistic reflexivity; Allen Thiher on 'das Man' in Heidegger; Alain Badiou on fidelity; and what has been called 'the recent turn to posthumanism in Beckett criticism' (Effinger, 'Beckett's Posthuman', 369).

[19] Laura Salisbury usefully tracks the fluctuating critical attention to Beckett's comedy (*Samuel Beckett*, 5–14); her own strong interpretation of the comedy of *The Unnamable* relates it to 'alimentary dysfunction' (78). Although Gibson calls the plight of the Unnamable 'quintessentially comic' (*Beckett and Badiou*, 191), his account of the work (186–97) gives no sense of its laugh-aloud moments. Sheehan makes the important point that Beckett's humour is undecidable rather than affirmative (*Modernism, Narrative and Humanism*, 155, 172), though he doesn't develop it in his discussion of *The Unnamable*. Rabaté, more perceptive than most, writes of 'a pervasive hilarity, a human and posthuman comedy of sorts that finds its sporadic discharge in jokes, sallies, or witticisms' (*Think, Pig!*, 46).

these works are highly amusing while one is engaged in the labor of trying to come to terms with them critically' (*The Fiction of Samuel Beckett*, 136). It's not, surely, the content of this passage that makes it such a pleasure to read, and that makes me want to re-read it secure in the knowledge that that pleasure will not diminish with repetition. A paraphrase might retain the passage's strangeness but would lose that particular power to please. We need to examine what Derrida calls 'the remainder which remains when the thematics is exhausted', 'the composition, the rhetoric, the construction and the rhythm of his works.' Keeping the various thematic possibilities at arm's length, I want to focus on the experience of Beckett's words as they unfold in the event that constitutes their literariness, aiming to be as literal-minded as I can.

In the first place, perhaps, it's the sheer *momentum* of the language that compels me and moves me onward, so powerfully that sometimes I find myself reading the words for their movement and forget to take in their meanings, aware only *that* they mean but not *what* they mean. This momentum comes from several features of Beckett's writing.[20] One is the overriding of the rules of grammar and punctuation that insist on a complete sentence ending with a full stop, question mark, exclamation mark, or at the very least a semicolon or colon. Our example contains a number of full sentences strung together with commas, a feature that is typical of the work as a whole, especially its latter part. These short units create an underlying rhythm of phrasal units that keep on accumulating, well beyond any norm of 'good style'. There is some resonance here with the quality of verbal (and hence mental) movement Joyce achieves in the 'Penelope' episode of *Ulysses*, but the momentum is different, thanks to those short phrases and the repetitiveness they bring with them. (Coetzee speaks of 'a certain dancing of the intellect that is full of energy yet remains confined, a dancing on the spot' ('Homage', 9).)

This repetitiveness is partly a matter of rhythm: many of the phrases have only two stresses, though longer units provide frequent variation. Beckett often uses a sequence of phrases of increasing length to generate a sense of (comic) climax, as he does twice in this passage. First:

> ... business trips, pleasure trips, research expeditions, sabbatical leaves, jaunts and rambles, honeymoons at home and abroad and long sad solitary tramps in the rain ...

[20] McDonald refers appropriately to the 'propulsion' of the final stretch of the novel, but I am less persuaded that it's 'deterministic' or 'mechanical' (*The Cambridge Introduction to Samuel Beckett*, 108).

Then the sequence of movements begins again with another steady increase in length:

> ... athletics, tossing in bed, physical jerks, locomotor ataxy, death throes, rigor and rigor mortis, emergal of the bony structure ...

The rhythmic repetitiveness of the phrases is intensified by verbal repetition – for instance, the series 'Would it not suffice ... would it not suffice ... would not a little stir suffice ...' and then, after a long stretch, concluding the sentence as it began, 'that should suffice'.

The Unnamable's momentum is also a matter of expectations aroused and either satisfied, postponed, or disappointed. 'Would it not suffice', even without the question mark that should follow it, makes us look ahead, syntactically and semantically, but the sentence gets distracted, and the question has to be repeated, and then the whole thing fizzles out in a manner typical of the voice's failure to make progress: 'would it not suffice to, to what, the thread is lost ...' But the voice is not dismayed, and jauntily starts again: 'no matter, here's another, would not a little stir suffice ...' And then we have the extraordinary sequence of bodily movements, getting ever more ambitious, from mere locomotion to a variety of trips and on to energetic physical activities, and finally descending to death and decay, always pulling us onward to find out what comes next.

Also important is the distinctive and engaging modulation of tone and register. The norm is elevated language and seriousness of purpose; but this seriousness is always in danger of being undermined, by tinges of pomposity, by inappropriateness to the subject at hand, or by shifts into a more demotic style. (There is something of the first part of the 'Nausicca' episode of *Ulysses* here.) Take this question: 'Would it not suffice, without any change in the structure of the thing as it now stands, as it always stood'; out of context, this would be bland officialise without any implication of physical posture, but here the 'thing' is a hairless ball, and the idea of its 'standing' doesn't seem quite right. The apparently passionless precision of the description that follows – 'little stir', 'tiny subsidence or upheaval' – is challenged by the momentary jollity of 'the ball would start a-rolling' (in French it's a 'boule de neige', or snowball (160)). Since the voice has represented itself as a ball, the idiomatic expression hovers alarmingly on the edge of literal description. But seriousness, with a slight touch of affectation, returns with 'trips properly so called', though this quickly becomes mock-seriousness, thanks to the over-explicit listing of activities in a variety of registers.

The voice of the self-important lecturer gets funnier and funnier – 'I indicate the main trends' – and then the mordant humour breaks out as movement turns into the final rigidity: 'athletics, tossing in bed, physical jerks, locomotor ataxy, death throes, rigor and rigor mortis, emergal of the bony structure . . .'. The French is just as funny: 'sports, nuits blanches, exercises d'assouplissement, ataxies, spasmes, rigidité cadavérique, dégagement de l'ossature'. 'Nuits blanches', or sleepless nights, doesn't have the sexual suggestiveness of 'tossing in bed', but 'exercises d'assouplissement', 'exercises to increase suppleness', is, for my money, even funnier than 'physical jerks'. Beckett's excruciating *doubles entendres* are so characteristic of his writing that one perhaps has to consider them part of the minimal reading I mentioned earlier. Some of the funniest parts of the English version have no equivalent in the French, including 'honeymoons at home and abroad', while the generalised 'promenades sentimentales et solitaires' is expanded to the weirdly specific and suddenly lyrical 'long sad solitary tramps in the rain'. Again there is a Joycean echo, this time of the ridiculously detailed lists of the 'Ithaca' episode, but again transformed into a distinctive Beckettian mode. And after the series of items leading all the way from youthful energy to decomposition in the grave there is the laughable understatement of 'that should suffice'.[21]

At times the diction is absurdly and comically recondite. 'Rigor' on its own is not an American spelling but a technical term for a 'sudden and violent shivering attack accompanied by a rise of temperature', as one of the *OED* citations has it. (This is another of the elaborations added in the English version.) 'Locomotor ataxy' would normally be 'locomotor ataxia', but this is an explicit nod to Joyce: one of the prostitutes in the 'Circe' episode utters this phrase – to which her companion responds, 'O, my dictionary' (1986, 425). And as for 'emergal'! The *OED* has no knowledge of it, and Google suggests that when it's used in English sentences it's a mistake for 'emergence'. Beckett had already used the word in *Dream of Fair to Middling Women*, but its meaning there is hardly clearer – we are told of the mind's 'recondite relations of emergal' (Beckett, 1993, 16). *L'Innommable* has 'dégagement de l'ossature': a late stage of the corpse's decomposition as the skeleton starts to come apart. Beckett's signature style, then, is wholly recognisable and yet always springing surprises on the reader.

To look at a short passage is to highlight the local operation of the language, but it says nothing about another important feature of the work: its length. That the momentum I've spoken of can be maintained for well over a hundred pages is an important aspect of the book's power: the voice's sense of a compulsion to speak, and its yearning for a final silence that only

---

[21] The series is another echo of Joyce, perhaps; this time of the four-stage Viconian sequences in the *Wake*.

speaking will produce, is made real by the continuation, page after page, of its self-interrogation, its telling of tales and spinning of imagined possibilities. I won't offer a solution to the conundrum of the ending – are we to imagine the voice continuing after the printed words have stopped?[22] – except to note that the obvious device by which to imply endless continuation, an arrested sentence that is completed at the start of the book, was unavailable to Beckett, thanks to Joyce's having got there first.

To read *The Unnamable*, then, is to participate in the voice's dilemmas, to follow its tortuous reasonings, to take part in its ironic musings, to share its anger and frustration, to laugh at its absurdities, to savour its sheer energy and persistence. It's to recognise and enjoy an intelligence, a caustic wit, a verbal facility, a linguistic inventiveness, a sureness of touch. It's to be taken on a tonal roller-coaster, a journey with an ever-receding terminus, an emptying-out that never results in emptiness. And all this arises from the event of reading, the experience of the text as it unrolls its words and sentences. Of course, we continue to pay attention to content, to the puzzles enunciated as the work's opening questions, but our enjoyment emerges from what *happens* to this content, how it fades in and out of view, how it is asserted and undermined.[23]

Many years ago, I published an argument about *Finnegans Wake*, rather brashly claiming that Joyce's last work should stand, not as an anomaly on the edges of the literary universe but at its centre, since it exploits to the full the resources of the language and the literary tradition (*Peculiar Language*, 7). Could one argue something similar of *The Unnamable*, in spite of its huge differences from the *Wake*? Joyce seized upon literature's deployment of the referential and symbolic capacity of language, its ability to bring into being richly detailed worlds, both subjective and objective, and pushed it as far as he could take it. He enhanced the capacity of lexical items to resonate with multiple meanings by eroding the fragile limits that constitute single words and distinct languages and capitalised on the echoes and reduplications among the world's myriad stories, packing into a few syllables a host of concepts, historical allusions, and narratives. Beckett was taken by the

---

[22] Weller offers some astute remarks on the 'paradox of the ending of *The Unnamable*', suggesting that any answer to the question must come, impossibly, from outside the text (*A Taste for the Negative*, 112).

[23] Hill, in *Beckett's Fiction*, is not alone in picking up the text's use of the term 'aporia' to emphasise its constant undoing of its own propositions. In a valuable re-reading of the aporetics of *The Unnamable*, Amanda Dennis draws on Derrida's understanding of aporia to argue that it functions not as closure but as an opening to unthought possibilities ('Radical Indecision').

other side of this property of literature: the fact that the inner and outer worlds it conjured into being so readily could be dissolved with equal ease. He made use of language's capacity to unmake what it has made, a capacity that many earlier literary works had tentatively exploited, from lyric poems drawing attention to their own verbal constructedness to novelistic narrators insisting on the fictionality of their narratives, but that none had turned into a central principle.

With these claims that the work concerns the operation of language and of literary conventions I may seem to have fallen back into the thematic mode. But these are not philosophical arguments. What *The Unnamable* does is to *stage* these paradoxes, to take readers through them as oscillations and self-cancellations that actually happen as they read, and make of this an engaging and entertaining work rather than a mental exercise. The literary force of the work, its singularity and inventiveness, the space of otherness it opens beyond our closed world of habitual thought and feeling, emerge only from the event of reading, and from the reader's painful, pleasurable experience of that event.

Post-script

I write this sentence, here at my computer, looking out through my study window at an unusually blue sky, and what I write is full of meaning, my meaning as a human subject with a dense personal history alive at a particular place and time. But now that I have written it, it has lost that plenitude of meaning; it has become a record of a moment in another place at another time; and it could easily be spoken by someone else, further dislocating it from that origin. And not only has it lost that fullness of meaning, there can be no guarantee that it ever had that kind of meaning. Was it perhaps written by an inebriated friend, you may ask? Was it produced by a computer program into which a number of words were fed? Is it a quotation from a novel? You have no way of knowing. The voice of *The Unnamable* addresses these questions in many places. Here is one such:

> These things I say, and shall say, if I can, are no longer, or are not yet, or never were, or never will be, or if they were, if they are, if they will be, were not here, are not here, will not be here, but elsewhere. (11)

Our daily use of language is designed to fend off such doubts, and fictional literary works, while taking advantage of the separability of language from both producer and referent, usually try hard to maintain the illusion of an unshakeable bond. Beckett saw that there was a kind of bad faith in this doubleness, and *The Unnamable* is his most ambitious attempt to meet it head on. The challenge, of course, lay in writing a work that exposes the duplicity of literary language without simply demolishing itself after a sentence or two – and further, to write an extended work that would grip and please a reader from start to finish. Part of Beckett's solution was to make a comedy of sorts out of what could have been mere negativity, to create a voice that could enunciate, in multiple ways, the fundamental untrustworthiness and autodestructibility of language through its repeated efforts to establish some sure ground of bodily existence in a specific place and time, or at least a mental existence as a thinking subject, while searching for some means to achieve a coincidence of language and its referent, its goal being the silence that represents the only sure way of escaping the deceptions of language – and to do all this with a wry sense of its risibility, a buoyant humour giving way at times to distress or to anger. Since the only assured existence the voice has is as utterance, it can't simply stop. Which might be an argument for taking the ending not as the achievement by the voice of its goal, but simply an acknowledgement that books, like chapters, have to have conclusions.

CHAPTER 7

Multilingualism and Translation: W. F. Hermans' *Nooit meer slapen*

Multilingualism and Minor Languages

In writing *Finnegans Wake* Joyce exploited to the full the possibilities of multilingualism. No writer after him has drawn so extensively on the world's languages, but some have found a resource in the freedom to move between one language and another. Sometimes this switching occurs without comment, as in Cormac McCarthy's use of Spanish in many of his novels or the occurrence of Dutch and English in some Afrikaans novels (to be discussed in the following chapter),[1] but occasionally it becomes part of the thematic point of the work. One such novel is W. F. Hermans' 1966 novel *Nooit meer slapen*, one of the best-known Dutch novels of the second half of the twentieth century, a staple in Dutch classrooms and a work that has been widely translated.[2] The English translation, under the title *Beyond Sleep*, is by Ina Rilke.

The conceptualisation of singularity that I have sketched in earlier chapters is a response to the distinctiveness among all human productions of the making and receiving of art, and to its non-instrumental relation to human actions. But unlike most versions of the autonomy of the artwork, an emphasis on singularity recognises the inseparability of the work of art from its contexts of production and reception,[3] and the freedom it implies is

---

[1] The inclusion of fragments of another language in a literary work has been termed 'non-translation'; see Harding and Nash, eds, *Modernism and Non-Translation*. The collection includes two chapters on Joyce, as well as discussions of, among others, T. S. Eliot, Ezra Pound, and William Carlos Williams.

[2] According to Britz, there have been fourteen translations (review of *Nooit meer slapen*).

[3] See Attridge, 'Context, Idioculture, Invention'.

not a freedom from the constraints of economics, politics, culture, or society but rather an ability to exploit those constraints as resources to enable what they occlude to be heard and seen.[4]

One of the most important contexts within which the singular work is constituted is *language*: the particular language a writer uses brings with it a host of resonances and implications, including its ethical and political resonances and the implications arising from its role in the power relations that necessarily operate in relation to other languages (and, behind languages, cultures). This fact alone prevents the literary work from having impermeable boundaries; it's always engaged, overtly or covertly, with the larger world of linguistic relations. A work in a minor language may seem to ignore the major languages of the world, but in so doing makes a claim about the relationship between them; and if the work is translated into a major language (with or without the author's involvement) the relationship becomes all the more evident.[5] If, on the other hand, a writer in a minor language chooses to foreground the interplay between that language and others, the singularity of the work will reside partly in these linguistic operations, while the ethical responsibility of the reader – and the translator – lies in doing justice to the complexity of its handling of languages. An outstanding example of a work which achieves singularity in this manner is Hermans's *Nooit meer slapen*, and the challenge its multilingualism poses to the translator highlights this achievement.

Languages in *Nooit meer slapen*

The novel begins with an epigraph: Isaac Newton's famous account of his self-image as 'a boy playing on the sea-shore', diverting himself with pretty pebbles and shells. Or to be more precise, the novel begins with Newton's original account written *in English*. So much the easier for the translator, one might think, who has no work to do at all on this page. This is not the case, however, as becomes evident as soon as we contemplate the difference between a book in Dutch that begins with an epigraph in English and a book in English that begins with an epigraph in English. It certainly wouldn't do to translate Newton's English into Dutch in order to preserve

---

[4] See Ruiter and Smulders, Special Issue of the *Journal of Dutch Literature* on 'The Ethics of Autonomy'.

[5] 'Minor' and 'major' are not, of course, objective categories, but it wouldn't be contentious to say that Dutch and Norwegian are minor in terms of global use and importance, while English is major. The next chapter is concerned with writing in, and translations of, an indisputably minor language, Afrikaans.

the distinction between the languages. Hermans thus alerts us at the outset to the importance in his novel of the status of English, and of the question of language difference more generally; and Rilke has no way of conveying this feature of the original to her readers. (A note stating 'In English in the original' would seem excessive.) We can see immediately that the translator's responsibility to the work of the author is an impossible one – though, as Derrida has argued, the impossibility of ethical responsibility could be seen as what makes it possible at all.[6]

The novel proper opens as follows:

De portier is een invalide.

Op het eikehouten bureautje waaraan hij zit, staat alleen een telefoon, en door een goedkope zonnebril staart hij roerloos voor zich uit. Zijn linkeroorschelp moet afgescheurd zijn bij de ontploffing die hem verminkt heeft, of is misschien verbrand toen hij neerstortte met een vliegtuig. Wat er van het oor is overgebleven lijkt op een slecht uitgevallen navel en biedt de haak van de bril geen houvast.
    —Professor Nummedal, please. Ik heb een afspraak met hem.
    —Goodday, sir. Ik weet niet of professor Nummedal binnen is. (7)

The singularity of this opening includes the immediate uncertainties into which the reader is plunged, notably the question of who is narrating this story and from what perspective this scene is being witnessed. For it's clear at the outset that this *is* the view from someone's perspective: to refer at once and without preamble to 'De portier' is to imply that a person through whose eyes we are looking has arrived at a particular building and is now face-to-face with the individual controlling entry. And the rest of the sentence registers the most salient fact about this porter. Literature is full of odd figures creating obstacles to admission, from the drunken Porter in *Macbeth* to Browning's 'Childe Roland' ('My first thought was, he lied in every word, / That hoary cripple') to the gatekeeper in Kafka's 'Before the Law' with his 'large pointed nose and his long, thin, black Tartar's beard'. And beyond these resonances lie the many mythological figures who

---

[6] See, in particular, Derrida, *The Gift of Death*, chapters 3 and 4. Derrida is building on Kierkegaard's *Fear and Trembling* in arguing that the ethical decision is one that occurs beyond all calculations of right and wrong. Translation that remains within the realm of the possible – translation that could be undertaken by a computer – does not involve ethical responsibility. See the following chapter for further discussion.

combine power with disability, such as the various versions of the wounded Fisher King.

What makes the sentence resonate all the more is its shortness and its placement as a separate paragraph (in fact, it occurs as one of the book's super-paragraphs, signalled not by indentation but by a line's worth of white space). The sentence itself functions, that is, as the guarded entryway to the novel; and if the individual who lets us in is not whole, what deformities may lie within? We note, too, that the statement is in the present tense; we are invited to look at the disabled porter at the same moment as the focalizer does. All this happens as an event in the reading, a little explosion of meaning and affect (apprehension, curiosity, anticipation?) that already takes us to a mental place not quite like any we have experienced before.

Our questions about the focalizer receive no answer in the paragraph that follows; instead we learn more about the porter and his setting. But our sense of the consciousness we are inhabiting grows stronger, as we are made privy to its speculations – 'moet afgescheurd zijn' ('must have been ripped off') suggests a process of deduction on the part of the speaker, as does the alternative explanation introduced by 'misschien' ('perhaps'). And the scene before us is an unsettling one: our focalizer can't avoid eyeing the misshapen ear, so much so that the small detail of the unsupported glasses hook becomes the dominant focus of attention. Then without further introduction we're given an utterance, which we must assume is spoken by the narrating presence to the porter, and which is, surprisingly, in English. (We normally expect a novelist to represent speech in the novel's own language, even when we're aware that it's 'really' being uttered in a different language.) Hermans is clearly relying on the familiarity most of his Dutch readers will have with the English language. However, the speaker moves from English to Dutch, as does his interlocutor, which puts us in a quandary – are these Dutch sentences meant to be understood as English too? Or are we in a linguistic environment in which a speaker may freely switch from English to Dutch? The name Nummedal doesn't immediately support this second hypothesis, though there's nothing to prevent a Scandinavian professor from moving around the world.

When we turn to the English translation of this opening, the language problem disappears – but so does the experience of linguistic uncertainty that is part of Hermans' writing.

The porter is disabled.

The oak reception desk at which he sits, staring through cheap sunglasses, is bare but for a telephone. His left ear must have been ripped off in the explosion that caused his disfigurement, or possibly it was burnt in a plane crash. What is left of the ear resembles a misshapen navel and offers no support for the hook of his dark glasses.

'Professor Nummedal, please. I have an appointment with him.'

'Good day, sir. I don't know if Professor Nummedal is in.' (1)[7]

Readers of the translation have no way of knowing what language is being spoken here: it may be English, or the English of the text may represent another language. Once more, translation is impossible.

A surprise is in store as we read on, however, for the next sentence in the original is: 'Zijn Engels klinkt langzaam of het Duits was' (7) ('His English sounds slow, as if it's German' (1).) It seems, then, that the two people have been conversing entirely in English, but that this is not the porter's native tongue. From the comment, we might conjecture that the scene is taking place in Germany. After another remark from the narrator about his appointment, however, we are given a sentence that clears up part, at least, of the mystery:

Onwillekeurig kijk ik op mijn polshorloge dat ik gisteren bij aankomst in Oslo gelijk gezet heb op Noorse zomertijd. (7)

(Automatically I glance at my watch, which I adjusted to Norwegian summer time upon my arrival in Oslo yesterday. (1))

So: we're in Norway – Oslo, to be precise, it is summer, and the voice we've been hearing all this while is the first-person voice of a narrator, narrating events (impossibly) as they happen. He (we now know his gender from the porter's 'sir') is not Norwegian, and in fact six lines further on we learn that he was given a letter to bring with him by his professor 'in Amsterdam'. At last we understand the use of English: it's a lingua franca that makes communication possible between a Dutch individual (we won't learn his name until the end of chapter 6) and a Norwegian interlocutor. In this scene,

---

[7] I don't intend to comment on the strengths and weaknesses of Rilke's translation, but it's perhaps worth noting that something of the singularity of Hermans' prose is lost when the second sentence is rearranged from two statements about the telephone and the porter to one about the desk; especially regrettable is the disappearance of 'roerloos' ('motionless') from the English version.

then, when a Dutch character is represented as speaking Dutch, we are to take it that he's speaking English – though his thought-processes, recorded in the narrative, presumably take place in Dutch. This Babelian juggling with languages is not a momentary game to keep us on our toes at the start of the novel but reflects a concern of the whole work, which will keep coming back to the question of what language is being spoken and how languages relate to one another – itself part of a larger question the novel explores about the role of small nations (like the Netherlands and Norway) in relation to dominant ones.

Leaving the porter – who turns out to be blind as well as maimed – the narrator reaches Professor Nummedal's office and knocks:

In de kamer roept iemand een woord dat ik niet versta. Ik open de deur, met gesloten, maar mummelende mond repeterend wat ik zeggen moet. Are you professor Nummedal . . . Have I the pleasure . . . I am . . .

. . . Where are you, professor Nummedal? (9)

(From inside a voice calls something I don't understand. I push open the door, rehearsing my English phrases under my breath: Are you Professor Nummedal . . . Have I the pleasure . . . My name is . . .

. . . Where are you, Professor Nummedal? (3))

Hermans underlines the awkwardness felt by his character not only by means of punctuation and layout but by representing his hesitant English in English. Nummedal replies in English – recorded in the text as English – and the narrator explains his mission 'in het Engels'. Nummedal's next utterance is given in Dutch – '—Mijn secretaresse?' – but this is followed immediately by the comment, 'Zijn Engels is alleen met grote moeite te onderscheiden van Noors dat ik niet versta', so we know that he has actually used English. (The translation has '"My secretary?" His English is very hard to distinguish from Norwegian, which I don't speak' (3).)

Nummedal's speech in what follows, though presented largely in Dutch, is sometimes given in poor English, to remind us both that he's speaking English and that his command of it is not good: 'Where does you come from?'; 'You is a Nedherlander, you is . . .' (10). (These remarks are unchanged in the translation.) The second of these statements includes a Dutch word (the normal English term would be 'Dutchman'), pronounced, as indicated by the inserted *h*, in the Dutch manner, something of which the narrator shows his appreciation. But then there's another linguistic twist:

> —Kunt u mij volgen? Of wilt u mischien liever dat wij Duits spreken?
> —Dat . . . dat is mij hetzelfde, zeg ik in het Engels. (10)

> ('Can you follow me? Or do you prefer to speak German?'
> 'It is . . . all the same to me', I say. (4).)[8]

That our narrator answers in English, and somewhat hesitatingly, suggests that he is not in fact quite at home in German; nevertheless, Nummedal responds in that language (rendered, of course, as Dutch on the page), praising the Dutch for their grasp of 'alle talen' ('all languages'). An attempt to switch back to English on the part of the narrator fails, and Nummedal continues in German, a fact that is both stated and enacted at the end of his little speech by the sudden insertion of a German sentence.

In translation, as we have seen, almost all of this happens in English, although the sentence in German is retained unchanged. By a convention of translation, the translator's task is to turn into English only the Dutch words, on the assumption, presumably, that English readers will respond in the same way as Dutch readers to other languages in the text. (To the extent that Nummedal's praise of the linguistic ability of Dutch speakers is true, this might be an unsafe assumption.) There is one anomalous moment in the translation when Nummedal's word 'Nederlanders', in Dutch on the page but said to be uttered 'in het Duits' ('in German'), is rendered by the translator directly in German as 'Niederländer'. In the original, their conversation is rendered continuously in Dutch, with only one reminder in this chapter that it's actually taking place in German: the narrator says, 'Ik weet niet of wat ik gezegd heb correct Duits mag heten' (13) ('I am not sure what I just said rates as correct German' (7)).

The following chapter provides another reminder of the language in which the conversations are taking place, when the narrator thinks of a reply to Nummedal but doubts that he could express it in German. We might wonder why Nummedal, in a little speech mocking Holland, gives the wording on the airport control tower in English (18) ('Aerodrome level thirteen feet below sea level', unchanged in the translation); is it really in English, or is he switching from German to English because he doesn't know Dutch?

---

[8] Rilke's version doesn't translate 'in het Engels', though without this addition we can't be sure what language the narrator is speaking.

There is more linguistic comedy in Chapter 3 when the couple enter a restaurant and Nummedal shouts (in Norwegian) for a waitress and for the cured salmon he is seeking: 'Frøken!' and 'gravlaks!' He has little success, and suddenly switches to English with '—No gravlaks in this place' (the normal English word would be 'gravlax', though the translation has 'grav-lachs' (15)) and then offers an apology in German, rendered in the text as German, for speaking English: 'Entschuldigen Sie dass ich englisch gesprochen habe. Kein Gravlachs hier!' ('Apologies for having spoken English. No gravlachs here!') (Rilke, presumably doubtful whether her English readers will comprehend so much German, summarises instead: 'Next he apologises to me for not having spoken in German, and repeats, 'Kein gravlachs hier!') The narrator replies that he has understood the English statement – in fact, has just replied in English: 'I understand. It's not important' – but does so in German, again rendered on the page as German: 'Ich verstehe. Ich verstehe' (22). Rilke retains the German here.

A few moments later, a local customer approaches, speaking in English (rendered first in English and then in Dutch) and, assuming the visitor is from Britain, apologises for the poor quality of Oslo restaurants. He reappears at the end of the chapter, uttering a speech which is given in a hilarious mixture of English and Dutch and continues the theme of the inadequacy of Norwegian culture, now in comparison with New York and Paris as well as London. The translation loses much of the comedy of this chapter, since everything is given in English apart from a couple of phrases in German.

Throughout the remainder of the novel the reader is made aware of the shifting relationships among languages, and often of the power disparities that these arise from and entrench. Alfred – we can now give him his name, revealed on a postcard he writes – has been sent to Trondheim in search of the aerial photographs he considers essential for his venture into the far northern territory of Finnmark. He encounters one Professor Oftedahl, whose English is flawless and who finds Alfred's English good enough not to suggest they use another language. Again, the occasional English sentence, easy enough for Dutch speakers to deal with, reminds us that the Dutch we are reading is a representation of English: 'It must have been a very quick story!' (56); 'We are very sorry' (59). And again, there is no way the translator can convey the same information; we just have to remember that the English we are reading is English, not, as it was with Nummedal, German, or, as with Alfred's postcard, Dutch. (Though, interestingly and surely unjustifiably, Rilke 'translates' the English word 'story' in the original as 'business'.) Norwegian, however, which is as obscure to Alfred as it is, presumably, to the average Dutch or English reader, remains Norwegian, as when Alfred overhears Oftedahl on the phone (after which we receive a little lesson in the linguistic complexities of Norway, with its three versions of Norwegian).

If the importance of language relationships and translation to *Nooit meer slapen* were not already evident, it would become unmissable in Chapter 10, which is largely taken up with a conversation between Alfred and a fellow Dutch passenger on the flight to Tromsø about the difficulties of the English language for Dutch speakers. It would take a long time to analyse the toing and froing of languages in this passage, but it's worth noting that even when Alfred tries to explain English word-order to the other man, he gets it wrong: 'Als de Engelsen iets vragen, dan vragen ze niet: "Gaat Alfred naar de races?", maar "Doet Alfred naar de races gaan?"' (66).[9] Of course, 'Does Alfred to the races go' is just as incorrect as 'Goes Alfred to the races?' (The fact that Dutch uses an English word for 'races' is not commented on.) Faced with this linguistic knot, the translator gives up, simply writing: 'When the English ask something, they use "do" to activate the verb. Not like the Dutch' (59).

Language difference continues to be foregrounded throughout the novel. Amundsen's note left for Scott at the North Pole is said to have read 'De groeten van Amundsen and good luck to you, sir' (71).[10] The American woman Alfred meets in Tromsø chatters on in what we know must be English, though only a couple of phrases are given in this language (73–5). The different degrees of competence in English displayed by Alfred's three Norwegian companions on the journey are noted, and at one point – though only one – Mikkelsen's poor pronunciation is indicated by spelling: '—Of course, zegt Mikkelsen, you may look at ze pictures if you like. Iet ies my pleasure' (207). (In the second sentence, the translator uses the spelling more usual in English representations of foreign pronunciation: 'Eet ees' (199).) Arne, the most sympathetic of Alfred's companions, laments the unimportance of Norwegian and the dominance of English (87). There is a conversation with Qvigstad, the third of the group, in which the challenge of representing one language by another is revealed: Alfred notes that Qvigstad, though speaking English, has used the Norwegian word 'bensin' instead of 'gasoline', but on the page we have just read 'benzine', the Dutch

---

[9] No mention is made of the coincidence of names between the character and the grammatical example; it's one of many curious correspondences – and failed correspondences – that befall the hero (actually an anti-hero if ever there was one) in his strange odyssey.

[10] The note was in English, and did not include these words; see http://scottvsamundsen.blogspot.com/2012/01/thursday-18-january-1912.html.

word, since his speech is given in Dutch; and there follows a conversation about the origin of the Dutch word. (The translator substitutes the rare spelling 'benzin' for both words.) When Alfred, after a terrible ordeal in the rugged emptiness of Lappland, returns to civilisation, the language issue is not foregrounded; he speaks to a doctor and a girl on the bus with ease, and so presumably in English, but there are no indications of this. Only when he meets the American woman again is language highlighted: she speaks 'Amerikaans', and gives a short lecture on the unwarranted hegemony of English.

One of the major themes of *Nooit meer slapen*, as I suggested earlier, is the vexed relation between 'minor' and 'major' cultures, a theme not only stated at several points but enacted in the play between languages we have been tracing. The singularity of the novel, then, lies not in its self-enclosed autonomy but in its openness to a number of languages and the cultures they embody and support. It brings into the world a fresh insight into language difference, not as knowledge we have acquired when we have read it, but as an experience we undergo during the reading. As we have seen, translation is an active process in the text, and the kind of translation undertaken by Ina Rilke is not a conversion of one single, discrete object into another one, but a continuation of a process that had already started within the original. The responsibility of the translator is to be open to the text's strangenesses, including its inventive dances with languages, and to create a work that provides the reader who has no access to the source language with some sense of those strangenesses. Where the dance takes place between Dutch and English, the translation into English inevitably fails to do justice to the singularity of the original. Is this Hermans's way of fighting back on behalf of languages like Dutch and Norwegian against the apparently all-conquering power of English?

CHAPTER 8

Afrikaans Modernism and the Anglophone Reader: Etienne van Heerden's *30 nagte in Amsterdam*

The Afrikaans Language and Afrikaans Literature

What would it mean to claim that a *language*, any language, is singular, in the sense I have sketched in earlier chapters? The singularity of any language would be evinced not by a unique lexicon and set of phonological, morphological and syntactic rules that set fixed boundaries but by the practice of a group of language users in a particular historical, geopolitical and social context, a practice that is constantly changing as that context changes. Singularity in this sense implies not resistance to translation but openness to translation: since the language has no unchanging essence and no fixed boundaries, it invites translation – and is in fact always implicated in translation, from dialect to dialect, idiolect to idiolect, old forms to new forms, indigenous terms to borrowed terms, and so on.

The language I am focusing on in this chapter is Afrikaans. Afrikaans is spoken as a first language by just under seven million people in South Africa, and a small number elsewhere (principally Namibia). The larger proportion of these Afrikaans-speakers would have been classified under apartheid legislation as 'Coloured,' that is, so-called 'mixed race' peoples, living mostly in the Western and Northern Cape.[1] Somewhat less than half speakers of Afrikaans are 'white' Afrikaners, for the most part descendants of early Dutch settlers with an admixture of later German and French immigrants. A small number of indigenous Africans speak Afrikaans as a first language. This makes Afrikaans the third most common mother tongue in

---

[1] The name 'Coloured' (and 'Cape Coloured' for the largest community so named), though historically tainted by its association with state racism, has been widely embraced, often with a lower case to signal a distance from apartheid classifications. I will follow this practice.

the country, after the indigenous languages isiZulu and isiXhosa, but ahead of English – though English is spoken as a second or third language by a very large number and is the dominant lingua franca in urban areas.[2]

These figures alone might suggest a fairly significant reading public for literary works in Afrikaans. But a large segment of the Afrikaans-speaking population lives in considerable poverty and suffers from inadequate education; the number who read fiction is small, and the number who read 'literary' fiction even smaller. In spite of these facts, many of the most ambitious and important South African novels of the past fifty years have been written in Afrikaans, and some of them, I would argue, merit comparison with the best fictional writing anywhere in the world. Surprisingly, perhaps, given the conservative bent of the white Afrikaner establishment, many of these works explore unconventional subject matter in formally inventive and linguistically bold works. Afrikaans is a relatively young language, and although strenuous efforts were made during the twentieth century to standardise a 'pure' form, it has in practice always been involved in an interchange with other South African languages; and perhaps these two facts have something to do with the continuing creativity of its writers. Although the reading and purchasing public for literary fiction in Afrikaans is small, it is loyal; Afrikaans novelists don't suffer from the global competition experienced by South African writers in English, and as a result their books sell more widely than those of the majority of their Anglophone counterparts in the country.[3] The Afrikaans of the large Cape Coloured community – commonly known as Kaaps – had very few successful writers during the apartheid era, owing to the systematic material and educational deprivation of the period; the major exception was the poetry and drama of Adam Small, who died in 2016 at the age of 80. More recently, several contemporary writers have laid claim to Kaaps as a literary language and produced highly successful work.[4]

[2] See the figures from the 2011 census at www.statssa.gov.za/census2011/Products/Census_2011_Census_in_brief.pdf, p. 26. The results of the 2022 census were not yet available at the time of writing. For a comprehensive account of South Africa's languages, see Mesthrie, *Language in South Africa*.

[3] In 2015, 450,000 copies of South African novels in Afrikaans were sold, compared to 75,000 in English (Anon, 'The shocking number of books'). In 2010, Afrikaans trade fiction had a market share of 78.6% while English had 20.7% (and all African languages 0.7%) (Le Roux, 'Book Publishing Industry Annual Survey').

[4] In poetry, the work of Nathan Trantraal and Ronelda S. Kamfer has set high standards; see Attridge, 'Untranslatability'. Other active poets are Ashwin Arendse and Ryan Pedro, while recent novelists writing in Kaaps include Chase Rhys (*Kinnes*, 2018), Olivia M. Coetzee (*Innie Shadows*, 2019), and Kamfer (*Kompoun*, 2021).

Afrikaans literature developed with an eye constantly on European traditions and with very little attempt to engage with indigenous literary cultures, and it was successive waves of European influence that brought about its major transformations. The first occurred in the 1930s, with the work, above all, of N. P. van Wyk Louw (who held a chair in Amsterdam for eight years), and the second in the 1960s, with the writing of the group of writers known as 'die Sestigers' – 'the Sixties' – who outraged the Afrikaner establishment with their sexual explicitness, political outspokenness, unrepentant blasphemy, and formal experimentation. After a tremor produced in 1956 by Jan Rabie's innovative short story collection *21*,[5] the full seismic shock arrived six years later with André Brink's *Lobola vir die Lewe* ('Brideprice for Life') and Etienne Leroux's *Sewe Dae by die Silbersteins* (translated as *Seven Days at the Silbersteins*). These writers were influenced above all by surrealism and existentialism and by French avant-garde fiction – Brink's *Orgie* (1965; 'Orgy'), for example, is set out to be read with the pages arranged top and bottom rather than side to side. South African fiction in English of the time had nothing to compare with this body of work in its challenge both to generic and formal conventions and to social and ethical norms.

Brink continued to be prolific in both Afrikaans and English, and to utilise a range of different fictional devices, from postmodern metafiction to realist narrative. Another writer associated with the Sestigers who has switched effortlessly between Afrikaans and English, and has been inventive in both languages, is Breyten Breytenbach. His most innovative work is *Mouroir*, published first in 1983 in a mixture of Afrikaans and English and the following year in English only, presumably in Breytenbach's own translation. We should also note an Afrikaans novel by a writer better known as a poet: Wilma Stockenström's *Die kremetartekspedisie*, a linguistically dense monologue of a 15th-century slave woman living in a hollow tree published in 1981 and translated as *The Expedition to the Baobab Tree* by J. M. Coetzee (1983). Also becoming prominent as a novelist the 1980s was Etienne van Heerden: consistently inventive in plot and character, Van Heerden's work – including *Toorberg* (1987; translated as *Ancestral Voices*) and *Die swye van Mario Salviati* (2001; translated as *The Long Silence of Mario Salviati*) – sometimes uses the techniques of magic realism to upset temporal continuity and narrative logic.

Arriving somewhat later on the scene were two women writers whose work, in very different ways, has renewed the possibilities of Afrikaans

---

[5] Etienne Leroux's recently reprinted 'first trilogy', *Die Eerste Lewe van Colet* (1955), *Hilaria* (1957), and *Die Mugu* (1959), also shows signs of the impending challenge to convention; see Louise Viljoen's review.

as a literary language. The first is Ingrid Winterbach, who has cultivated a mode of ironic detachment and understated but subversive humour unusual in Afrikaans literature, in an extensive series of novels.[6] The second is Marlene van Niekerk, the Afrikaans writer whose claim to belong to the pantheon of world literature is perhaps strongest, in spite of (or rather because of) the remarkable situatedness of her work in specific South African settings – settings that are linguistic as well as geographic, social and economic. Her first novel was *Triomf*, a sizeable work published in the year of the first South African democratic elections, 1994, and set in the run-up to those elections. It's a novel whose originality lies in both in its subject matter – the hilariously repulsive goings-on of a violent, dysfunctional Afrikaner family living in the poor white Johannesburg suburb of Triomf – and in its language, a hugely creative version of Afrikaans drawing on non-standard usages with frequent switches between Afrikaans and English, and an uninhibited use of slang and obscenity.[7] *Agaat*, published in 2004, is an even weightier volume that is both a homage to the tradition of the Afrikaans *plaasroman* or farm-novel and an exposure of the racism and exploitation on which the farm celebrated in that tradition was based. At the same time it's both a minutely detailed playing-out of the shifting power relationship between a farm matriarch and an adopted Coloured girl and a mystery narrative in which dark family secrets are gradually revealed. As with *Triomf*, the achievement of the novel is in large part owing to the virtuoso handling of language; hence the enormous difficulty of the translator's task.[8] A third novel, *Memorandum*, which adds to linguistic complexity the combination of verbal and visual art, will be discussed in Chapter 11.

[6] The novels published under her own name are *Niggie* (2002; *To Hell with Cronjé*, 2007), *Die boek van toeval and toeverlaat* (2006; *The Book of Happenstance*, 2008), *Die Benederyk* (2010; *The Road of Excess*, 2014), *Die aanspraak van lewende wesens* (2012; *It Might Get Loud*, 2015), *Vlakwater* (2015; *The Shallows*, 2017), *Die troubel tyd* (2018; *The Troubled Times of Magrieta Prinsloo*, 2019), and the untranslated *Voorouer. Pelgrim. Berg* (2021). Winterbach has also published five novels under the name Lettie Viljoen. See Attridge, '"A Pinch of Salt"'.

[7] See Devarenne, '"In Hell You Hear Only Your Mother Tongue"'.

[8] *Triomf* was translated into English by Leon de Kock, working with van Niekerk; two versions were produced, one for the South African, the other for the international, market. *Agaat* was translated by Michiel Heyns, again with the collaboration of the author, and published first under the title *The Way of the Women* and later under the original title. See Attridge, 'Contemporary Afrikaans Fiction in the World'.

Singularity and Translation

In order to enter that world arena, of course, Afrikaans novels have to be translated, most importantly into English.[9] Unlike many novelists who rely on English translations to reach a global audience, most Afrikaans writers have an excellent grasp of the other language; as we have seen, some write in English as well as in Afrikaans,[10] and if they do turn elsewhere for the translation, it's usually not a matter of handing the text over and hoping for the best, but of working closely with the translator (who is often someone with a distinguished reputation in the world of English letters in South Africa) to produce a version that satisfies both. Novels primarily in Afrikaans frequently use a great deal of English, in the knowledge that this will cause no trouble for their readers (though the practice creates headaches for translators of the sort discussed in Chapter 7) and that it reflects colloquial spoken Afrikaans.

Like the singularity of a language, the singularity of a literary work is realised in practice: in the events of reading whereby it is sustained but also constantly remade anew. All these events involve some variety of translation, whereby the opacities in the text are re-formed within the reader's habitual framework of understanding, which itself has to undergo some degree of transformation as it absorbs the newcomer. The work in its singularity thus calls out for translation, both the minor translations of readers who are at home in its original language, and the major translations undertaken to make the work available to other readers. Fully translingual translation is a distinct event of reading, one that makes an especially important contribution to the survival of the work, changing it while preserving its complex identity, preserving its identity *by* changing it (which is what all readings do, if only in a small way). Translingual translation is also, of course, transcultural translation; the very specific place of Afrikaans within South African culture has no equivalent in other languages, each of which will have its own political and social specificity. This, too, is part of the singularity of the work, and of its translations.

Derrida asserted on more than one occasion that translation is both *possible* and *impossible*; or, in a variant of this statement, that *everything* is

---

[9] Leon de Kock discusses the importance of translation in South African culture in "'A change of tongue'".

[10] Another author who publishes works in both Afrikaans and English is S. J. Naudé (*Alfabet van die voëls* (2011) /*The Alphabet of Birds* (2015); *Die Derde Spoel*/*The Third Reel* (both 2017); *Dol heuning* (2020)/*Mad Honey* (2021). Like Brink's, Naudé's two versions are not identical; both are powerful contributions to the literature of their language.

translatable and *nothing* is.[11] In one sense, the possibility of translation is a fact that is evident all around us, and even the possibility of exhaustive translation is thinkable: all the depths, complexities and nuances of any text in one language could, in theory, be transferred to any other if there were no limit on the time of the translator and the space occupied by the new text. The result, however, would look nothing like a translation as we usually understand the word; it's not enough to exhaustively chart all the meanings of a text, because we expect equivalence in *length* as well as *sense* (and, in literary translation, other qualities as well). This double demand or double-bind means that no translation succeeds in living up to the ideal of translation, but every translation contributes something to that impossible task.

If singularity names the translatability of both languages and literary works, it also names their untranslatability. That is to say, the process of translation is not a process of exhaustive replication: even exact repetition doesn't produce an exact equivalence, since repetition always takes place in a new context, and singularity, as I've said, is always open to context and changes in context. This is not an admission of defeat, however. As Derrida remarks, 'What remains *untranslatable* is at bottom the only thing *to translate*, the only thing *translatable*' ('Ulysses Gramophone,' 257–8). One way of understanding this paradox is to think about what is called machine translation. It's sometimes said that in the foreseeable future, nothing will be beyond the capacity of the best translation software, which has improved in leaps and bounds in recent years. Whatever one may think about this assertion, it's surely the case that in principle just about everything in any text could be translated – or let us say converted – into another language by a sophisticated enough computer, and that to the extent that the human translator is dealing with these elements of the text they are behaving like a machine. What demands a human translator are those elements that require the translator to make *decisions*, in the sense of that word as used by Derrida. A decision is not of the order of the calculable but is the leap one finds oneself taking when all possible calculations have been made, when the alternatives before one remain undecidable. And it's only the untranslatable aspects of the work that demand translation, understood as the

---

[11] See Derrida, *Monolingualism of the Other*, 56, and 'What Is a "Relevant" Translation?', esp. 178–81. (Note, however, that the crucial sentence in the former work is mistranslated; it should read 'Nothing is untranslatable, if only one gives oneself the time necessary for the expenditure or expansion of a competent discourse that measures itself against the power of the original'.) For an illuminating account of Derrida's understanding of translation, see Davis, *Deconstruction and Translation*.

making of decisions, and only these that *can* be translated – rather than merely being mechanically converted.

The challenges and decisions facing the translator of literary works have often been enumerated. In particular, the question of 'domestication' has been much discussed, from Goethe and Schleiermacher to the present. Is the task of the translator to produce a version in the target language that reads as if it had been originally written in that language (what has been called *covert* translation), or is it to develop strategies that keep the reader aware that they are reading a translation (in *overt* translation)?[12]

There can be no simple answer to this question, since translation is not a single activity carried out for a single purpose. A novelist who wants their books to sell widely in foreign markets will not thank a translator who makes reading uncomfortable as a result of oddities of phrasing or vocabulary designed to suggest the original language. (It's obviously meant as praise when a popular reviewer says 'This work doesn't read like a translation.') And a covert translation of this kind is more faithful to the singularising event of the original in that it creates for the foreign reader an experience equivalent to that of native reader. On the other hand, a novelist who wants their work to be appreciated for its exploitation of the singular textures of the language in which it was written may seek out a translator who is keen to evoke those textures in the translated text, giving rise to a feeling of strangeness for the foreign reader that corresponds to nothing in the native reader's experience. When the original work already foregrounds the processes of translation operating within the source language and culture, however, the issues are more complicated, as we saw in the case of Hermans's *Nooit meer slapen* in the previous chapter; the translator may use overt translation to retain some of these features, or seek for comparable effects within the target language and culture. Many of the Afrikaans novels I have mentioned pose a challenge of this sort.

Etienne van Heerden, *30 nagte in Amsterdam*

Some of the most innovative writing in recent Afrikaans fiction is in Van Heerden's 2008 novel *30 nagte in Amsterdam*, which was translated by

[12] *Overt* and *covert* are the terms proposed by Juliane House (*A Model for Translation Quality Assessment*); I prefer them to the more commonly used 'domesticating' and 'foreignising' translation (see, for instance, Lawrence Venuti's many publications on translation, including *The Scandals of Translation*, *Translation Changes Everything*, and *The Translator's Invisibility*). Philip E. Lewis, in 'The Measure of Translation Effects', speaks admiringly of *abusive* translation, but this term has unfortunate connotations.

Michiel Heyns as *30 Nights in Amsterdam*. (Heyns worked closely with Van Heerden and with the latter's agent Isobel Dixon.) The novel moves between the third-person narrative of Henk de Melker, a buttoned-up small-town museum curator in post-apartheid South African who is summoned to Amsterdam to claim a legacy he has been left by his Aunt Zan, and the first-person narrative of the said Zan, starting in the 1960s when she and Henk, then a boy, lived in the same house in the small Karoo town of Graaff Reneit. Zan is epileptic, a wayward member of a cell of an equally wayward liberation movement, and a free spirit whose interior monologue is linguistically exuberant and inventive, mingling dialectical Karoo idioms with nonce compounds and portmanteaus. Here's a typical passage from near the end of the book. Zan (or Xan) has travelled to Pretoria in disguise as a Dutch gentleman, Zondernaam Zuiderzinnen, to attend the trial of her cell comrades, and is staying in a boarding-house near the courtrooms. She decides on an expedition of sexual provocation to the nearby South African Airforce base at Voortrekkerhoogte:

Ek gaan julle opsoek seuns van die wolke julle. Bedfordryers julle. Pille oor die linkerskouer gegooi vir die dag soos vlugsout en met 'n wens. Vandag is ek kaalgat net ek ek Xan sonder boerebedrog. Pielevlegters ek is op pad, ek het julle gesien op Johannesburgstasie!

Maar eers tog maar omieklere aantrek rustig eet, Engelse ontbyt twee eiertjies asof uit die hand van Kytie-ek-issie-jou-mytie en nou eers Zuiderzinnen speel en vryf met sy roosterbroodjie daardie spekvetjies op, klap die Hollandse lippe ai douvoordag! Bedank die houer van die pan die draer van die kokshoed.

Dan by die hotel uitstap en winkel gaan soek. Vrouplek. Ruik poeier so 'n winkel. Ek koop 'n rok soos g'n rok nie so ene met 'n slit en het nog die bene. Hou die roksak toe. Ek koop 'n dit en dat en in die aantrekkamer sing ek deuntjies uit die Amsterdamse kroeg dis verbode om to verbied, en daardie ene niks moet alles kan.

(401)

In Heyns's translation:

I'm going to pay you a visit, Biggles & Co you. Bedfordbumboys you. Chucked pills over the left shoulder like spilt salt and wished a wish. Today I'm bare-arsed just me Xan, Biggles Get it Up Reach for the Sky. Cockchafers I'm on my way. I saw you on Johannesburg station.

But first get into the old gent's clothes have a leisurely meal, English breakfast with two little eggs as if from the hand of Katie and now first play Zuiderzinnen and swab the dribbles of bacon fat with my crust of toast, smack the

Dutch lips ai breakofday! Thank the wielder of the pan the wearer of the chef's hat.

Then walk out of the hotel and go look for a shop. Womanplace. Powdersmell such a shop. I buy a frock like no other frock one with a slit and still have the legs. Frock of ages cleft for me. I buy a this and a that and in the dressing room I sing tunes from the Amsterdam bar it's forbidden to forbid, and that one: nothing must everything can. (401–2)

The singularity of Zan's internal speech lies in its fertile exploitation of the resources of several varieties of Afrikaans (and some Dutch), effecting its own translation of familiar scraps of Afrikaans culture and spoken slang into a rich literary language. The result is clearly untranslatable – and therefore open to translation, to an inventive transposition into another language rather than mechanical conversion. My purpose is not to assess Heyns's version – in my view, he has done as well as could be imagined given the scale of the task – but to explore the problems and opportunities this singular literary performance raises for the translator.

For a start, there is the danger that an English version of Zan's monologue may sound too much like an echo of Joyce, in the verbal high jinks (including the deformation of proper names), the unpunctuated sequences, and the frequent sexual allusions. Heyns, I believe, succeeds in skirting this danger by creating a distinctive English of his own. (In Afrikaans, there is no such major precursor, which makes Van Heerden's games with language all the more innovative.) Then there is the challenge of finding equivalents for the original's inventive vocabulary. 'Pielevlegters', for instance, is a derogatory term used for men involved in backroom machinations, but in translating it as 'cockchafers' – and turning the schemers into beetles – Heyns picks up the subterranean sexual implications, since the term literally means 'prickbraiders'. Sometimes, on the other hand, literal translation is called for, such as in the case of the two aphorisms Zan remembers from an Amsterdam bar, redolent of sixties hedonism: 'dis verbode om to verbied' and 'niks moet alles kan'. In reading 'It's forbidden to forbid' and 'Nothing must everything can' one has to recognise that these stand in for Dutch originals.

References to Afrikaner culture abound, requiring inventive translation. Zan recalls the traditional Afrikaans song, 'Hou die roksak toe', where *roksak*, or placket, is clearly a metaphor for the vagina. Heyns's substitution, 'Frock of ages cleft for me', works brilliantly, sharing with the original its reference back to the slit dress, even if we might wonder how Zan would know such a quintessentially English hymn. A reference which could be to August van Oordt's young readers' futuristic novel *Seuns van de Wolke* or to the South African film of the same name would be translated literally as 'sons of the clouds', which would mean nothing to the non-Afrikaans reader; Heyns has to introduce another somewhat unlikely reference to Biggles, substituting British stiff upper lips for half-naked Afrikaner bodies.[13] I can't explain Heyns's little riff that replaces 'sonder boerebedrog' (literally 'without farmer's trickery') with 'Biggles Get it Up Reach for the Sky', but the phrase has its own appeal and does introduce more male military heroics.

The multilingualism characteristic of the daily use of Afrikaans surfaces in the frequent use of Dutch and English vocabulary. When Zan uses the English word 'slit', for instance, it signals the spoken form of the language – an effect that is, inevitably, completely lost in translation. There are other places where Zan's economical colloquialisms give way in translation to lengthier and more stilted language. 'Kaalgat' is a colloquial expression (literally 'barehole'); 'bare-arsed' conveys the meaning, but not the slanginess, of the original (and sounds a bit too literal). The single word 'omieklere' (literally 'little uncle's clothes') becomes the over-explicit 'old gent's clothes', while 'spekvetjies' becomes 'dribbles of bacon fat', again capturing meaning but not the ease with which Afrikaans creates such compounds. (Would an English reader accept 'baconfatlets'? Probably not.) 'Wielder' for 'houer' works better, though, than the more literal 'holder' would, since Zan adopts a more formal register here, and the echoing of 'wielder' and 'wearer' is entirely appropriate. Other aspects of the language's particular idiom pose problems for the translation: an example here would be *julle*, the Afrikaans second person plural, which can be used after a noun for emphasis. A reader of the translation who knows Afrikaans will recognise the source of the pronoun in 'Biggles & Co you. Bedfordbumboys you'; a touch of overt translation that to the non-Afrikaans reader may simply seem strange. But 'Bedfordbumboys' captures nicely the sexual implication of 'ryers', literally riders in Bedford trucks.

Heyns's translation is both licensed and thwarted by the singularity of the Afrikaans text. In no way a substitution for the original, it takes advantage of the inventiveness of the source text to find its own inventive way forward, leaving behind many features of the Afrikaans but sometimes replacing them with its own linguistic innovations. *30 Nights in Amsterdam* is itself a singular work, not a mere copy of *30 nagte in Amsterdam*.

---

[13] In an article on the representation of homosexuality in South African cinema, Botha states that the film, which was distributed in Anglophone countries as both 'Wing Commander' and 'Fighter Pilots', 'presented audiences with vague homoerotic images of half-naked men' ('The Representation of Gays and Lesbians').

Triomf, Agaat, and *30 nagte in Amsterdam* are bold attempts to redeem Afrikaans, to acknowledge not only its impurities and porous boundaries but also the fact that impurity and porousness are among its greatest strengths. The endeavour to remove all traces of the original language in a translation is a misguided one, therefore: even if we encounter them in English, it's important that we read these novels as both occurring in, and engaging with, Afrikaans. The English translations don't, of course, participate in this enterprise of remaking Afrikaans, which makes them from the start very different works; but if they are read *as* translations, as a counter-signatures to Van Niekerk's and Van Heerden's signatures, validating and affirming those signatures, they may offer a glimpse of the work the novels are doing in their own language.

Translation and Untranslatability

Translation is a form of interpretation, and the responsibility of the translator, like that of any interpreter, is to do justice to the singularity of the work – the work as text but also the work of the author in creating that text. The work's singularity is, as I've stressed, its untranslatability: that is what calls out to be translated not by a machine but by an equally singular human. This is the impossible but necessary task of the translator. But note: the singularity of the work is not a fixed thing; it varies from time to time, place to place, reader to reader, reading to reading; it's the product of an encounter between the reader's idioculture and a set of signs encoding a historical creative act. This is why there can never be a final translation (as opposed to a machine conversion) just as there can never be a final interpretation.

Furthermore, the work's singularity is itself multiple, if that's not too much of a paradox; it often includes its own translations of itself – its own repetitions and rewritings, metacommentary and reflexivity, and internal linguistic borrowings. It also translates the language and culture within which it is written, a language and culture which are themselves products of ongoing translation. So translation into another language is only a continuation of what the work does when we read it, and what we do when we read the work.

To allude to Derrida one final time, he stresses that a work *lives* only if it *lives on*, if it survives;[14] and it can only survive if it's open to change, if, in fact, its very existence as what it is depends on openness to change. A text that is totally tied to the time and place of its origination would quickly become unreadable. Translation is one of the ways in which works survive:

---

[14] Derrida, 'Living On/Borderlines', 102–3.

translation and retranslation, transmedial and transcultural translation as well as translinguistic translation, covert as much as overt translation. The works I've been discussing are living on within Afrikaans culture, where they have been much discussed (translated into commentary, if you like), and within Anglophone culture, both in South Africa and in the wider world (and, of course, within the other linguistic cultures into which they have been ushered by the work of translators). Given the close involvement of Van Heerden himself in the translation by Heyns, it might seem that the usual view of translation as interpretation is inappropriate, but there's no reason why the author's own interpretation as reflected in his or her input into the translation process should be considered differently from that of the translator proper. The interaction between the two creative minds undoubtedly produces fresh insights and helps to reinvent the work anew.

30 nagte in Amsterdam is untranslatable, like any important work of literature, which is to say it is *only* translatable and retranslatable. The reader who can move between original text and translation, source language and target language, is in a particularly privileged position; not because they can search for errors (though that can be a source of satisfaction, as long as it isn't one of irritation) but because a new work arises out of the act of comparison. One begins to understand what Benjamin meant in 'The Task of the Translator' when he remarked that translation 'ultimately serves the central reciprocal relationship between languages' (72). For the reader who has access only to the translation, there is loss but there is also gain: exposure, thanks to the efforts of the translator, to an otherwise inaccessible world, with the flavours of a different linguistic culture and literary tradition.

There is a debate going on within the fields of comparative literature, translation studies and 'world literature' about the values and dangers of translation. Some see it as contributing to the effacement of minor languages, as the vast majority of translations are from minor to major languages, and to English in particular (though Chinese may be vying for the top spot); others see it as a way of bringing to the attention of the speakers of those major languages important cultural productions in minor languages, which they are never going to learn.[15] I'm swayed more by the latter argument than by the former: the existence, and dissemination, of these translations of novels that deserve their place on the world stage is vital to the flourishing of Afrikaans. Writers like Van Niekerk and Van Heerden are more likely to pursue their difficult craft if they know that able

---

[15] See Emily Apter's discussion of this debate in *The Translation Zone*, 4–5. For a defence of English as a lingua franca on empirical grounds see House, 'English as a Lingua Franca'.

translators are willing to take on the often thankless task of translation – and that readers are willing to take the risk of entering upon and living with a translated work. It's the responsibility of readers who are able to cross the language boundary in question to assess and comment on translations, comments that will, ideally, lead to new translations that will bring out different aspects of the original. All these processes are crucial to the living on of these extraordinary achievements in a minor language from a corner of Africa.

CHAPTER 9

Crossings of Place and Time: Zoë Wicomb's Fiction

The Troubling of Place

Joyce, in spite of his own peripatetic existence, set his first three works of fiction solidly in Dublin, even naming his short story collection after the inhabitants of the city; there are repeated intimations of lives lived in other places, but the distinction between 'here' and 'there' is consistently maintained. Although other modernist writers registered the experience of travelling to a foreign environment – Richardson's *Pilgrimage*, a work about England if there ever was one, begins in Germany and moves to the Swiss Alps in the volume *Oberland*, for example – geographical rootedness remains a common feature of their fiction, as it had been for their Victorian predecessors. This strong concern with location is inherited by the South African-Scottish writer Zoë Wicomb, but she complicates it by exploring the ways in which spaces can overlap or collide in the consciousnesses of those whose existence has a global dimension.[1]

Mercia Murray, the Namaqualand-born central character of Wicomb's 2014 novel *October*, is on the train back to Glasgow after a rather unsuccessful trip to Edinburgh when she passes through the small town of Falkirk. Seeing the name on the station signs she reflects, 'No escape from home there'. An explanation of this unlikely association between provincial Scotland and provincial South Africa follows: 'Falkirk was the name stamped in relief on the three-legged cast-iron pots at home, pots manufactured for the colony, for Africans to cook their staple mealiepap over an open fire' (112). This is no mere verbal coincidence of the sort Joyce exploited to the limit

---

[1] Driver provides a full and perceptive account of the role of location in Wicomb's writing ('Zoë Wicomb's Translocal'). See also the collection *Zoë Wicomb & the Translocal*, ed. Easton and Attridge, which opens with Driver's essay.

in *Finnegans Wake*, but has a basis in the real world: Falkirk Foundry (later Falkirk Iron Company) was established in 1810 and grew to be a leading supplier of cast-iron goods to the Empire; by 1914 it had 1500 employees, and it stayed in business until 1981.[2] Falkirk pots were successfully marketed in South Africa to the indigenous population to replace the clay pots that had traditionally been used for cooking.

This is one of many moments in Wicomb's fiction when the history of colonialism makes itself felt as a vivid impression experienced by a character, suddenly fusing the here and now with a distant reality thanks to links forged a century or more earlier. But, as Mercia is well aware, not only is the 'traditional' African pot in fact an import from the imperial centre, it's now being purchased by middle-class South Africans to be used in 'fashionable braais' as a marker of their imagined anti-colonial endorsement of native tradition (112).[3] The imprint of history is not a static presence in Wicomb's fiction but is constantly changing, creating new connections while obliterating others. Geography, too, is not a matter of maps and miles, but a lived reality, now shrinking, now expanding. These moments of translocal association are always infused with a complicated array of feelings and always raise the question of 'home', a concept subject to particular stress in the migrations that are the aftermath of colonialism: on this occasion Mercia unselfconsciously uses the word to refer to the country she left over two decades earlier; at other times she agonises over the meaning of the word, and over the relative claims of Kliprand in Little Namaqualand, where she grew up, and Glasgow, where she has lived for two and a half decades, to occupy the emotional space of 'home'.

Wicomb conveys brilliantly the affective complexity of these experiences, using fictional means to register the personal consequences of the long history of colonial exploitation. Her novels and short stories abound in South Africans who, for one reason or another, have travelled to Europe, and very few of them feel entirely comfortable in their new surroundings. In one of the linked stories of Wicomb's first fictional work, *You Can't Get Lost in Cape Town* (published in 1987), her semi-autobiographical character Frieda Shenton, back in South Africa after having lived for more than ten years in England, says that her view of the latter country will always be 'the view of a Martian' (130). She has returned to her native country because she is 'tired of being stared at' (119), and one of her strongest memories of England is of her tears as she watched the drops falling from her leaking kitchen roof. In *David's Story* (2000), the visit to Glasgow by the South

---

[2] See 'Falkirk Iron Co' in *Grace's Guide to British Industrial History*.

[3] 'Braai' is short for 'braaivleis', or barbecue.

African ANC guerrilla David Dirkse proves deeply troubling for him: he gets nothing out of a visit to the magnificent Burrell Collection – not even remembering the name of the gallery – and is profoundly disturbed by the ghostly apparition of a painted-out slave in the Glassford family portrait hanging in the People's Palace, an apparition that conjures up the unsavoury practices upon which the city's wealth was built.[4] Marion Campbell, in Wicomb's next novel, the 2006 *Playing in the Light*, going on a grand European tour after the revelation of her parents' racial history, finds the world 'all aslant' (187) and cries continually while she is in London, spending much of the time reading the South African novels recommended to her before her departure by a saleswoman in a Cape Town bookshop.

Several further versions of these experiences of affective dislocation in the metropolitan centre occur in Wicomb's more recent short stories. In the title story of *The One That Got Away* (2008) the young South African Jane, on her honeymoon in Glasgow, is driven out of Princess Square by a group of local girls whose speech she can't understand (42) and in 'There's the Bird that Never Flew' (a story which also takes place during that honeymoon) some of her anxieties are listed: 'her fear of fumbling with the unfamiliar, her hatred of being conspicuous, of being stared at, of shop assistants speaking slowly, loudly, to accommodate her foreignness, of children pointing' (68). 'Nothing Like the Wind' is focalized through Elsie, whose discomfort after having moved with her father and brother from the Karoo to Glasgow includes her uncertainties about class: her father, she feels, 'does not know that it is different over here: that difference, no longer simply identified by surface, the colour of skin or texture of hair, is hidden' (136). Another young female expatriate narrates 'My Name is HannaH'; she has moved from the Karoo to Nottingham with her father, and finds herself identifying with the South African poet Arthur Nortje among his Oxford student companions: ill at ease, but pretending to be at home. Dorothy Brink, in 'In the Botanic Gardens' is repeatedly subjected to confusing and alienating encounters – the incomprehensible speech of a kilted British Council representative, a foul-mouthed taxi-driver, the apparent coded message on a Clydesdale Bank banknote. And among the resonances of the title of *October* is Mercia's dislocating experience of that particular month in Glasgow as a time of autumnal melancholy rather than joyous spring. All these characters, from Frieda Shenton to Mercia Murray, are coloured, in the South African sense of the word, and their discomfort

---

[4] For an account of the Glassford portrait, and a reproduction of the barely visible head, see https://glasgowmuseumsslavery.co.uk/2018/08/14/john-glass-fords-family-portrait/.

clearly has much to do with the racially-tinged perceptions of those they encounter in Europe, and especially in the context of the predominantly white culture of Scotland.[5]

The discomfort of relocation and non-belonging is also something that comes up repeatedly in interviews with Wicomb herself. Born in remote Namaqualand in 1948, she left her native South Africa for the UK in 1970, and in 1990, at the beginning of a three-year stint back at the Cape, she said to Eva Hunter, 'In some ways I have acculturated in Britain – I'm middle class, educated and in a sense grew up there – but in another sense I will always be an outsider' (87). In an interview published in the *Scotsman* in 2006 she said, 'I have a ghost existence here: my whole intellectual and emotional life is in South Africa,' and to Stephan Meyer and Thomas Olver she commented in 2007, 'It's not possible for me to belong in Scotland: one couldn't in a place where one's difference is so salient'(182). In a 2001 interview, Hein Willemse asks her – in connection with a discussion of her willingness to raise challenging questions about the ANC liberation struggle in *David's Story* – if she could 'define (her) freedom to write brought about by the physical distance from South Africa' and Wicomb replies, 'I don't know whether that distance affords me any freedom. I really doubt it, because I'm in denial about living abroad' (150). On reading Rushdie's *The Ground beneath Her Feet*, she says, 'I suddenly realized I can't be a writer and keep on living in Scotland. I can't continue living on childhood experiences. A good third of *David's Story* is based on childhood experiences: people I've known, people I've spoken to. You can't go on writing if you're not living close to the place that you're writing about' (151).

In her important essay on 'Setting, Intertextuality and the Resurrection of the Postcolonial Author' Wicomb again expresses her doubts about being able to continue to mine her memories of the place she grew up in, but she also offers an interesting theoretical account of the difficulty of writing about the place to which she has transplanted herself. She uses Kaja Silverman's notion of 'proprioceptivity' to provide a rationale:

> If the foreigner is marked by her visual salience and the natives' focus on her difference, the imagined envelope of space will not fit her snugly; she will

---

[5] Among the numerous discussions of this aspect of Wicomb's work are Marais, 'Bastards and Bodies'; Macmillan and Graham, 'The "Great Coloured Question"'; Robolin, 'Properties of Whiteness'; Dass, 'A Place in which to Cry'; and Jacobs, 'Playing in the Dark/ Playing in the Light'. Van der Vlies summarises the apartheid context of Wicomb's writing in 'Zoë Wicomb's South African Essays'. Wicomb provides a penetrating account of colouredness in South Africa in 'Shame and Identity'.

necessarily have difficulty in setting her fictions in that space or in pressing her characters into ill-fitting envelopes that would render then posturally disfigured. ('Setting, Intertextuality', 239)

However, in a 2017 interview, Wicomb observes that with the passage of time, her position has shifted:

Whilst I am not visually salient in the Cape, there is increasingly the sense of being a stranger there as well. This formulation is perhaps an exaggeration, but what I think I'm trying to say is that the condition of being a stranger is probably not such a bad thing for writing. ('Zoë Wicomb in Conversation', 209)

Several critics have written illuminatingly about Wicomb's challenge to any notion of a comfortable cosmopolitanism, stressing that, as in her life, her work presents no easy crossing of geographical boundaries.[6] And numerous novels and short stories by other South African authors treat of the experience of displacement as a result of global travel, forced or willing – I think of Etienne van Heerden's *30 Nights in Amsterdam* (discussed in the previous chapter), Coetzee's semifictional memoir *Youth*, Nadine Gordimer's *Burger's Daughter*, S. J. Naudé's *The Third Reel*. The singular feature of Wicomb's treatment of this subject to which I wish to pay particular attention is her compelling evocation of the emotionally powerful experience of finding the familiar in the midst of the unfamiliar, connecting distant places and times in a single word or sight, as occurs in *October* with the name 'Falkirk'.

In a number of Wicomb's works, the uncanny feeling that the unfamiliar has suddenly revealed itself to be familiar is often both comforting and unsettling at one and the same time. Thus David, in *David's Story*, notices how many Scottish place names are familiar to him from their South African duplicates, an onomastic product of colonisation:

Everywhere the names of places at home: Kelvingrove, Glencoe, Aberdeen, Lyndoch, Sutherland, Fraserburgh, Dundee. There was no danger of feeling lost in Scotland, except that he felt dizzy with the to-ing and fro-ing between rain-sodden place names and the dry, dusty dorps at home. (188)

For both the British and the South African reader these names are familiar – but they refer to very different places. He can't enjoy the beauty of Glasgow's

---

[6] See, for instance, Driver, 'Zoë Wicomb's Translocal'; Gurnah, 'The Urge to Nowhere'; Parsons, 'Zoë Wicomb's Telescopic Visions'; and Scully, 'History, Critical Cosmopolitanism, and Translocal Mobility'.

sandstone buildings because 'the city began to haunt him with its history of elsewhere, so that the majestic structures would, from time to time, before his very eyes, disappear into a fog' (188).[7] The Clydesdale Bank has the same name as the farm that featured importantly in Abraham le Fleur's land claims on behalf the Griquas, whose history he is researching (189);[8] the Kelvingrove Museum brings back memories of the exclusive Cape Town club where he caddied as a student (189); and the Winter Garden at the People's Palace recalls District Six's long destroyed Winter Garden Hall, where Le Fleur once gave speeches (190). The Glasgow city councillors themselves appear to believe in the significance of verbal coincidence: visiting the working-class area of Govan, they tell David they expect a visit of the ANC leader Govan Mbeki, father of Thabo Mbeki (188), immediately on his release from Robben Island.[9]

Although David's experience grants the new a mantle of familiarity, which might seem reassuring, it's in fact powerfully unsettling: 'In this friendly foreign city, his visit had become an exercise in recognizing the unknown, in remembering the familiar that cast its pall over the new' (189). Yet when an old Glaswegian says repeatedly, 'Ye ken . . .', David's response is positive: 'That *ken*, soothing for being also the Afrikaans word for *know*, quite made up for everything' (188). And David takes 'unexpected pleasure in the tender green of the hothouse versions' of familiar Cape plants – 'palm trees, begonia, poinsettia, hibiscus, and strelitzia' (189). It seems that one can't be sure whether the links between present and past, here and there, strange and familiar are going to produce comfort or unease, and this uncertainty itself adds a further layer to the sense of dislocation. (There's a nice reversal of the familiar/unfamiliar trope when David tells the amanuensis who is ghost-writing his story that according to a brochure in the Winter Garden, 'strelitzia was discovered by a Scots gardener' (194): the joke here is that this flower was already well-known to indigenous South Africans – David's Griqua ancestry goes back to the time before

[7] Richter, in 'Zoë Wicomb's Ghosts', discusses David's Glasgow experience in the appropriate terms of spectrality and 'hauntology'.

[8] See Beinart and Bundy, *Hidden Struggles in Rural South Africa*, 57–8.

[9] Or perhaps one of the councillors has done the necessary homework and discovered that the association is more than merely verbal: Govan Mbeki was named after Edward Govan, a member of the Glasgow Missionary Society who in 1841 founded the Lovedale Missionary Institute, which became one of South Africa's most important black educational institutions. It's likely that the surname Govan – one of the oldest Scottish surnames – derives from the name of the Glasgow district (http://www.alastairmcintosh.com/kandinsky/A-History-of-Govan-to-2011.pdf).

European colonisation – but was unfamiliar to the Scot Francis Masson, who 'discovered' it in 1772. There's a further irony, this time not David's, in that poinsettia and begonia are in fact not native to South Africa.[10])

In *Playing in the Light*, one exception to Marion Campbell's failure to be stimulated by the great cities of Europe is an exhibition in Berlin:

> There was a room filled with photographs of farmhouses, and she could have sworn it was the Karoo: poor-white or perhaps coloured houses, and in one of them an image of a young man in profile, holding a set of handles of something that has already disappeared around the corner of the building. Drawn in that stark, unambiguous light, the figure made her think of her father, pushing an absent wheelbarrow. Marion found tears trickling down her cheeks. (188)

And in London, too, it's the connection between the unfamiliar and the familiar that's most unsettling:

> It's in the assumed familiarity of London that she is invaded by the virus of loneliness. It's here that Marion experiences the world in reverse, feels the topsy-turviness of being in the wrong hemisphere. . . . Believing that at some level she knows the country, or the language, she is shocked to find herself a stranger, so very different from the natives, although the motley crowds about her can hardly all be natives. The sensation of a hole, a curious, negative definition of the familiar emptiness develops in her chest, and she feels compelled to see a doctor. (188–9)

Turning to the short stories in *The One that Got Away*, Jane, in 'There's the Bird that Never Flew', is also struck by the echoes of South African speech in Glaswegian utterances: the cleaner in the hotel says 'yous' (68) for 'you', and her pronunciation of the word *world* provokes two associations: 'The woman pronounces the word like a Xhosa-speaker, inserting another vowel so that it sounds almost like the Afrikaans "wêreld"' (74). The former echo is said to be 'comforting', and the other two provoke no comment; nevertheless, whatever comfort is provided is shadowed by the distance emphasised by the very coincidence.[11] In 'Nothing Like the Wind', Elsie's

---

[10] See Richter, 'Zoë Wicomb's Ghosts', 380 n41.

[11] In *October*, the use in both South African and Scotland of 'stay' where the English would use 'live' is ascribed to the former's 'having inherited the language from the Scots' (14). In 'My Name is HannaH', the narrator – another coloured expatriate from the Karoo feeling out of place in the United Kingdom – deliberately uses this word to refer to her habitation in Nottingham, much to her father's annoyance (199).

sense of dislocation in her new home is manifest in her hearing the Karoo wind in the noise of Glasgow's Great Western Road traffic, even though, as the opening sentence tells us, 'The sound of traffic is nothing like the wind'. The two sounds fuse in a single sentence, which conveys what has been left behind:

> Just about by the post office, she guesses, there is the business of changing gear, of vehicles revved up and whining towards Byres Road, so that the wind whooshes with a whistle across the veld, across the yard, through the out-buildings and the workers' shacks, the rickety deal-wood of doors with cracks and gaps through which it weeps like an orphan. (137)

Elsie manages to avoid asking herself why this unlikely association is occurring to her in such a vivid form ('something like a mathematical calculation, or a grammatical exercise' (135)), but there are times when she is overpowered by a different feeling, reminiscent of the one that causes the buildings of Glasgow to disappear into a fog for David: 'Only sometimes, no doubt to throw her off the track, another world engulfs her, a vague distant one where things remain out of focus' (135). Dorothy Brink, in 'In the Botanic Gardens', is happy to find familiar flowers in the Kibble Palace – the great glasshouse in the Glasgow Botanic Gardens – though they too are in a strange situation, 'sitting pertly behind glass if you please' (491). She is perturbed by the combination of familiar and strange when she sees a photograph of the High Commissioner for Papua New Guinea that strikes her as an image of her missing son Arthur, causing a chill to 'creep up from her feet and spread through her entire body' (171). The fusing of the known with the unknown also furnishes the story with its climax: months afterwards Dorothy remembers, or believes she remembers, the guard who had lifted her to her feet speaking comforting words to her – in Afrikaans.[12]

Mercia's response to the Falkirk signs is also mixed: she 'smirks' at the thought that there is '(n)o escape from home' and finds the petunias and begonias in the hanging baskets – also reminders of South Africa – 'ugly' (112). A little later she finds herself 'unable to leave her seat' when the train arrives in Glasgow; 'Her heart seemed to break over and over again' (113). Mercia also experiences this familiarity within unfamiliarity in the 'wide plains of dry earth and sparse growth' on the island of Lanzarote; she finds the place 'uncannily like that of her childhood', with plants that remind her of the plants of '[g]ood old Kliprand' (205), though they are more lush.

---

[12] McCann discusses the fusion of sameness and difference in 'Nothing Like the Wind' and 'In the Botanic Gardens' in 'Broadening and Narrowing Horizons'.

And again in Macau, 'so many flowers are those of the Cape: bougainvillea, hibiscus, poinsettia, oleander. Perhaps even jacaranda, which, like the frangipani she does recognize, is not in flower' (232). There is also a South African version of the experience of the familiar/unfamiliar involving a flower that many of Wicomb's travellers abroad undergo. In the veld outside Kliprand Mercia remembers the official name of the flower locally known as kalkoentjie (literally, small turkey), *Gladiolus alatus iridaceae*, and it's the Latin, not the Afrikaans, that makes her eyes prick. A question – is it just rhetorical? – follows: 'Does Mercia know that what threatens are tears of self-pity, that she is touched by her own difference, her distance from home?' (39). Kalkoentjies are endemic to the Western Cape, and a strong marker of locality; and the puzzling tears, it seems, are caused by Mercia's sense of her own alienation from that locale, signified by her scholarly knowledge. What might at first appear to be a comment about far-away Glasgow – 'her distance from home' – is, surely, a comment about her feeling of distance from her 'own' language and people of Little Namaqualand. Mercia's inability to write her memoir stems from the same disparity between her scholarly, language-oriented self and the practical lives of her family.

The twinge of recognition produced by names, by flowers, by an individual's speech, by the similarities between far-distant cities, is not arbitrary but the result of the history of global movements of people, languages, and botanical specimens, and of the transplantation of the streets and buildings of towns and cities. Wicomb's characters, feeling even more out of place when we might expect them to feel more comfortably *in* place, seem to register unconsciously the history of suffering that underlies these unexpected chimings. Literary technique here is placed at the service of historical and political understanding.

The Troubling of Time

The events of *Ulysses*, famously, take place over a day; Woolf's *Mrs Dalloway* follows suit. Other modernist novels, however, make freer with time; in Woolf's case, for instance, rapidly passing over the period between two days that occurred ten years apart in *To the Lighthouse*, or spanning centuries, as with *Orlando*. Even in *Ulysses*, time is not linear from the start: the first three episodes take place over the same period as the next three. In *Finnegans Wake*, of course, all times from the Fall to the present are juxtaposed, and often fused; just as places around the globe are amalgamated along with the languages spoken in them.

David's Story combines the troubling of location with a troubling of chronology that shows a certain allegiance to modernism; not only do the sections of the novel move back and forth (or to and fro) between 1991, the present of the novel, and the earlier history of the Griqua people – there are sections headed 'Kokstad 1917' and 'Beeswater 1922' – but David's narrative linking of the Huguenot settler and Griqua forebear Madame la Fleur with the zoologist Georges Cuvier and his prize exhibit Saartje Baartman is avowedly impossible, since there is a century between them (a disparity commented on by the narrator). Moreover, there is plenty of scepticism on the part of the narrator about the very project of constructing such a genealogy. David's exploration of his Griqua roots is made fun of by his sensible wife Sally – 'Don't try to fob me off with nonsense about roots and ancestors, she shouts. Rubbish, it's all fashionable rubbish' (27) – and by the narrator – 'Well, well, I mock. Here we have the true descendant of the Griqua chief, the green-eyed visionary who can make a canvas cough up its secret' (194). The very notion of a Griqua 'identity' is shown to be a dangerous delusion when the treks and edicts of the colourful Griqua leader of the late nineteenth and early twentieth centuries, Andrew Abraham Stockenstrom le Fleur, lead to a conception of ethnic purity that goes hand in glove with the evolving doctrine of apartheid. Wicomb herself has written of the 'mythical excess of belonging or exorbitance of coloured identity . . . denying history and fabricating a totalizing colouredness' ('Shame and Identity', 105).

Yet we cannot forget, once we are aware of the fact, that Wicomb was raised in a Griqua community.[13] She was born, as she puts it in an interview with Eva Hunter, 'in a little, remote Griqua settlement,' which she names as Beeswater (81) – the settlement which is specified in *David's Story* as the unpromising promised land of one of le Fleur's treks.[14] In an interview, she commented that her parents encouraged her to look down on Griqua individuals who engaged in a search for their roots ('Zoë Wicomb in Conversation', 213). But her own researches into, and retelling of, Griqua history cannot be the product of mere distaste. Perhaps the author's stake in the search for Griqua roots is not unconnected with her comment on David's motivation in the interview with Willemse: 'He is still very drawn to some of those notions that he knows are retrogressive' (146). The novel acknowledges, both in its content and the very fact of its emergence from Wicomb's pen, the compulsion to seek for a historical and genealogical

[13] Wicomb's earlier collection of stories, *You Can't Get Lost in Cape Town* (1987), also mixes autobiography and fiction, and provides some vivid vignettes of life in a small Griqua settlement.

[14] Beeswater is near Vanrhynsdorp in Namaqualand, Northern Cape. In 2019, President Ramaphosa presented title deeds to members of the Beeswater community who had been forcibly removed in 1960 under the apartheid laws.

grounding for one's sense of identity, even as it offers a telling critique of such enterprises.

This exploration of genealogy has become a common feature of post-apartheid South African novels, no doubt reflecting a need to complicate the myths of purity, linearity, and separation on which apartheid was founded. The year of *David's Story*'s publication, 2000, was a bumper year for such novels, whose concern with genealogy is often indicated by a family tree. Among the South African novels published in that year was Etienne van Heerden's *The Long Silence of Mario Salviati*, which begins with 'The Yearsonend Blood Tree'.[15] This complex diagram shows the interconnected lines of descent of several of the present-day inhabitants of the Karoo town Yearsonend, a mingling of Khoi, Xhosa, Dutch, and British, with later admixtures of Indonesian and Italian, that makes any attempt at racial classification ludicrous. (Interestingly, Van Heerden's 1986 novel *Toorberg* – translated in 1989 as *Ancestral Voices* – also begins with a family tree, but in this case a heavy dividing line separates the Afrikaner Moolman family from the so-called 'skaamfamilie' (shame family) of coloured relatives.) A second example from the same year is Zakes Mda's *The Heart of Redness*, which opens with a genealogical tree entitled 'The descendants of the headless ancestor', connecting a Xhosa family of the mid-nineteenth century, at the time of the Great Cattle-Killing, with a parallel family in ANC-governed South Africa. Another novel published in 2000 that could well have started with a family tree, as its title suggests, is Elleke Boehmer's *Bloodlines*: however, the unfolding narrative depends on a gradual revelation of generational connections – in this case between an Irish volunteer fighting with the Boers in the Anglo-Boer war at the start of the 20th century and a coloured ANC member who detonates a bomb in a Durban supermarket in the early 1990s – and a family tree would probably have given away too much at the start. And David's story begins with a family tree that links Adam Kok I, the eighteenth-century Griqua leader, to the late twentieth-century family of David and Sally Dirkse.

It can't be sheer coincidence that these four novels exploring the challenges of post-apartheid South Africa, written at the same time but by writers with very different backgrounds (to use somewhat reductive labels: Afrikaans, Xhosa, English/Dutch, and Griqua/Scottish) all concern themselves with a generational history stretching back to a period well before the apartheid era, which began with the election of the Nationalist government in 1948. The effect of this long perspective is that the apartheid years are situated within a larger historical context which was much more

---

[15] I am quoting from the English translation, published in 2002.

difficult to grasp when the racist state loomed large, entirely filling the vision of most writers. Now it's easier to see the apartheid era as a phase – less than two generations – in a much longer history of racial oppression and resistance, one which did not begin in 1948 and did not end in 1994. It's also significant that three of the novels have central characters who are coloured – people whom the apartheid classifiers categorised as 'mixed-race' – since the use of these characters enables the genealogical narrative to explore the dissolving of racial boundaries that was characteristic of South Africa at least from the arrival of Europeans in the seventeenth century. As a result, the ideology of racial purity that emerged in the nineteenth century and dominated political life in South Africa for half of the twentieth century stands out all the more clearly as not only an appalling evil but also, and more encouragingly, a historical anomaly.

Genealogical history and modernism are perhaps not obvious bedfellows, but I think it's true to say that all four of these novelists have learned from modernism, though with significant differences among them. Van Heerden employs magic realism in *The Long Silence*, although in all other respects he writes in a traditional manner in this work. Mda's novel, too, has a touch of magic realism, when his distant generations fuse into one, and his temporal dislocations and juxtapositions, like Wicomb's, belong more fully to the modernist heritage. Boehmer also draws on the repertoire of modernist techniques in her collage of documents in *Bloodlines*, interrupting and complicating the narrative. But it's Wicomb who exploits most fully the possibilities, and conveys most forcefully the new uncertainties, that we associate with the early twentieth-century innovations of modernism and their long heritage. [16]

The Troubling of Representation

It might seem odd that a story should be called *David's Story*, but it becomes quickly clear that this is indeed the story of a story – of the telling and the writing, and also of the withholding, of a story. It is, from the title on, both

---

[16] Kaelie Giffel demonstrates the modernist impulses at work in *David's Story*, noting its references to Joyce and Conrad ('Historical Violence and Modernist Forms'). Wicomb's most recent novel, *Still Life*, also travels across centuries with ease: the twenty-first century writer is haunted by the ghosts of three nineteenth-century figures – Thomas Pringle, the Scottish poet and abolitionist, Mary Prince, whose autobiographical account of slavery he helped write, and Hinza Marossi, the African boy he adopted at the Cape – who take on a very concrete existence, along with a fictional character from Woolf's *Orlando*, Nicholas Greene, who is already a time-traveller.

strongly committed to and unsettlingly sceptical of, the power of narrative, a scepticism shared by its author: Wicomb observes in her interview with Olver and Meyer, 'I have used historical sources, but since there is no simple or fixed process of transferring those to my page – different writers will produce different texts from the same sources – and the very fact that I set out to use these in the service of what is to some extent a pre-conceived project, necessarily turns it into faction' ('Zoë Wicomb on *David's Story*', 132–3). David Dirkse, who is carrying out undercover work in the Cape for the ANC (even though the ANC is no longer a banned organisation) has come to the unnamed narrator, a woman who is sympathetic to but not a participant in the organisation's military campaign, because, rather like Susan Barton in Coetzee's *Foe*, he wants his story told. When the narrator asks him 'why he wants his story written – which is to say, have it read' he replies that 'it is not that he wants to be remembered; rather, it is about putting things down on paper so that you can see what there is, shuffle the pages around, if necessary, until they make sense' (140).

The story of *David's Story* is, then, first of all the story of the telling of the story (including the reluctance that marks the telling), and of the writing of the story. At several points in the novel, the ghost-writer describes her meetings with David, whose story, to make things more complicated, moves on between meetings. We never know to what extent the story we're reading is the fabrication of the narrator, filling in the gaps left by David or letting her imagination develop the hints he has dropped, since we get only a few direct quotations of David's speech and some puzzling doodles from his hand (as well as a reproduction of the aforementioned family tree that he has drawn).[17]

Like the geographical and temporal crossings discussed earlier, the troubling of representational certainties in the novel is not simply a modernist cliché implying the fallibility of all communication and the slipperiness of all language, however; it's a direct product of the ambiguities and conflicts of the historical time at which and the place in which the novel is set. In the year 1991, when apartheid is crumbling, various players are jockeying for position in the rapidly changing political arena, and many unspeakable deeds are being done in the hope of gaining advantage or with the aim of settling scores; these are what the novel calls 'days of treachery and flux and things being all mixed up' (13). Just as the instability and confusion in Europe in the period immediately after the Second World War is captured

---

[17] This family tree, like David's historical narrative, has an error in its marking of centuries; Adam Kok I is shown as having died in 1875, which is around a century too late.

in the fluid and perplexing narrative of Pynchon's *Gravity's Rainbow*, so the uncertainties of the period of transition from apartheid to democracy produce both David's desire to make sense of his own part in the struggle and the thwarting of that desire as the narrative slides around, falters, and, quite literally, explodes.

This, then, is not the familiar tale of bad white South Africans (with their black lackeys) against brave, usually black, opponents (understandably the dominant narrative of black writers in the apartheid years). The bad white South Africans are scarcely present, except in a generalised way as the old enemy now in retreat. David's secrets, that he does and does not want to divulge, concern events *within* the liberation movement.[18] Wicomb has chosen to place at the centre of her novel – albeit a shadowy centre – a part of South Africa's recent history that many who, quite rightly, wish to celebrate the achievements of the ANC would prefer to leave unexamined: the treatment of individuals and groups who did not conform to the requirements laid down by the Movement. She is especially interested in the position of female and coloured combatants, and in the treatment of dissidents, in Umkhonto we Sizwe (Spear of the Nation), the guerrilla wing of the ANC. If one of the roles of the postcolonial novel is to rewrite official history in order to reveal what has been occluded by it, *David's Story* undoubtedly deserves the label. Yet in probing the official history not of the colonial masters but of a triumphant liberation movement she is doing something that at the same time tests the values and norms of postcolonial writing. The experience of reading the novel is far more than finding out about deliberately obscured areas of history.

David's task in the transition period is to work out 'how to maintain an army while officially dismantling it' (108). He is thus involved himself in the subterfuge and dishonesty characteristic of the political negotiations in progress, as they have been characteristic of the years of racist government and resistance to it. To give one small example, at one point the narrator asks David: 'So in the New South Africa militarised men and women will enter civic positions without declaring themselves as the military?' He answers: 'What else can we do. . . . Such lives that have always, necessarily, been wrapped in secrecy can't be unwrapped at this stage' (79). But it emerges that, although a highly respected leader in the Movement, he has

---

[18] Dorothy Driver, in her Afterword to the Feminist Press edition of the novel, spells out some of what is known about the treatment of dissidents and suspected traitors in the ANC; she also provides useful background information about the history of the Griqua people.

some black marks against him – his support for the mutineers in the ANC camp in Angola where dissidents were held in the 1980s, the now notorious Quatro camp; an imprudent conversation in Glasgow with a South African intelligence agent, observed by his own side's security personnel; and the fact that he and another high-ranking coloured cadre, a woman named Dulcie Olifant, appear to be working together in defiance of the Movement's rules. One of the most gripping threads of the plot concerns David's visit to Kokstad (a town, now in KwaZulu-Natal, founded by Adam Kok III in 1863), during which he becomes increasingly aware that a trap is being laid for him, not by the white security forces – who play no part in the story – but by his own comrades. The worry that runs through the novel is expressed at one point by Dulcie (or in the words the narrator imagines might occur to Dulcie): 'if on the edge of a new era, freedom should announce itself as a variant of the old' (184).

David's fascination with the history of the Griqua people stems in part from the stories told to him by his grandmother, Ouma Ragel, stories that link her to Le Fleur. It's a straw he grasps at as all the old certainties begin to disappear, a straw that seems particularly appropriate as he suspects that his racial identity is partly behind the suspicion in which he is held by his comrades now that black majority rule looks like a real possibility. (The incipient racism in the ANC is parallel to that which David experiences among his own community, and which motivates, in part, his research into their history: his father, for instance, distances himself from 'the kaffirs and the Hotnos' and is proud to have shaken off 'the Griquaness, the shame and the filth and idleness' (23).) A substantial part of the novel relates the tale of le Fleur's campaigns on behalf of the Griqua people, ending in his disastrous endorsement of apartheid ideology.

And so we get two unfolding narratives, separated by three-quarters of a century: the story of Le Fleur's dealings with the old South African powers, providing, at least at moments, comic relief from the uneasy story of his descendant's dealings with its new powers. However, the nexus of the perplexities and searchings that pervade the book is the figure of Dulcie, about whom David is reluctant to speak but around whom his thoughts constantly circle. The reality of her experience is conveyed with extraordinary intensity, and yet it's one of the most doubtful realities in the book. It tests, more strongly than anything else, the limits of narrative as a conveyor of truth.[19]

---

[19] 'Truth' is a word that becomes oddly defamiliarised in the scribbles David has given the narrator: he changes it to 'the palindrome of Cape Flats speech' – TRURT – and repeats it over and over (136).

As leaders of separate cells, David and Dulcie have rarely met, but they have fallen in love – even though they have never spoken of their mutual attraction and, apart from handshakes, the only physical contact they have had is an occasion when David put his hands on Dulcie's shoulders, an occasion they both remember vividly. (This, at least, is the story the narrator constructs.) It's hinted that they have both objected to the treatment of coloureds in what was primarily an African guerrilla movement. Both bear the scars of torture, perhaps undergone in the Quatro camp. They are now both subject to surveillance by the movement to which they belong, even as they go about their political activities on its behalf.

But for Dulcie, there is worse than surveillance. She is being tortured in her home at night by a troop of unidentified people, and the descriptions of these visits are among the most chilling pages of the novel. I can give only a couple of extracts:

> The men in balaclavas come like privileged guests into her bedroom, in the early hours, always entering the house by different routes. . . . One of them carries a doctor's Gladstone bag filled with peculiar instruments and electrical leads. (81–2)

> They do not speak unnecessarily. For special operations she is blindfolded. They grunt and nod in a shadow play of surgeons, holding out hands for instruments, gesturing at an electrical switch. A woman, who does not always come along, performs the old-fashioned role of nurse – mopping up, dressing wounds. Once, as she left, even lifting the edge of the mattress to tuck in the sheet in a neat hospital fold. (178)

These and other passages detailing a meticulously planned and executed program of torture present a host of conundrums. Are these Dulcie's comrades? (She feels at times that she recognises them.) What crime, in their eyes, is she paying for? (On the first visit, the one in charge says to his colleagues, 'Not rape, that will teach her nothing, leave nothing; rape's too good for her kind' (178).) Why does her torture seem so like a surgical operation? Why is she not told the reasons for what is being done, if it's meant as a lesson? (She deliberately does not ask for an explanation, since she knows she will be lied to.) Why is the torture repeated night after night? Why can she do nothing about it? (Occasionally, we learn, she is left with enough strength to pursue and shoot, always successfully, at her visitors (181); but she is unable to prevent the repeated intrusions.) What is the connection, if any, with David? (She associates the visits with her relationship with him, though 'she does not know why or how' (184); while he draws versions of her mutilated body (205).)[20] Dulcie herself speculates on the ambiguity of these visitations: there is something in her torturers 'that makes them both friend and foe as they tend to the cracks and wounds carefully inflicted on parts of the body that will be clothed' (179); Dorothy Driver calls them her 'lover-torturers' (240). Dulcie has no doubts or regrets about her own past actions – 'She has done nothing less than her duty, nothing less than fighting for freedom and justice – even though these words have now become difficult' (179). She knows they are trying to drive her to suicide, and she triumphs over them by staying alive.[21]

These accounts are so vivid that while we read them we forget that they are written, within the fictional frame, by a story-teller trying to piece together the bits of David's life. If David is so reluctant to talk about Dulcie, who, then, has provided the information about the nightly visits, so chillingly described? And if it is David, how does he know about them if he is not implicated himself? Or is our narrator fabricating a terrible story to answer some need of her own? After a conversation in which he has been more open than before about the possible reasons for punitive behaviour by their comrades – including the mistaken belief that, as two coloureds with similar views, they were working together in opposition to the leadership – he whispers, 'It's here in close-up, before my very eyes, the screen full-bleed with Dulcie. Who? Is it you put it in my head? The terrible things happening to Dulcie? It's here, in close-up – and he stumbles to his feet with a horrible cry, knocking me over as he charges out' (201). But the next day he is prepared to talk about Dulcie's fate in a way that suggests the narrator was on the right track all along:

> Yes, she's grown too big for her boots and they've had enough of her. She must give up her power, hand over her uniform, make way for the big men. But that is not enough. She knows too much; knows the very fabrications, the history of every stitch against her. She must – and he stops abruptly. (204)

The narrative itself stops abruptly a few pages later, when an unknown marksman fires a bullet into the computer on which it's being typed. The violence that had looped its way through David's and Dulcie's story, driving the former to his death and seeking to do the same to the latter, and that has recently begun to touch the narrator, has finally destroyed the story itself –

[20] There is also the strange business of the hit list: David scores out her name, adds a comment, and finally passes it to the disguised security operative.

[21] Meg Samuelson discusses the scenes of Dulcie's torture in a perceptive essay on Wicomb's concern with the female body in 'The Disfigured Body'.

except for the backup copy which, we learned a little earlier, she always slips into her pocket when she leaves the computer. Although it would be a mistake not to keep narrator and author separate, we cannot make an absolute distinction between the story contained on the narrator's disk in Cape Town and the one on Wicomb's disk in Glasgow. They consist, after all, of exactly the same words.

Wicomb's fiction, from the stories of *You Can't Get Lost in Cape Town* (where the death and subsequent reappearance of the heroine's mother suggests that the mode is not-quite-realism) to the time-travelling ghosts of *Still Life*, presents a highly distinctive take on modernism: relishing the licence it offers to ignore the constraints of time and place, it nevertheless locates this freedom, and the amalgamations and juxtapositions it facilitates, in the concrete worlds of her characters, exploring the formations and deformations of their – and our – historical and global situatedness.

CHAPTER 10

Form and Content:
Eleanor Catton's *The Luminaries*

Organic Form

Criticism of the novel is concerned, above all, with meaning – and, most often, meaning understood as a noun, something that can be extracted from the text or something outside the text to which it refers. Character, plot, scene, motive, development, crisis, recognition, reversal, and other features of the world brought into being by the text are the staple of most accounts of fictional works. Less often, criticism concerns itself with the *experience* of meaning, how the text does its work of meaning as it is read (which, to my mind, is a better way to think of literary meaning). In either case, when the question of form is being addressed in studies of the novel, and when it's not simply being described, it's almost always assumed to have as its sole *raison-d'être* the enhancement or complication of meaning in this sense – what we can call 'referential meaning', or content. When Samuel Richardson writes *Clarissa* in the form of letters, it's in order to convey a sense of immediacy and authenticity in the writing; when Dickens switches between first-person and third-person narration in *Bleak House* it's in order to achieve a contrast between subjective and objective views of the world – these, at least, are the kinds of explanation usually given. And if a critic raises the question of the pleasure to be gained from literary form – a question not often asked, but in my view a crucial question, one which underlies all our reading – the answer is usually also given in terms of its contribution to the referential meaning of the work.

Literary form is most often discussed in terms of the dictum that form and content are inseparable, that the former arises 'naturally' from the latter, an idea that goes back at least to the Romantics. The notion of 'organic form', introduced most influentially into English literary criticism by

Coleridge (in the footsteps of A. W. Schlegel), continues to surface right up to the present. Statements about the inseparability of form and content could be culled from a wide range of critical and theoretical texts, ranging from introductions for students to philosophical tomes. The hugely influential model of interpretation favoured by the founders and proselytisers of 'close reading' in Britain and the USA – T. S. Eliot, I. A. Richards, William Empson, F. R. Leavis, W. K. Wimsatt, Reuben Brower, and many others – took this inseparability as a fundamental axiom. Yet there is also an ancient tradition – more ancient, in fact – of proposing form alone as a source of pleasure, without being the subsidiary partner in a form-content marriage. Music and the visual arts are obvious domains in which this tradition flourishes, and some lyric poems might be said to possess formal arrangements that please in their own right. I wish to follow up the thought that form – sonic, visual, structural, rhetorical – can operate in ways other than as a reflection, or enhancement, of the content established by the referential function of the words. By approaching the question in terms of the reader's experience, it's possible to explore how form can not only be a source of pleasure in its own right but can make a singular contribution to the operation of the text as a work of literature taking place in the world.

Before going any further, it's necessary to clarify what exactly is meant by these two terms, *content* and *form*, in the argument I am making. I take content to be the world which the words of the text bring into being for the reader, including the dictionary meanings of words, the referents of proper names (where these are non-fictional), the images conjured up by both literal and metaphorical verbal collocations, and the characters, narrator(s), places and events in a narrative sequence. Form, by contrast, comprises all those features of the text that don't point to the extra-verbal world of people, things, events, and places: its material properties (such as sounds and rhythmic movement), its repetitions and patterns, its adherence to or deviations from established conventions, its structural articulations, and its lexical and syntactic characteristics. What is termed 'style' is the consistent use of certain formal properties, say the employment of arcane vocabulary, the preference for short sentences, or the repetition of particular grammatical structures.

The use of rhetorical figures is an aspect of form, some (traditionally called *figures of speech*) involving the verbal surface, such as alliteration, anaphora, or archaism, others (*figures of thought* or *tropes*) having a more direct relation to the content, such as metaphor, personification, or bathos. In making this distinction, it's helpful to think in terms of the reader's experience. A rhetorical figure is a moment of disturbance in the smooth processing of language: in the case of a figure of speech, it's a linguistic feature (like a rhyme) that momentarily makes one aware of the words' material composition; in the case of a figure of thought, it's an eddy in the seamless passage from language to meaning (as when a metaphor requires an act of interpretation). With a figure of thought, the result is a modification of the content; with a figure of speech, the relation to content is less obvious.

Although my concern in this book is not with poetry, we can turn to the features of regular verse to challenge the idea that form always relates to content. Does every metrical line forge a union between form and content? Can every rhyme be justified as contributing to the referential meaning of the poem? Although much critical ingenuity has been deployed in making such connections, the vast majority of lines don't exhibit close unity of form and content. The history of Western poetry in the twentieth century illustrates the abiding impact of the doctrine of organic form at the same time as it highlights the inorganic nature of traditional verse form: poets who threw off what they saw as the shackles of meter and rhyme often did so in the name of an increased organicism. In doing so, however, they removed one of the sources of readerly pleasure. As children, we enjoyed rhyme and meter for their own sakes, or perhaps for their assault on the semantic operation of language; as adults, we should not pretend we have lost that ability to enjoy the patterned dance of words.[1]

To make this point is not to devalue the power of form as a component of the meaning of the literary work, in all the ways critics have pointed out (although this is an area in which fanciful claims tend to proliferate). Nevertheless, I want to suggest that to appreciate fully the revolution in literary fiction carried out by Joyce we need to raise the question of what I'm calling 'inorganic form': that is, the contribution made to the reader's experience (and, I would add, pleasurable experience) by formal properties operating with a degree of independence – without, that is, playing second fiddle to content.

---

[1] A recent assertion of the importance of recognising that the formal properties of verse don't necessarily contribute to meaning comes from Jonathan Culler: 'Rhythm, repetition, sound patterning [are] independent elements that need not be subordinated to meaning and whose significance may even lie in a resistance to semantic recuperation' (*Theory of the Lyric*, 8). The history of drama in European languages also reveals the operation of formal constraints, such as observation of the classical unities, the division into five acts, or the *liaison des scenes* preventing the stage from being emptied of characters. For an even more obvious indication of the capabilities of form divorced from semantic content, we need think only of the power of non-verbal music.

Inorganic Form in *Ulysses*

The use of innovative formal devices in order to enhance the reader's experience of content was, of course, a significant marker of modernist fiction. Dorothy Richardson's use of stream-of-consciousness narration in *Pilgrimage* captures the movements of Miriam Henderson's mind; the repeating cycle of narrative voices in Virginia Woolf's *The Waves* represents the fluidity of human awareness; Joyce, in developing the technique of interior monologue in *Ulysses*, was able to express the constant flux of an individual's inner life with unprecedented immediacy. And many of the novels labelled 'postmodern' or 'late modernist' similarly find inventive ways of extending the fictional use of language in the service of more precise, more intense, or more humorous representations. In Chapter 12, I discuss three different fictional styles: Eimear McBride's tortured syntax in *A Girl is a Half-formed Thing* and *The Lesser Bohemians*, the grammatically continuous, spatially punctuated, prose of Mike McCormack's *Solar Bones*, and the imaginative dialogues of Kevin Barry's *Beatlebone*. Other recent examples would include the onrush of mental fragments in Patrick McCabe's *Poguemahone* ('If you're looking for this century's *Ulysses*, look no further', wrote Alex Preston in the *Observer*), and what has been called the 'stream-of-fractured-consciousness' of Will Self's Busner trilogy – the novels *Umbrella*, *Shark*, and *Phone*.[2]

But what are we to say about Joyce's parade of prose styles tracking the history of writing in English in 'The Oxen of the Sun' episode of *Ulysses*? Or the lengthy lists of phrasal permutations in Beckett's *Watt*? Justifications in terms of content can, and have, been given for these: the development of English prose in Joyce's text mirrors the stages of gestation and thus relates to the context of the maternity hospital, for instance, and Beckett's lists reflect the narrator's obsessive attempt to control all possibilities of articulation. Such interpretations are all well and good, but they may themselves reflect a Wattian desire to control the excesses of form, the places where formal devices seem to operate in distinction from – or even in defiance of – content. If we focus on the way we experience these formal features we have to admit that any contribution they may make to our appreciation of the characters, places, and events we are being asked to imagine is not part of the reading process whereby we engage with content.[3] We don't, as we read 'Oxen of the Sun', keep an image of a developing foetus in mind while

---

[2] See Preston, 'Fiction to look out for' and Leith, 'What could be saner?'.

[3] In *The Rhythms of English Poetry*, I distinguished between two ways in which language can be iconic: *mimetic* and *emblematic*. Emblematic devices 'provide relations between the linguistic substance and the larger world only by means of a conscious intellectual act' (288). See p. 44, note 23 above.

turning the pages; it's much more engrossing to trace the manner in which Joyce has met the self-imposed challenge of capturing the stages of prose style while relating relatively banal content. And how many of us actually read every word of those prolonged permutations in *Watt*? Once we see how the pattern is operating, the temptation to skip is almost irresistible – something that would result in a loss of potentially valuable information in fiction that is entirely taken up with the task of representing the world.

In the history of the novel, Joyce's decision to write each of the later chapters of *Ulysses* in a distinct style constituted a major break, freeing novelistic form from its age-old servitude to content. What was especially momentous about this decision was that the style didn't necessarily emerge naturally from the content of the chapter. Although critics – under the enduring influence of the idea of organic form – have consistently looked for justifications of the style of each episode (so the wordy infelicities of 'Eumaeus' are supposed to reflect Bloom's 'tiredness', when in fact there's evidence of considerable mental energy on the part of the represented consciousness; or the catechistic over-explicitness of 'Ithaca' is said to indicate his 'detachment', when he is clearly engrossed in the utterances of his companion), these distinctly *post hoc* accounts don't stand up to serious scrutiny.

The appearance of *Ulysses* was a moment from which there was, and is, no going back: in showing us that our pleasure in representational fiction is not lessened when we are enjoying other features of the writing that have little to do with those representations, Joyce transformed the field for future authors. One could say the same, in fact, of the whole Homeric scheme of *Ulysses*: it's fun to trace the parallels between events and characters in the *Odyssey*, but they don't contribute to our direct comprehension of Leopold Bloom's and Stephen Dedalus's inner lives on 16 June, 1904.

Important as this breakthrough was, Joyce built into *Ulysses* an even more radical challenge to the subservience of form to content, a challenge I discussed in Chapter 2: there are moments when, in a reversal of the normal relationship, the *style* chosen for an episode appears to have an influence upon the *content*. Joyce allows the designated Homeric counterparts in a chapter to infiltrate the narrative and even affect the way characters think and speak, so that terms relating to death or the heart proliferate in the 'Hades' episode, references to wind abound in 'Aeolus', and words that have musical meanings are everywhere in 'Sirens'. The pleasure we derive from these correspondences is not one of enhanced realism; on the contrary, it's enjoyment of the formal device independently of the content. As noted earlier, this kind of pleasure is ubiquitous in *Finnegans Wake*. To take one small example, when the Lord's Prayer is transmuted into a song of praise for Anna Livia (both woman and river) – 'haloed by her eve, her singtime sung, her rill be run, unhemmed as it is uneven!' – we may find the implicit blasphemy amusing or shocking, but above all we take delight in Joyce's exploitation of verbal echoes where we would least expect them.

We could describe many of these Joycean effects as the operation of *rules*, chosen with a degree of arbitrariness, upon the style and other formal properties of the text, over and above the rules governing grammar, genre, and sense. *Ulysses* as a whole, for instance, is subject to such rules as 'relate each chapter to an episode in Homer's *Odyssey*; give the main characters Homeric equivalents; make every chapter correspond to an organ, an art, a "technic", etc.' (In some cases, however, it's likely that Joyce decided on the correspondence after having written the chapter.) Individual chapters are subject to other rules: 'Where there is a choice of terms, choose the one that suggests a death/the heart/flowers/wind/music . . . etc.' Although some commentators have sought to attribute these rules to the work of a hidden originator,[4] there's no need to invoke a human figure at work deploying them – except that we are aware of Joyce's own presence behind the verbal games, smiling rather than paring his fingernails (a point I shall return to at the end of this essay).

The pleasure we take in noting Joyce's successful implementation of his self-imposed rules is in part an appreciation of his *craft*. As I noted in the Introduction, the element of craft is something works of art share with other well-made artefacts; it doesn't elicit the same kind of response as the work's singular inventiveness, taking the reader into new mental and emotional terrain, and thus doesn't have the potential to change their grasp on the world, but it does provide real enjoyment coupled with admiration for the artist's skill. To say that the formal arrangements of a literary work can please in their own right is to draw attention to the value of craft. Once we notice the flower words in 'Lotus-Eaters' or the musical terms in 'Sirens' we're likely to smile inwardly each time they occur; they are a kind of pun, and puns are, potentially at least, a pleasurable linguistic effect.

There may be more to this aspect of *Ulysses*, however; to say that these features operate independently of the work's content is not to say that they have no significance other than as a source of pleasure in the writer's skill. To find external imperatives governing content is to have the assumptions on the basis of which we usually read fiction challenged: it's to be reminded that the words we are engaging with are all the result of deliberate choices, and that there are rules governing even the most transparent realism that

---

[4] The best-known of these suggestions is David Hayman's 'Arranger' (*'Ulysses'*). This Arranger has human agency; for instance, Hayman refers to the 'intrusive and puckish arranging impulse' (125).

the writer has to follow in order to achieve the effects desired. There are also more specific rewards: the word-choices in *Ulysses* and the matches between Joyce's novel and the *Odyssey*, for instance, function to fuse elements of the perceived world normally kept apart: we see new patterns and new alignments, just as we do in a successful metaphor. The basic principle of organic form thus slips in by the back door: no formal is arrangement is *completely* meaningless, though its meanings may have nothing to do with the obvious content.

Inorganic Form after Joyce

Joyce's liberation of form from content didn't have many parallels or immediate successors in modernist fiction, and his practice of allowing form to influence content even fewer. (As I've suggested, the story of poetry is different: notwithstanding the popularity of theories of organic form, formal features are always foregrounded to some degree in verse, and don't in every case make a contribution to content – though it has to be said that a great deal of poetry criticism in recent decades has proceeded with no attention at all to formal questions, as if, that is, the text were in prose.) However, if we think of Joyce as writing *Ulysses* according to rules he devised himself one can identify a few descendants. Samuel Beckett, in *Lessness* (1970),[5] for example, composed a work of 120 sentences in which the first 60 sentences are repeated, but in a different order. In a further self-imposed constraint, he allowed himself only 166 different words.[6] In such a text, part of the reader's pleasure is in the successful resolution of the conflict between language's propensity to flow freely and the tight limitations under which it's being made to work (something we're very familiar with in regular verse, of course).[7] Film also furnishes examples: in Peter Greenaway's *Drowning by Numbers* (1988), for instance, each of the numbers from 1 to 100 either

---

[5] Originally in French as *Sans*, 1969.

[6] I take this figure from an essay by another novelist who was fascinated by numbers: J. M. Coetzee, 'Samuel Beckett's "Lessness"'.

[7] Allowing form to control content is not a twentieth-century invention; Late Antiquity, in particular, was a period that seems to have looked favourably on ingenious linguistic artifice (see Attridge, *The Experience of Poetry*, chapter 6). There is also a long history of numerologically structured literary works; these are, for the most part, poems, but claims have been made for the influence of number symbolism on prose fiction as well. One example is Douglas Brooks's detection of numerological organisation in Fielding's *Joseph Andrews* ('Symbolic Numbers').

appears visually or is spoken by a character, mostly in the correct sequence –
a structure, notes Greenaway, 'independent of any internal plot, story or
narrative.'[8] Noticing the numbers as they appear is part of the fun the movie
has to offer the viewer.

Turning to languages other than English, the most extensive body of
literary works written in obedience to arbitrarily chosen rules is that associated with the *Ouvroir de littérature potentielle* (Workshop of Potential Literature), or Oulipo. Founded by Raymond Queneau and François Le Lionnais
in 1960, Oulipo fostered a huge variety of literary writing in which the
normal generic rules were supplemented (or contradicted) by additional
constraints.[9] The most famous Oulipian works are Queneau's 1947 *Exercices
de style*, in which the same short anecdote is given in ninety-nine different stylistic versions,[10] and Georges Perec's 1969 *La Disparition*, a 300-page
novel in which the letter *e* is missing.[11] Perec was influenced by the less
readable *Gadsby* (1939), by Ernest Vincent Wright, subtitled *A Story of Over
50,000 Words Without Using the Letter 'E'*. Perec used a more complex determining structure in *La Vie mode d'emploi* (1978), in which the actions of
the many characters are generated by the figure known as the Graeco-Latin
bi-square, and the order of the chapters follows the Knight's Tour Problem
in chess. Other English examples include Walter Abish's *Alphabetical Africa*,
in which the initial letter of the words of each chapter is controlled, allowing only words beginning with *a* in the first chapter, *a* or *b* in the second,
and so on, until the process is reversed after chapter 26.

There exist many anthologies and surveys of Oulipian writing, in
both prose and verse (in the latter field, such writing is sometimes called

---

[8] Conway, '30 Years of Drowning by Numbers'. Musical forms, of course, depend
on the observation of rules, such as those of Western harmony or those of twelve-
tone serialism. Translation could also be considered a type of writing-according-
to-rule, in which the original text governs the procedures of the translator.

[9] Jan Baetens makes two important clarifications in discussing 'constrained writing' such as that associated with Oulipo: the rules must be supplementary to the
existing rules, whether those of the language or those accepted by convention,
such as rhyme in standard forms of verse, and they must be applied systemati-
cally ('Oulipo and Proceduralism'). Baetens gives a convincing account of the significant implications of Oulipean writing, which are also insightfully discussed
by Anna Kemp in 'Oulipo, Experiment and the Novel'.

[10] Raymond Queneau, *Exercices de style*, translated by Barbara Wright as *Exercises in
Style*. As the date of publication indicates, the work was Oulipian *avant le lettre*.
Queneau explicitly declared the importance for him of Joyce's work; see Duncan,
'"Joyce, un pornographe"', 352.

[11] Georges Perec, *La Disparition*, translated by Gilbert Adair as *A Void*.

'procedural poetry'), and writers continue to create new constrained texts and to invent new constraints.[12] To take one remarkable recent instance, Christian Bök's 2001 book *Eunoia* consists of five chapters, each of which is composed of words that use only one vowel, in the sequence *a, e, i, o, u;* moreover, each chapter – made up of from five to nineteen 12-line sections, describes 'a culinary banquet, a prurient debauch, a pastoral tableau and a nautical voyage' (103) – a sequence that could be read as alluding to the *Odyssey*.[13]

Some anthologies include examples of what has been called 'anticipatory plagiarism': works (like Queneau's *Exercises de Style*) that pre-date Oulipo but display similar characteristics.[14] One of many specimens is the tradition of the *cento*, a poem made up solely of quotations from other poems. An early instance of this genre is the fourth-century poet Ausonius's 'Nuptial Cento', a sexually explicit description of a wedding day – and night – made up entirely of lines and half-lines from Virgil. *Ulysses*, with its Homeric framework and its episode-appropriate events and vocabulary, undoubtedly deserves a place as an anticipatory Oulipian work. The compendium of rhetorical figures in 'Aeolus', for instance, operates very like an Oulipian text,[15] as do the various rewritings in particular styles – the parodies in 'Cyclops', the pastiches in 'Oxen of the Sun', and the distinctive uses of language in episodes like 'Circe', 'Eumaeus', and 'Ithaca'. *Finnegans Wake* is less obviously Oulipian on account its free-ranging linguistic inventiveness, but – as with the river names in the ALP chapter – there are numerous local examples of the application of transformation rules that turn normal language into a comic echo-chamber.

Another technique that provides formal pleasures from self-imposed limitations are books that are created out of other books. The painted pages

---

[12] Some examples of anthologies in English are Motte, ed., *Oulipo: A Primer of Potential Literature*; Brotchie and Mathews, eds, *Oulipo Compendium*; Monk and Becker, eds, *All that Is Evident Is Suspect*; and Terry, ed., *The Penguin Book of Oulipo*. For a spirited defence of procedural poetry, see Perloff, 'The Oulipo Factor'. Terry, in *The Penguin Book*, lists over seventy-five different Oulipian constraints used by writers (515–20).

[13] Additional constraints observed by Bök include the use of at least 98% of the available vocabulary for each letter and the total exclusion of the letter y. I have not been able to locate a copy of another extraordinary Oulipean fiction of recent times: Doug Nufer's *Never Again* (2004), a 40,000 word novel whose every word is used only once. See Katz, 'Exercises in Wile', 157–8.

[14] See, for instance, Terry, *Penguin Book*, xvii–xviii and *passim*.

[15] As an appendix to their annotations to *Ulysses*, Gifford and Seidman provide a listing of well over a hundred figures of rhetoric in 'Aeolus' (635–43).

of the many versions of Tom Phillips's *A Humument* that have appeared since 1973 all start with the same Victorian novel and allow a story to emerge from the words that escape obliteration by paint. (The cover of this book shows one example of a page.) A similar, though less visually appealing, method was used by Jonathan Safran Foer to create *Tree of Codes* in 2010: he cut out large sections of each page of Bruno Schulz's *The Street of Crocodiles* to create a new narrative from the remaining words. In these examples, the constraint is the set of existing words on each page from which the new creation has to be drawn, and the reader's enjoyment is derived partly from seeing how that challenge is met. Such works also afford an insight into verbal narrative by liberating one story from another in which it was invisibly encased, and raising the possibility that a thousand different narratives could nest in what seems like one. (The multiple versions of *A Humument* begin to show how this might happen.)[16]

It has often been said that after *Ulysses*, novelists were presented with a choice: to write as if it hadn't happened or to embrace the new possibilities it opened up. However, for the writer taking the latter course, there was, and there remains, a further choice: to build on Joyce's inventive use of formal devices for the purpose of enhancing meaning in the traditional way, or to take on board in addition his exploitation of the possibilities offered by inorganic form. A revealing counter-example is from the pen of B. S. Johnson, whose 1963 novel *Travelling People* follows *Ulysses* in using a variety of styles and thus might seem to follow the second path. However, Johnson boasted that he had improved on Joyce 'by allowing the subject matter of each particular series of events which form one chapter to determine organically the style chosen', completely missing the point of the earlier author's formal breakthrough.[17]

Innovative fiction in recent years, much of which is indebted to Joyce, uses form in both these ways. In other chapters I discuss examples of contemporary Irish and South African novels that intensify immediacy and affective power through verbal innovation; these defy the normal rules that govern fiction, but they don't introduce rules of their own. Other examples would include Kate Atkinson's *Life after Life* (2013), which looks on the page like a normal novel but plays with the conventions of narrative form to allow her heroine to follow several alternative life trajectories, George Saunders' *Lincoln in the Bardo* (2017), which mixes documentary quotations

[16] Phillips died while this book was in production. I am deeply grateful to him for allowing me to use a page from *'Humument' Images to Accompany James Joyce's 'Ulysses'* for the cover.

[17] Letter to George Greenfield, 18th October, 1961; in Coe, *Like a Fiery Elephant*, 115.

about the illness and death of Lincoln's son with the imagined voices of the recently dead and sets them out on the page in identical fashion, and Nicola Barker's *H(a)ppy* (2017), which uses varied fonts, coloured print, and other visual devices to complicate the reader's experience.

A different experience is invited by novels governed by an initial formal decision made by the author, whether a fixed scheme that determines the unfolding of the work, as in Beckett's *Lessness* or Bök's *Eunoeia*, or a looser structure that depends on a selection from a potentially much larger series of governing principles, as in *Ulysses*. Donal Ryan's *The Spinning Heart* (2012) has twenty-one chapters each of which is spoken by a different character: the skill with which Ryan unfurls the narrative through the constantly changing narratives is something to relish, while the sequence of voices conveys the role of talk in the community. A related technique signalled by the same metaphor in the title is the weaving of disparate storylines in Colum McCann's *Let the Great World Spin* (2009): the interlocking but very different narratives are held together by their characters' acknowledgement of a feat that is never described (though preparations for it are): Philip Pettit's high-wire walk between the Twin Towers in 1978. We shall return in Chapter 13 to the craft evident in Kamila Shamsie's *Home Fire* (2017) and Damon Galgut's *The Promise* (2021). In all these cases the reader is aware of the mediating presence of the author, telling the tale not just 'as it happened' but according to a predetermined scheme; and yet the illusion of real events being narrated is never shattered. Many other recent examples could be cited, but for the remainder of the chapter I shall concentrate on one remarkable work.[18]

Eleanor Catton, *The Luminaries*

I first encountered Eleanor Catton's *The Luminaries* as an audiobook. I had read very little about the novel and didn't know what I was letting myself in for, though I could see I was in for the long haul. Each of the book's parts, as I listened to it, began with a title, a date (at first all of them in 1866), and a grid reference. Within those parts the chapter headings were intriguing but puzzling; such phrases as 'Mercury in Sagittarius', 'Saturn in Libra', and 'Sun in Capricorn' meant very little to me other than to signal a connection to astrology. It was quickly clear, however, that what I was hearing was a pastiche of a Victorian novel, including brief summaries at the start of each

---

[18] There is a sense in which genre fiction also involves the following of rules: the reader beginning a detective story or a Harlequin romance expects plot and characters to conform to familiar norms – although often the greatest pleasure is to be experienced when those norms are subjected to minor challenges.

chapter. What became very noticeable as the recording went on was that the parts became shorter and shorter, and that towards the end the sections within the parts also shrank. This formal device certainly contributed to the experience of meaning: a sense of the speeding up of the action and of the revelations that explained some of the earlier mysteries. The most condensed account of the major events of the narrative occurred as the lengthy preliminary summary to the last part, which itself consists of just a few lines of dialogue. Another formal device, a time-shift that allows the book to end at a moment just before the beginning, added to the revelatory character of the closing. And the intricacy of the plotting, as nuggets of information pass from character to character and are thus revealed to the listener, was part of my pleasure in the author's craft.

It was only when I bought a hard copy of the book that I realised how complex and determining of the action the astrological structure is.[19] The decreasing length of the parts could now be seen as a carefully calculated construction: each of the twelve parts is about half the length of the previous one, and each part is made up of a diminishing number of chapters, from twelve to one. Part One is 360 pages long; Part Twelve just over a page. Observed on the page, the character chart at the start of the book is easier to make sense of than when heard in a recording: twelve characters under the heading 'STELLAR', each with a 'related house'; seven characters under the heading 'PLANETARY', each with a 'related influence'; and one character headed 'TERRA FIRMA' with the note *deceased*. Thus, for example, the first stellar character is 'Te Rau Tauwhare, *a greenstone hunter*', whose related house is 'The Wells Cottage (Arahura Valley)', while the first planetary character is 'Walter Moody', whose related influence is 'Reason'.

What the audiobook couldn't reproduce, and what explained these categories, was the astrological chart prefacing each of the book's parts, showing the position of the seven planets, identified with the seven 'planetary' characters, in relation to the twelve signs of the zodiac (or 'houses'), identified with the twelve 'stellar' characters. Every one of the twenty major characters, that is, is identified either with a zodiacal constellation or a planet, apart from one, who is dead when the book begins; and their interactions are governed by the placing of the planets within the zodiacal houses on the particular date and at the particular locality of the chapter in question.[20]

---

[19] The audiobook does articulate the 'character chart' at the start, but this passes the ear very quickly, and only provides limited information anyway.

[20] When I tried to replicate Catton's zodiacal charts using the online generator available at www.astro.com, the results didn't tally with hers. If it turns out that the novel's charts are not accurate, would this matter?

Furthermore, the personalities and occupations of the characters reflect the supposed qualities of their astrological equivalents.

To give one example: the opening chapter is titled 'Mercury in Sagittarius', and the chart indicating the stars at this locality on this date indeed shows the symbol for Mercury in the slice of zodiacal pie labelled with the sign for Sagittarius and the name of the character Thomas Balfour, the Sagittarian. It's not difficult to work out that the character represented by Mercury is Walter Moody, a lawyer just off the boat in the small gold-prospecting town of Hokitika on the West coast of New Zealand's South Island, whose conversation with the aforesaid Balfour takes up much of this first chapter. The opening scene also relates to the chart: the twelve men associated with the twelve zodiacal signs are all in the smoking room of the Crown Hotel, and as the chapters of this part proceed, they reveal their own knowledge of the events that have brought them together in conclave: the discovery of the dead man, the disappearance of another man, and the apparent attempted suicide of a woman, all occurring on the same evening two weeks earlier and all involving one or more of the characters identified with the planets. These events remain at the heart of the narrative, among the many mysteries with which the reader is tantalised.

The question I want to ask is this: what does the complex structural apparatus contribute to the reader's experience of the novel? What kind of pleasure does it provide, what insights does it offer?[21] I enjoyed the audio-book immensely, as an intricately woven mystery story in which the competing impulses of greed and love energise and twist human behaviour, in which the desire for gold, sex, and opium drive the diverse characters to different ends, and in which the distinction between truth and fabrication remains unresolved to the end. (The television adaptation, by contrast, was unsuccessful, unmooring the complex narrative strands from the continuous narrating voice.) It would seem, then, that knowledge of the astrological armature is unnecessary, however useful it might have been to the author in writing the novel. Yet my feeling is that my second experience of the

---

[21] It goes without saying that the mere presence of a complex formal structure doesn't guarantee a pleasurable experience for the reader, something Catton herself is very aware of, as this comment on a novel structured on a Tarot spread illustrates: 'I wondered why it was that novels of high structural complexity were so often inert, and why it was that structural patterning so often stood in the way of the reader's entertainment and pleasure. Did structure have to come at the expense of plot? Or could it be possible for a novel to be structurally ornate and actively plotted at the same time?' ('Eleanor Catton on how she wrote *The Luminaries*').

novel, in which I was aware of that armature and during which I could turn back to the information at the beginning of the book or the part in order to check parallels and conjunctions, was the richer, and did fuller justice to Catton's achievement.

Like Joyce's Homeric parallels, Catton's astrological framework is an example of inorganic form. As with Joyce's Homer, there's no limit to the connections we can draw between that framework and the book's content – I've already mentioned the mapping of the characters onto the Zodiac – but this is not a matter of the formal structure as a secondary element that enriches the primary meaning. That Moody's encounter with Balfour mirrors the appearance of Mercury in the sector of Sagittarius in the Hokitika sky on that particular night doesn't enter into our experience of the narrative, as the audiobook version demonstrates; rather, like those words for death in 'Hades' and wind in 'Aeolus', the formal conditions *require* that the encounter take place.[22] (The closest thing to a forebear is, perhaps, Perec's *La Vie mode d'emploi*, with its multiple characters behaving according to a complex pattern – a novel that can also be read in complete ignorance of that pattern.) Likewise, the lengths of the parts are determined not by the content but by an external scheme, which we can relate to the waning of the moon (an interpretation encouraged by the series of lunar images on the book jacket) but which doesn't in itself contribute to the meaning. We enjoy the formal arrangements for their ingenuity, their playfulness, the reminder they provide that we are reading a fiction, not a historical report. They are part of our sense of what I have called elsewhere the *authoredness* of the work: the knowledge that it's the product of the inventive labour of an artist, not the world itself speaking.

The Experience of Form

I've argued in the past that form and meaning are not two separate properties of the work, but rather that, in the experience of reading, the sequence of formal events produces a mobilisation and staging of meaning (*Singularity of Literature*, 152–3). Literary meaning, that is, is not simply a matter of a verbal sequence that sends the reader to a series of referents (there's nothing wrong with reading a literary work in this way, but it would not be treating it as literature); it's an *enactment* of referring, a process in which the work's formal properties play a crucial role. This

---

[22] The mapping of the night sky onto the relations among characters is not mechanically carried through, however; it's done selectively, allowing a sense of freedom of choice to survive.

account needs qualification, however: what I've been calling 'inorganic form' doesn't participate in the staging of meaning. The relation between Joyce's Homeric schema or Catton's zodiacal patterning and the referential meanings of the text – or, for that matter, between those formal structures and other formal properties that *do* operate to mobilise the content as we read – can be thought of as one of *layering*, an additional stratum that the creative reader can treat in a number of ways (or ignore). Think of the relation between a painting and its title, or between a programmatic musical work and the verbal programme: these elements of the work have to be taken in separately, and the manner in which they are used by the viewer or listener in enriching the experience of the work is not prescribed in advance.[23] (There are, however, traditions in which formal elements contribute to the reader's experience in a predetermined way – some types of medieval number-symbolism, for instance.)

Although there's no necessity for formal arrangements of this kind to be relatable by an act of conscious interpretation to content, there's a particular sense of satisfaction to be had when such mirroring can be detected. The subject matter of works associated with Oulipo often reflects the constraints observed by the writing: for instance, the narrative of the *e*-less *La Disparition* concerns the disappearance of a character by the name of Anton Voyl (derived from *voyelle*; in the English translation he is Anton Vowl.) This mirroring adds to the reader's enjoyment of Perec's ingenuity rather than fusing form and content in the experience of reading; it is, in other words, like many examples of Oulipean works, an example of craft. The chapters of Bök's *Eunoia* not only obey a rule that requires them to deal with the four topics enumerated earlier, but 'must allude to the art of writing' (103). I've already mentioned the familiar strategy of linking Joyce's chosen style to the content of the episode, and it could be argued that the use of the zodiac in *The Luminaries* reflects the characters' helplessness in the face of the fates that ensnare them.[24] Such parallels are not necessary to the operation of inorganic form, however, and their identification is sometimes the product of critical ingenuity after the fact rather than a genuine report on the reader's experience. And when form appears to influence content, the familiar illusion of unmediated reference to an existing world is profoundly disturbed.

Of course, from the point of view of the writer, these constraints often function effectively as generative principles rather than limitations, just as

---

[23] See the discussion of non-linear or 'ergodic' fiction in Chapter 11.
[24] Anna Kemp points out that many Oulipean works reflect 'the disorienting experience of late modernity: one in which individuals are caught in abstract systems that are opaque to them' ('Oulipo, Experiment, and the Novel', 551).

a requirement to rhyme can be a spur to creativity in verse. But from the reader's point of view, it's not clear how aware of a formal feature of this type one needs to be in order for it to be effective. If knowledge of the rules is required to fully experience the work and can be acquired only by going outside it, we have another challenge to organic theories of form and content, according to which every work should contain within itself the reason why it is so and not otherwise. For the most part, Oulipean texts wear their constraints on their sleeves, and it's impossible to avoid the zodiacal charts in the printed version of *The Luminaries*. But without Bök's note explaining the additional constraints of *Eunoia*, few readers would appreciate them, and, as I noted in Chapter 2, without Joyce's schemata we might still be in ignorance of some of the formal features of *Ulysses*. Do readers unaware that the organ of 'Hades' is *heart* or that of 'Sirens' is *ear* nevertheless subliminally register their frequent occurrence?[25] I suspect not – and in any case, to the extent that this unconscious effect does take place, the feature is no longer operating inorganically.

Inorganic form, then, complicates the idea of the literary work as a linear temporal experience in which all aspects are geared toward the representation of a single world, however complex. But it's still part of the literary experience: it contributes importantly to the pleasure to be gained and has the potential, as an important contributor to the work's singularity, to alter, however slightly, the reader's apprehension of their own world and the relationship of language and discourse with it. As I've suggested, it's not as if formal devices can operate without any meaningful effects at all; even a resistance to interpretation carries meaning of a kind. One aspect of the reader's experience of inorganic form is enjoyment of the author's wit (if I may resurrect an older critical term), a quality especially evident when formal arrangements can be seen as influencing content. The apparently mechanical operation of many Oulipian procedures masks their human origin; but to attend fully to the Homeric parallels or the zodiacal framework of the novels I've been considering is to enrich one's reading by entering, as it were, the workshop of the writer, a place of mental delight and verbal creativity, and thus to augment one's engagement with the work's human dimension.

---

[25] Interestingly, the frequency of the word 'dead' in 'Hades' is not reflected in the schemata; it's up to the reader to notice it – or not.

CHAPTER 11

Reading and Choice: Ali Smith's *How to Be Both* and Marlene van Niekerk's *Memorandum*

The Ergodic Text

Most works of fiction call for a linear reading from title to last word, and, although the codex form of the modern book allows for easier checking backwards and forwards than the papyrus roll it supplanted and the e-book adds to this facility the capacity for searching by means of words or phrases, the basic assumption that governs the processing of fictional prose is that the text unfolds continuously from start to finish. However, a different mode of semantic enrichment may happen when the visual layout of the page or the organisation of the book includes elements that ask to be taken in separately, at a moment of the reader's own choosing. Texts of this kind invite a reading process that is the opposite of the inorganic works discussed in the previous chapter: rather than learning or deducing and following out the special rules obeyed by the text, the reader has an unusual amount of freedom in deciding how to engage with it. Espen J. Aarseth, in a discussion of cybertexts, provides a full discussion of this issue, coining the term 'ergodic literature' for texts in which 'nontrivial effort is required to allow the reader to traverse the text'; by contrast, traditional texts, which require only 'eye movement and the periodic or arbitrary turning of pages', are 'non-ergodic' (*Cybertext*, 1). Ergodic literary productions are one example of multimodality, a phenomenon that is receiving increasing attention in studies not only of literary texts but other art forms and games.[1] In this chapter, I wish to explore the reader's experience of this type of fiction.

---

[1] See, for example, Page, ed., *New Perspectives*, and Sachs-Hombach and Thon, 'Multimodal Media'. A comprehensive survey is provided by Gibbons, in *Multimodality, Cognition, and Experimental Literature*.

Before *Finnegans Wake*, Joyce was content to observe linearity in his fiction. The introduction of headlines in the 'Aeolus' episode of *Ulysses* is an example of multimodality, but not one that requires the reader to deviate from a continuous progress through the text. In his last work, however, he broke decisively and influentially with linearity: the 'Nightlessons' chapter includes a drawing that catches the reader's eye as soon as the page is turned (293) and is studded with both footnotes and sidenotes. The reader is thus faced with choices: Does one stop in midsentence to study the diagram, or start with it, or come back to it? When does one read the sidenotes, which are not keyed to the text? Does one move immediately from the footnote reference to the footnote, or does one wait until a suitable punctuation mark?[2] Joyce was not the first to introduce marginal notes into a fictional text – Jonathan Swift (in *A Tale of a Tub*) and Laurence Sterne (in *Tristram Shandy*), much cited in the *Wake* – were among his predecessors, but none had made such conspicuous use of them.[3] After Joyce, examples proliferate; William Denton lists well over a hundred, most of which are later than 1939 ('Fictional Footnotes and Indexes').

Joyce's diagram in 'Nightlessons' and the use of sketches in the footnotes belong to a long tradition of illustrations that break the flow of the text, from medieval illuminated manuscripts to Sterne's graphic interpolations in *Tristram Shandy* (1759–67) to the nineteenth-century illustrated novel. Readers of European novels from the eighteenth to the early twentieth century (which were often first published in serial form) expected them to be illustrated, thus breaking the continuous flow by their invitation to the reader to divert attention from text to image. If, as was often the

[2] The two complete recording of the *Wake* treat the non-linearity of this episode very differently. Patrick Healey reads down the page, jumping to the sidenotes rather randomly, then going on to the footnotes in an unnumbered sequence, so that the arbitrary division created by the page break becomes a large gap in the performance (see Attridge, Review of *James Joyce's Finnegans Wake* read by Patrick Healy). The unabridged Naxos recording by Barry McGovern and Marcella Riordan (2021) is more circumspect: McGovern introduces the sidenotes at appropriate points in the main text, and pauses at each footnote reference, the note itself being read by Riordan. (The abridged version, read by Jim Norton, omits this chapter.) For discussions of the notes in 'Nightlessons' see Lipking, 'The Marginal Gloss', and Benstock, 'At the Margin of Discourse'.

[3] Factual footnotes were relatively common in earlier literary works, especially poetry. For an extensive list, see Miriam Lahrsow, *Self-Annotated Literary Works*. Probably the most creative use of the marginal gloss in poetry is represented by Coleridge's additions to *The Ancient Mariner* when he published it in *Sybilline Leaves* (1817).

case, the illustrations were on separate pages, this movement from one set of signs to another occurred at a moment determined not by the author or illustrator but by the reader. Although in the twentieth century the illustrated novel became associated with children's and young adult literature, various types of graphic supplement to novel texts continued to appear, such as W. G. Sebald's frequent use of photographs, Jennifer Egan's Powerpoint chapter in *A Visit from the Goon Squad*, and, in a different mode, the collaboration between the novelist Ivan Vladislavić and the photographer David Goldblatt in *Double Negative/TJ*. And, of course, in the graphic novel the visual dimension often plays a more important role in the reader's experience than the verbal.

Among the most inventive use of the footnote is Samuel Beckett's *Watt* (1953) (such as 'Haemophilia is, like enlargement of the prostate, an exclusively male disorder. But not in this work (100)), Flann O'Brien's mock-scholarly apparatus in *The Third Policeman* (1967), and David Foster Wallace's resourceful exploitation of the endnote in *Infinite Jest* (1966). B. S. Johnson employs side-notes as running commentary in one section of *Albert Angelo* (1964) and a further development of visually simultaneous narrative threads occurs in J. M. Coetzee's *Diary of a Bad Year* (2007), with its triple bands of text. An intriguing recent example of the use of a scholarly apparatus in a novel is Kirsty Gunn's *Caroline's Bikini*, with its many footnotes referring the reader to sections at the back of the book on such topics as narrative technique, the personal history of the (fictional) writer of the novel, and literary background and context. Perhaps the fullest exploitation of the text plus notes format is Vladimir Nabokov's *Pale Fire* (1962), which allows the reader a number of different reading experiences, depending on what route is chosen between the poem and its lengthy apparatus.

The readerly choice evident in the inclusion of non-verbal material is also manifest when alternative routes through a novel are provided. *Finnegans Wake* could be said to be an early example of this mode, since the sentence that runs from the end of the book straight back to the beginning might be taken to imply that the reader can start the text at any point. A well-known Spanish example is Julio Cortázar's 1963 *Rayuela*, translated into English as *Hopscotch*, which provides instructions for an alternative ordering of the chapters; and even more extreme are those novels published in boxes with loose leaves or chapters, like Marc Saporta's *Composition No. 1* of 1962 and B. S. Johnson's *The Unfortunates* of 1969. Other extravagant games with visual layout include Mark Z. Danielewski's *House of Leaves* (2000), with its dizzying array of typefaces and spatial arrangements, footnotes and footnotes to footnotes, index, diagrams and photographs, and J. J. Abrams and Doug Dorst's *S.* (2013), a narrative that unfolds in handwritten marginal notes to a printed novel which has every appearance of being a library copy of a 1949 novel called *Ship of Theseus* by one V. M. Straka, complete with loose inserts. In these examples, the reader has multiple choices in sequencing his or her reading (and, of course, difference decisions produce a different book). And when we leave the category of the printed book for electronic media, we find a new universe of multiple plots, readerly choice, and visual effects.[4]

I have argued elsewhere that to read a literary work responsibly is a matter of actively exercising interpretation (of language, of referential detail, of generic conventions, and so on) and at the same time passively allowing the text to operate upon one – and, if the work is a powerful one, allowing it to effect a change in one's mental and perhaps emotional world. The literary work, therefore, is not, to my way of thinking, an object but an *act-event*. Ergodic novels produce an increase in the reader's active engagement by making conscious choices necessary, but this increased activity is only valuable if it contributes to the work's effect upon the receptive reader. In all the examples I have cited, it's possible to make a case for the contribution made by the non-linear materials to the text's production of meaning; harder to account for, however, is the experience of non-linearity, and thus of choice, as *itself* as an element in the act-event of reading.

The question I'm asking, then, is this: is the enhancement or complication of the semantic dimension the only way in which this aspect of the reader's experience – the freedom to choose a pathway – can contribute to the work's literary operation, or can it make a contribution by functioning independently of meaning? Nicholson Baker gives a witty account of some of the pleasures of ergodic form in one of the many extensive footnotes in *The Mezzanine*, a novel that accepts the gauntlet thrown down by Joyce in *Ulysses* by taking place during a single lunch-hour. Footnoting writers such as Gibbon and Boswell, Baker writes,

> liked deciding as they read whether they would bother to consult a certain footnote or not, and whether they would read it in context or read it before the text it hung from, as an hors d'oeuvre. The muscles of the eye, they knew, want vertical itineraries; the rectus externus and internus grow dazed waggling back and forth in the Zs taught in grade school: the footnote functions as a switch, offering the model-railroader's satisfaction of catching the march of thought with a superscripted '1' and routing it, sometimes at length, through abandoned stations and submerged, leaching tunnels. (122)

---

[4] Two well-known examples are the hypertext novels Michael Joyce's *afternoon, a story* (1987) and Stuart Moulthrop's *Victory Garden* (1992).

Baker claims that the very act of choosing when to read a footnote is plea-surable, and that the 're-routing' that ensues is one of the rewards of this type of text. Linearity can come to seem a straitjacket, especially in this era of hypertext; the single-thread narrative can feel like an unnecessarily lim-ited use of the potential resources offered by the form of the book, a condi-tion even more evident in the case of narratives in electronic media. Being able to decide when to look at an illustration or a footnote, which thread to follow in a set of parallel narratives, how to treat spatial arrangements that complicate linearity are all ways in which the reader's freedom is enhanced. Making these choices impacts upon the experience of the novel as a nar-rative, of course, but the very fact of being given the choice is itself part of the experience that renders a given work singular. We are made aware of the book as a book, a material object, not an invisible medium through which we dive into a fictional world just like the one we live in. And we are made aware of an author making that book not only as a sequence of words pointing to their referents, but as an arrangement of words on pages. When handled subtly, these features enrich the reading process and heighten the reader's pleasure in responding to the art of the writer.

To explore the experience of reading an ergodic text I want to turn to two very different examples, one Scottish and one South African.

Ali Smith, *How to Be Both*

I have a copy of the Penguin paperback edition (2015) of Ali Smith's 2014 novel *How to Be Both* in front of me. The cover shows an apparently unposed photograph of two young women in a street; inside the front and back covers are full bleed reproductions of paintings of standing figures, the first a dark-skinned young man in tattered clothes with a rope serving as a belt, the second a richly-dressed person of indeterminate gender holding an arrow and a hoop. After the front matter, including a page of epigraphs, comes a page with the single word 'one' and a simple sketch of a security camera. The narrative that follows is an account, largely in free indirect dis-course, of the experiences of a teenage girl in contemporary Cambridge. We find ourselves seeing the world through the perceptions and memories of George (the character's preferred version of Georgia), living with her father and her younger brother and mourning the unexpected death of her mother four months earlier.

Particularly vivid among her memories is a visit to Ferrara with her mother and brother to see the frescoes by the fifteenth-century painter Fran-cesco del Cossa in the Palazzo Schifanoia. The trip, we learn, was prompted by George's mother's coming across a photo in an art magazine of 'a man

standing dressed in ripped white clothes and wearing an old rope as a belt'
(47), an image to be found in a room in the aforesaid palazzo. If we recognise this description as fitting the image inside the front cover, we may
respond to the invitation to page back and look at it: here we have one of
the novel's ergodic features, since we are equally free to continue reading.
Similarly, when the trio are in the room in the palazzo, George observes 'a
young man or a young woman, could be either, dressed in beautiful rich
clothes and holding an arrow or a stick and a gold hoop thing' (51); different readers will find out at different times in the reading process that this
image is at the back of the book, and can choose when to look at it and how
much attention to give it.

Another image that features significantly in George's story is a photograph given to her by her friend Helena, which is described in detail and
clearly refers to the image on the book's cover (81–2). If we don't know
who the two young women in the photograph are, we learn near the end
of George's story that one of them – whom George is said to look like –
is the French singer Sylvie Vartan (who is also the author of one of the
book's epigraphs); we might notice, too, that the back cover acknowledges
the source of the 'Photo of Sylvie Vartan and Françoise Hardy,' enabling us
to put a name to the other figure as well. (Alternatively, it's not difficult to
find the photograph on Google Images.) George also has a photograph of
an actress on her wall, whom it's not difficult to identify as Monica Vitti,
though George doesn't seem to know her name; in this case, there is no way
of seeing the image other than by moving outside the book.

As the sketch on the opening page suggests, one of the themes of this narrative is surveillance: George becomes preoccupied with a woman named
Lisa Goliard who appears to have been watching her mother, no doubt
because of the latter's political activities (but also perhaps because they
were in love). This motif of watching occurs in many variants: for instance,
George comes across a pornographic video of child abuse on her iPad and
forces herself to watch a few minutes of it as part of her daily schedule
(31–5). Late in George's narrative these references multiply: we find her in
the National Gallery in London watching people in front of Cossa's painting of St Vincent Ferrer, and (in a final look ahead) being surprised when
one of those with an interest in the painting turns out to be Goliard – after
which, she becomes in turn the watcher, installed outside Goliard's house.

George's story ends about halfway through the book; it's immediately
followed by another page with the single word 'one,' but this time with
a drawing beneath it of a flower stalk with eyes instead of blossoms. The
narrative that follows begins with pages of poetic prose in the first person
from which it emerges that the speaker is Cossa himself and that he has

travelled (painfully) across time to find himself in what we realise is the same room in the National Gallery where we recently saw George, who is standing in front of the painting of St Vincent and whom Cossa takes at first to be a boy. The account that follows is for the most part devoted to Cossa's reminiscences, from which we learn that she is in fact a woman who passed as a man (a feat of cross-dressing for which there is no historical evidence), and was thus able to pursue a career as a painter – including some of the frescoes in the 'palace of not being bored' (the Palazzo Schifanoia) (196 and *passim*).[5] We also learn, among much else, of Cossa's meeting with an 'infidel' worker in ragged clothes who obtains from her a rope to serve as a belt (283–5), perhaps prompting the reader to take another look at the inside of the cover. There is also a reference to Cossa's painting of St Lucia holding a stalk with eyes instead of flowers that chimes with the drawing at the opening of this section.

The remainder of the section has Cossa reporting on George's actions: she finds herself always in George's presence, though invisible, and we're able to translate her often bemused description of what she sees into the terms already provided by George's narrative: she observes Goliard's arrival in the room and George's pursuit of her, her few minutes watching the porn video on her iPad, and her games with her brother. In George's bedroom Cossa admires the photograph of Vartan and Hardy ('by a great artist surely in its patchwork of light, dark, determination, gentleness' (287–8)), encouraging us to shut the book and examine the cover again, and the one of Vitti (which she takes to be an image of St Monica, assuming that 'Vitti' is Latin for 'victims'). She accompanies George repeatedly on her mission to monitor Goliard's house and to capture Goliard's image on her iPad – here the story moves beyond the end of George's narrative – and witnesses what must be a reunion with Helena. As Cossa watches George and Helena paint eyes on the wall opposite Goliard's house, she feels herself dragged back 'to be / made and / unmade / both' (372).

---

[5] Some early reviewers speculated that Cossa's section of the novel represents George's reconstruction of the painter's life on the grounds that 'the palace of not being bored' in that section echoes George's mother's explanation that 'Palazzo Schifanoia' means 'the palace escaping from boredom' in the other section. Also cited as possible evidence is Cossa's use of the modern colloquialism 'just saying'. However, Cossa refers to another palazzo – probably the Palazzo Belfiore – as 'the palace of beautiful flowers' (196 and *passim*), so her translation of 'Schifanoia' is not exceptional. The idiosyncrasies of Cossa's account, such as her spellings 'Francescho' for Francesco and 'Cosmo' for 'Cosima,' require another explanation.

The ergodic features of this novel clearly contribute to its content: we can appreciate directly the force and beauty of Cossa's painting (to the extent that small photographic reproductions can do this) and are able to substitute image for words when the photograph of Vartan and Hardy is described. But the same result could be achieved by the simple use of Google or the more elaborate strategy of trips to the National Gallery or the Palazzo Schifanoia; what difference does it make that these images form part of the complex structure of the novel, and that the reader has a choice to make in accessing them? It surely increases the reader's enjoyment, enriching the experience of engaging with the text, adding a dimension to the purely verbal material of the narrative, continuing by other means the concern with seeing that persists throughout the book.

Another ergodic feature is implied by the occurrence of *two* section title-pages with the word 'one': the reader is offered the choice of reading Cossa's narrative before George's, which produces a very different reading experience. Read first, Cossa's account of the girl she finds herself watching after her time-travel throws up a number of puzzles: who is this girl? what is this room she finds herself in? why does she haunt a particular house? We might be able to deduce the identity of a few of the contemporary items Cossa is bemused by, such as George's tablet, before we find confirmation in the other half of the book. Though, admittedly, few readers are likely to read the sections in a different order from that in which they occur in print, *How to Be Both* could be said to continue the line of unorthodox fiction in which the reader has a choice in the matter of narrative sequence, like the boxed books by Saporta and Johnson. Although the doubleness of the novel's structure is one aspect of its thematic concern with doubles of all kinds – observable in the title, in the gender ambiguities in both sections, in the relation between original and copy, 'before' and 'after'[6]– it's also part of the innovative formal event that is central to the reader's experience. When George's mother poses a moral conundrum (arising from the historical Cossa's request for more pay in a rare surviving letter), George asks 'Past or present? . . . Male or female? It can't be both. It must be one or the other'. Her mother's answer is: 'Who says? Why must it?' (8). What the form of the novel allows the reader to experience is this 'bothness', an

---

[6]   'But which came first? her mother says. The chicken or the egg? The picture underneath or the picture on the surface?

The picture below came first, George says. Because it was done first.

But the first thing we see, her mother said, and most times the only thing we see, is the one on the surface. So does that mean it comes first after all?' (103).

experience that, though it can be related to the work's meanings, cannot be reduced to them.[7]

How to Be Both is even more extraordinary, however. I have another copy of the novel before me, which at first it looks identical: the same photograph on the cover, the same image inside it, the same front matter, the same single word 'one' – but in this copy, the drawing that accompanies the 'one' is that of the eyes on a stalk instead of the security camera.[8] And what follows is the Cossa section, after which we again find 'one' with the security camera drawing and then George's narrative. Smith arranged for the book to be published in two different versions, but with no indication in any particular copy that this was the case, or which of the versions it is.[9] Instead of a boxed book offering readers a choice we have two separate books, each of which provides a distinct reading experience (assuming a reading of the two sections in the order in which they are presented). In this way the theme of doubleness is carried through into the material publication process itself.

You might say that Smith has written two novels, and this would be true up to a point, since it's certainly the case that a reading of version one is a very different experience from a reading of version two. The catch is that no-one can read both novels, unless we imagine the second taking place after such a long interval that all memory of the first has been lost. The copy I bought happened to begin with Cossa's section; re-reading the novel, I began with George's, and although I registered consciously the differences this made, there was no way I could share the experience of a reader who first read the sections in this order. The full scope of the novel's (or novels') achievement is possible only when we consider it as being experienced by a *community* of readers – in fact, its singularity as a work of literature can be acknowledged only by means of such a community, since the existence of two different editions only becomes visible when readers compare their books. Readers of version one can have valuable discussions with readers of version two about their respective experiences of the novel, discussions which are likely to deepen the understanding and enjoyment of both.

---

[7] Elizabeth Anker offers a 'postcritical' reading of *How to Be Both* (which involves showing how the novel endorses a postcritical stance towards interpretation) ('Postcritical Reading'). Whatever one might think of the label, Anker's conclusion accords well with one of the central arguments of this book: 'These energies that I've characterised as postcritical above all return us to the status of the literary; to the fundaments of aesthetic experience; and to what it really means to see or encounter or immerse ourselves within a text' (37).

[8] Page references in this essay are to the version in which George's section comes first.

[9] The Kindle edition, however, begins with a statement that gives the game away.

Marlene van Niekerk and Adriaan van Zyl, *Memorandum*

Marlene van Niekerk is one of the most accomplished and important of contemporary novelists, writing strikingly innovative and ambitious fiction (as well as highly original poetry and drama); that she is not as well-known as she deserves to be is due to the language she writes in. Afrikaans, as remarked on in Chapter 8, is a minor language with a very small readership, and although Van Niekerk's fiction has been translated into several languages, the initial obstacles to global dissemination remain. Her two best-known novels, *Triomf* (1994) and *Agaat* (2004), are both large-scale dissections of central features of South African politics and culture – the promises held out by the Afrikaner nationalist government to their white supporters and the tradition of the farm as a white stronghold – that have global resonances. And both are strikingly inventive in their forms: the first a hugely creative version of non-standard Afrikaans with an uninhibited use of slang and obscenity, the second an interleaving of four narratives of different kinds, including the thoughts of an elderly woman who is nearing the end of her life as a result of motor neuron disease and is capable of communication only through blinking.

Van Niekerk's third novel is equally ambitious and innovative, but has not received as much attention as her first two, no doubt in part, at least, because of its radical use of non-linear form. *Memorandum: 'n verhaal met skilderye* (2006), translated into English by Michiel Heyns as *Memorandum: A Story with Paintings* (2006), is a joint endeavour with the painter Adriaan van Zyl, and it raises in sharp form the question of the reader's choices and procedures. I mean this less as an issue of description – how actual readers have gone about meeting the novel's challenges, a question that might be answered by a survey – than as an issue of readerly responsibility: what would it mean to do full justice to this extraordinary work, in which the possibilities of ergodic fiction are exploited to the limit?

The book, beautifully produced by Human & Rousseau in both the original and the translated versions, presents challenges to the reader from the very start. It opens with a triptych of paintings by Van Zyl and continues with 'Memorandum 3', identified at its head, as in an official document, as being by one J. F. Wiid, the 'Director of Parks & Playgrounds, Sanitation and Maintenance (1988–2004)' (6),[10] living at 17 Mimosa Flats in Parow

---

[10] I quote from Heyns's translation, referring to the Afrikaans original where appropriate. Further references will be given in the text. The pagination of the translation follows that of the original quite closely, being usually no more than one page apart.

(a somewhat cheerless Cape Town suburb).[11] Even the exact time is noted: '11 April 2006 19:20' (2006 being the year of publication of both the original and the translation). These meticulous details are followed by a heading in bold: **'To whom it may concern'** (6). This bureaucratic formalism at the outset of the work puts the reader on notice that generic expectations associated with the novel are not going to be fulfilled, as does the stilted, self-deprecatory tone with which Wiid begins his account, far from the vitality and vividness we might expect from a first-person narrator telling his story to an imagined audience.[12]

We quickly learn that the words we are reading are being written – within Van Niekerk's fiction – on the eve of Wiid's admission to Tygerberg Hospital (situated on the edge of Parow, and described by Van Niekerk as a 'sort of culmination of the Parow-esque'),[13] for a last attempt to save his life following the failure of both chemotherapy and radiotherapy to manage the cancer that has spread from his liver to his colon. Wiid, in his Parow flat with his suitcase packed, has decided to recount the events of his previous stay at Tygerberg a little over six months earlier, a single night with repercussions that have had a huge effect on his life and outlook. We also learn that Memoranda 1 and 2, which we can consult as 'Addenda' at the back of the book, are in tabular rather than discursive form, and that the account he is now writing is intended as an expansive explanation of these terse texts should the following day's intervention prove fatal, an outcome that is not unlikely. Memorandum 1 is a list of unusual words, both common and proper nouns, notated phonetically and then researched since the last hospital visit when he heard them spoken; Memorandum 2 consists of two tables setting out the conceivable futures that await Wiid the following day and beyond, the first assuming the operation will be the planned resectioning of the colon, the second that it will involve a colostomy, both of these futures holding out the hope of recovery as well as the possibility of death. The black humour that emerges in a few places in Memorandum 2 is all the more painfully funny in the context of the dry lists of facts entered under the headings 'Time', 'Place', 'Action', 'Agent', 'Outcome positive', 'Outcome negative'. In Table A, for example, the administering of anaesthetic produces as a positive outcome 'J.F.W.

[11] Van Niekerk, in an interview (in Afrikaans) with Etienne Britz, refers to the 'troostelose boustyle' ('comfortless building styles') of Parow ('Marlene van Niekerk', 23).
[12] Van Niekerk speaks of a 'verdunning' ('attenuating') of language in Wiid's style (in contrast to the 'verryking'('enriching') of her second novel, *Agaat*, and the 'vervuiling' ('dirtying') of her first novel, *Triomf* ('So-hede', 154).
[13] Britz, 'Marlene van Niekerk', 23.

passive operational unit' whereas the negative outcome is given as 'Hey, old Wiid. They beckon from the grave!' (Table A, 08:10). And there is the joking exclamation 'Humbaba!' in the cell describing the 'lower stomach incision' (Table A, 08:35) – Wiid's triumphant exploitation of his recently-acquired knowledge of the Mesopotamian god of the entrails. The last item in the book (other than a list of Van Zyl's paintings) is a letter from Wiid to the Superintendent of Public Libraries in the Western Cape dated two months after the earlier hospital visit.

The main body of the text – Memorandum 3 – consists of Wiid's account, written between eight o'clock in the evening on 11 April and a quarter past seven the following morning, of his experiences in hospital on that October night in 2005. It's presented as a memorial reconstruction, the only notes taken at the time (that is, on the following morning) being the aforementioned list of words. Memorandum 3 also includes details of the researches undertaken later in an attempt to make sense of the events of that night. Scholarly notes and references are added in footnotes, further complicating the reading process.[14] The memorandum ends with a short lyrical conclusion headed 'Passacaglia (for JSB)'. The experiences recounted in this memorandum – the Latin meaning of the term, '[a thing] to be remembered', is not far away – are largely a report on the conversation of the two equally bedridden patients between whom Wiid found himself placed on that night, men whom he refers to as X and Y and whose erudite vocabulary and wide-ranging knowledge has produced the list of words. X is a passionate bird-watcher whose feet are amputated and Y is a cynic, enthralled by cities and buildings, who has lost his eyes, or, as Wiid calls them, a 'fanatical poet without feet, who chattered about birds and birds' nests' and a 'blind mocker, who delivered one speech after another on antique building methods, the foundations of cities and on hospitals' (23). Van Zyl's paintings are interspersed throughout Wiid's text, which makes no specific reference to them.[15]

Memorandum offers no guidance on how to read it – or perhaps it offers too many suggestions. Do we proceed page by page as in a conventional

---

[14] Not all quotations are acknowledged, however; for instance, Goethe's 'Wandrers Nachtlied II' is quoted, with slight amendments (either as translated by its quoter or as recalled by Wiid) (47). Van Niekerk has said that she would have liked the book to have large white spaces at the foot of each page for readers to enter further notes and thus make the text endless (Britz, 'Marlene van Niekerk', 25).

[15] Van Niekerk explains that she and Van Zyl decided from the beginning that the text would not comment on or interpret the paintings, and the paintings would not function as illustrations of the text (Britz, 'Marlene van Niekerk', 21).

novel, enjoying the paintings when we reach them, taking in the footnotes when appropriate, and only reading the list of words, the table, the letter to the Superintendent of Libraries, and the titles of the paintings when we reach the end? Or do we start with Memoranda 1 and 2, and then proceed to the explanatory Memorandum 3? Do we pass over the footnotes on a first reading, and only come back to them later? And how do we read the paintings themselves, both intimately connected to the text and yet ignored by it?[16]

One way of reading the book is to treat it like a crossword puzzle, following Wiid's own investigation of the enigmatic utterances he heard from X and Y, using the footnotes and the explanations of difficult words and phrases in Memorandum 1 to develop an account of the contrasting views of buildings and living spaces held by the two interlocutors.[17] If we choose to read the snatches of hermetic knowledge provided in the word-list of Memorandum 1 in order, we find ourselves travelling erratically across the known universe; there is no apparent logic to the sequence, but the items are often entertaining and sometimes moving. In each case Wiid has written down a purely phonetic representation of what he heard, and only in consultation with the librarian in the Parow Public Library has he been able to track down the actual word. Thus he notes down Y's reference to 'wiele-rooi en bog' (to give the Afrikaans original), later to identify the phrase as 'Villeroy & Boch', the glass and ceramics manufacturer. And he adds, 'Vaguely I remember a little glass bowl of my mother's, perhaps it's still in my chest, must have a look' (135). The investigative reader is even given one item to track: Wiid has heard 'boo-requi-poo' but has been unable to work out what the word was, even with the librarian's help; 'Something to do with knotting of strings or embroidery' is all he can find (96, 136). Further research suggests that Y's phrase was 'boere quipu' – embroidery as the Afrikaners' equivalent of the knotted cords used by the Incas to record numbers.

---

[16] To say the text 'ignores' the paintings is to assume they are primary; this is in fact true of the process by which the book came into being, Van Zyl having proposed to Van Neikerk that she write a text to accompany his hospital paintings (Britz, 'Marlene van Niekerk', 12) – though I also mean it to suggest that at no point does the text acknowledge that it's being interrupted by images.

[17] The content of the bizarre exchanges between X and Y has received relatively little comment by critics and reviewers in comparison with Wiid's own account of his experiences, no doubt because of their obscurity. Van Niekerk makes no attempt to create a realistic representation of conversation, which is larded with allusions and rhetorical flourishes.

We are alerted early on to two key texts in the contrast between the outlooks of X and Y, the books by the two bedsides, Bachelard's *Poetics of Space* and Rykwert's *Idea of a Town*, the former appealing to X's poetic appreciation of natural spaces (birds' nests in particular), the latter to Y's interest in the built environment. Numerous further references both to published works and to historical, literary, archaeological, and ethnographic details augment the twin approaches to space and habitation. Although most of the references are authentic, Van Niekerk is not above the invention of convincing-sounding texts complete with spurious editors and publishers: specifically, Afrikaans translations of Homer's *Odyssey* (55, note 16) and Bach's chorales (69, note 19). In both cases, she takes the opportunity to satirise current Afrikaner concerns with the growing power of 'the Afro-National State' and 'Afro-centrists'.

This scholarly approach, though it has its rewards, taps into only a small part of the book's offerings. There is no escaping from the feeling that all this expert knowledge is being presented with a smile; that the tracking down of obscure references does not, in the end, count for much against the realities of love and death that run through the novel. These realities emerge from the story of Wiid's discovery of new meanings and values in his life; not from the accumulation of learning, that is, but from narrative sequences. In opting to concentrate on narrative, however, the reader faces a challenge, as there are four interwoven stories to follow. Three of these are textual, and all three reveal the manner in which Wiid's eyes have been opened to the limitations of his existence and the richness and beauty of what he has been blind to.[18]

We may consider as the *first* narrative the story of the night of 5 October 2005 in the Tygerberg Hospital Intensive Care Unit, from five o'clock in the afternoon when X and Y are brought in after surgery to the utterance of what are presumably their last words at some point during the night. (When Wiid wakes up in the morning, both beds are empty.) For all his bafflement at their abstruse and arcane utterances, Wiid is profoundly affected by the exchanges between his two roommates, as their physical conditions deteriorate. Wiid's positive response to these exchanges is not consistent – at one point he thinks, 'What a lot of gush! Two old spoonbills!' (110) – but his reaction to what might be the final moments of their lives is extremely moving:

[18] Interestingly, another highly inventive Afrikaans novel about the awakening of an inhibited, buttoned-up administrator when exposed to the wider world of cultural and human experience was published two years later: Etienne van Heerden's *30 nagte in Amsterdam*, discussed in Chapter 8.

Wake up, I prayed, wake up and feed me, speak your nourishing sentences to each other so I can rejoice in you.

And in the dark it truly came again, a soft fluttering in which I could distinguish single words. *Feather*, said one. *Stone*, said the other. *Breast*, the one. *Hand*, the other. (115)

These final, barely heard words are followed by a long exchange that is not presented as being actually spoken at this moment but as Wiid's own gathering up 'in a last cascade' the differing views on habitation held by X and Y, moving towards a concluding unity as they imagine, or Wiid imagines them imagining, living together in a reed hut like the Dioscuri.[19] We can take this final dialogue as Wiid's summing up of the understanding he reached that night, a dream of a 'home beyond the Styx', as X puts it, that is both house and nest.

A *second* narrative strand, interlaced with the first one, is the story of Wiid and Joop Buytendagh, the chief librarian of the Parow Public Library. It is a love story of sorts,[20] which begins when the former visits the library in December 2005 to carry out some research into the words he has written down after the night of X and Y's conversation. His initial response on encountering Buytendagh is spelled out in the letter – apparently unsent (25) – that forms Addendum 3 (138–40), in which he complains to the Superintendent about the loud Italian opera being played, the 'dirty teacups and half-eaten sandwiches on the issue desk', the cartoons in the men's toilet, the skewed, gaudy hangings, and, above all, the unprepossessing figure of the librarian himself, a figure as distant from the correct, tidy civil servant as could be imagined. And yet, Wiid has to admit, he is 'very well informed on his subject' and is able immediately to lay his hands on the desired facts (140).

The respect that glimmers through the irritation in this letter grows as Wiid keeps returning to the library, and much of the information provided in his Memoranda is the product of Buytendagh's researches. After a number of visits to the library, Wiid realises that the librarian revels in the research he is doing for him – in this case, finding poems in Bachelard's

---

[19] Van Niekerk refers to this sequence as a fantasy of Wiid's, a dream of both twinhood and dwelling representing the achievement of an intimacy he lacks (Britz, 'Marlene van Niekerk', 24). It's possible to mark the two (imagined) speakers in this sequence, but the absence of such markers on the page suggests that each might well have spoken what the other did.

[20] Van Niekerk herself observes that it's 'perhaps' a love story (Britz, 'Marlene van Niekerk', 24). Sanders treats this topic with tact and insight ('Mimesis', 118–19).

Poetics of Space that deal with wardrobes and cupboards (50).[21] A moment of intimacy occurs when Joop rests his hand on Wiid's shoulder on hearing the latter talk of dying; Wiid regards this as '[e]xtremely forward', but has to go home 'because after that I could not concentrate any more' (90). Writing his memorandum, he finds he has no desire to sleep, and at 03:40 the rather extraordinary thought occurs to him, 'Perhaps I should phone Joop' – though this is quickly qualified: 'Not that I've ever had the thought of phoning anybody. Least of all quarter to four in the morning' (91). The growing intimacy may not seem much, but for a man like Wiid it's a great deal: he writes a three-page Postscript in which he visualises going to the library the following day to pick up the Rykwert book, accepting, as usual, Joop's invitation to have tea in the little kitchen, and then, boldly, imagines inviting Joop over one evening for a meal. The whole passage is shot through with Wiid's cautious and tentative – but also thrilling – admission to himself of what, in the context, we can only call love.

The conclusion of this narrative is also the conclusion of the *third* narrative, upon which the first two are woven: the story of the night of writing, as Wiid recounts the experiences of the earlier night and the subsequent researches, as well as memories of his past triggered by those experiences, all the while facing the possibility that he will not live beyond the next day. He starts by describing his preparations, including the composition of the two tables of Memorandum 2 and the annotation of the word-list of Memorandum 1, then moves on to the main business: the composition of Memorandum 3. His stated intention is to bring 'music' into the description of the night of 5 October 2005, unlike the dry earlier memoranda (9). To help him in this endeavour – and, as he admits, to put off starting – he has listened to Bach's *Passacaglia in C minor* sixteen times. He marks the start of the memorandum proper with the time, 20:00, and, as his writing progresses, scrupulously notes the time at varying intervals thereafter.

The writing proceeds steadily as Wiid reports on his admission to Tygerberg and his two strange fellow-sufferers, summarising too his visits to Parow Public Library in consequence of that night. After undergoing a small psychological crisis, he composes a sentence that, as he says, he

---

21 Buytendagh has found a copy of the English translation of Bachelard's book, so the poems – one by Breton (unacknowledged in the text) and one by Rimbaud – are in English, and have been translated by him into Afrikaans. This, of course, poses a translation problem for Heyns, who provides his own re-translation into English of the Afrikaans translation of the primary English translation of the original French. An entire article could be written on the challenges *Memorandum* poses for the translator.

would never have written had it not been for 'that first strange night': 'The shabby stone pine with lengths of lamp post, a portion of pavement, lights of Cape Town and southern stars in its branches, the furniture of its dream' (64). And what follows is even more unlike Wiid the pen-pusher, and hints at a potential that, until now, had remained unfulfilled: allusions to Jesus in Gethsemane, memories of his parents putting a stop to his story-telling as a child, and reflections on the early death of his twin brother and his father. At 04:20 he returns from a walk round a few blocks, at the conclusion of which he had looked up at his flat and pondered its future without him. At 05:15 he hears 'the last of the night sounds' and records a memory of his parents' unexpected softness. 06:00 brings despair and more suicidal thoughts, but he goes on writing, culminating in the (invented?) dialogue between X and Y mentioned above.

The 06:40 Postscript, written as the morning light makes itself felt,[22] records a decision that arises from the process of thinking, remembering, and writing of the previous ten hours; 'One has to write', as Wiid says, 'to discover what has to be written' (120). He will not go back to the hospital; he will permanently cancel the operation and let the cancer do its work. There follows the account of his plans for the day to come, during which he will visit the library and, perhaps, invite Joop to join him for a simple meal. And he will give Joop the memorandum. The final entry is made at 07:15, which, thinking again no doubt of Bach's organ music, he calls a 'voluntary'.

The memorandum closes with the extraordinary page-long 'Passacaglia' imagining a walk through Parow (Wiid has discovered that the musical term comes from 'passer', 'to walk', and 'calle', 'street'(8)),[23] written in a rhythmic, heightened style as far removed as possible from bureaucratic prose. This passage serves as a conclusion to all three of the textual narrative strands: the debates in the hospital about housing and care, the broadening of sympathies through the relationship with Buytendagh, and the many hours of writing and thought that have produced the memorandum. It is headed '(for JSB)', and it's not clear whether the ambiguity – does it refer to Johann Sebastian Bach or Jeroen Sterrenberg Buytendagh? – is Wiid's or Van Niekerk's. Wiid, the erstwhile city planner, promises himself that he will walk his city's streets, drinking in all the details he sees, consecrating the boulevards, sanctifying the barbed wire and grey cement, unmaking in his heart what is unhospitable. With Mania, the goddess of the dead,

---

[22] Sunrise in the Western Cape on 12 April 2006 was at 07:03.

[23] He is not quite right: the Spanish word from which the first part of the Italian *passacaglia* derives is 'pasar', 'to pass'.

and the late hospital companions X and Y, he will traverse the squares and walkways of Parow until nightfall. The passage ends with an assertion of the hospitality that has been at the centre of much of the preceding book. Wiid's utilitarian home has now become a nest, its name conflated with that of the 'sensitive plant', the Mimosa tree, and the urban/natural opposition collapsed:

> And if I should by chance see a lonely tramp, before the last circuit, who like me has need of comfort, I shall be his friend and hospice and take him to Mimosa, to my nest already prepared for him as bequest, and to the end with him abide. (124)

The idea of 'comfort' ('troost') plays a central role in the work's concern with buildings, nests, the function of the hospital and the importance of hospitality.[24]

Then there are the sixteen paintings, telling their own story, which the reader is invited to relate in some way to the other narratives. They lead us from hospital entrance to waiting room, then from 'The Night Before' to the anaesthesia room and on to the operating theatre, and from there to the recovery room.[25] (The titles are given in the list at the back of the book.) The series ends with another waiting room, as if the process is going to begin again. The paintings provide us with stark images of hospital architecture, décor, and equipment, and in their utilitarian sparseness, muted colours, and lack of human presences speak of the kind of functional but cold environment for living beings opposed both by X in his discourses on nests and by the retired urban administrator Wiid at the end of his days. The formal, almost photorealist, style in which walls, beds, cupboards, and instruments are represented contributes to the atmosphere of efficiency and detachment, while the presence of mysterious objects behind glass doors adds to the sense of unfathomable processes. Wiid's text, without being an interpretation of the paintings, is greatly enhanced by these depictions of chilly, inscrutable hospital spaces; Van Niekerk's own suggestion about

---

[24] I noted earlier Van Niekerk's comment on the 'troostelose' style of Parow's architecture.

[25] Who arranged the paintings in this order? Van Niekerk states that they were placed in a narrative order by the painter (Britz, 'Marlene van Niekerk', 21). Yet the fact that 'Hospital Triptych II' begins the series, and 'Hospital Triptych I' occurs as the fourth painting suggests that Van Zyl envisaged a different order; or the numbering may simply reflect the order in which they were painted. The numbering of the other paintings is consistently sequential.

its relation to the images is that it's like the piano accompaniment in a Schubert song; it should not only mediate, but provoke, foretell, desire, and even impede. She remarks that for her what was most important was to preserve the enigmatic quality of the paintings, and therefore to let Wiid write something that bewilders him to the end, both as regards the content and the writing process (Britz, 'Marlene van Niekerk', 21). In another interview, she provides a somewhat different account of the relationship: '[T]he story consoles the paintings with intimations of friendship, care and sympathy, while the paintings remind the story of the grim and lonely business of bodily pain and suffering, the loneliness of facing death'.[26]

This story is complicated, however, by three of the paintings: two diptychs and a triptych in which hospital scenes are conjoined with outdoor scenes. Two of these, 'Hospital Triptych II' and 'Hospital Diptych III', show images of the sea, picking up the colours of the adjoining hospital images – brownish grey in the first case and leaden green in the second – to create a startling contrast of mood and atmosphere. Next to the rigid lines and angles of the hospital buildings the wind-blown sea suggests liberty of movement and escape from confines; and next to the ward's stilled machinery of linen and metal the rising swell speaks of the endless shifting of watery expanses. These marine images might be representations of dying patients' dreams of escape from the confines of hospital or of their memories of lost physical freedom; there is no way of closing down interpretation. The third outdoor image is of a nondescript urban landscape (Parow?) seen from a height at dawn or dusk, the sky's orange glow echoing the glow of the single lamp above the hospital bed in its partner painting. We may be looking through a hospital window on an upper floor (there's a suggestion of light falling on a windowpane), a view that, unlike the artificial time of the ward, permits diurnal changes to be seen and felt. In every painting, the immense care that has been lavished on the objects depicted – an attentiveness inherited from the long tradition of the still life – suggests that, despite the lack of a human presence, they are humanly of great importance, whether as instruments of recovery or focal points of fear.

We might guess, and a little research will confirm, that the paintings are of Tygerberg Hospital, based on photographs made when Van Zyl was being treated for cancer in that very hospital not long before his untimely death. There is perhaps a clue within the text, in the shape of the picture-book Wiid likes to look at when he visits Parow Public Library: a gathering of Manet's last sixteen paintings (the number is significant), still lives made when the painter's life was ending. Manet, like Van Zyl, died

[26] Van Niekerk, interview with Steyn, *The White Review*.

at the age of 49; the latter in 2006, the same year as the publication of the book.[27]

To return to my opening question, how are we to read these multiple interwoven narratives and the large amount of scholarly detail that buttresses them in attempting to do justice to the composite work? The answer must be that there is no optimal approach. A reading which proceeds from page 1 to page 140, taking in the footnotes when they occur, is feasible, allowing the paintings to come as a series of surprises as the pages are turned, and ending with the word-list, the tables, and, as something of an anti-climax, Wiid's letter to the Superintendent of Libraries. More likely, the mention of Memoranda 1 and 2 at the start will prompt the reader to check them out at once, though at this stage they are likely to be more puzzling than revealing and will need to be returned to frequently. (That Memorandum 2 precedes Memorandum 1 adds to the complication of the process.) A reading that follows this pattern will end, satisfyingly, at the 'Passacaglia'. Similarly, each time a word in bold comes up in the text, the temptation is to turn to the list for elucidation. There is also much to be said for enjoying the series of paintings as a separate encounter – though here again, the reader may want to flip to the list of titles at the back from time to time. (The paintings and the list of titles are the only element in the book not to form part of the fiction – unless we imagine Joop Buytendagh splicing them into Wiid's text for publication.) Each of these multiple possibilities will produce a different reading experience, or, to put it more strongly, will bring into being a different literary work. As with any ergodic work, *Memorandum* reminds us that all texts are nothing but inert sets of signs until the reader turns them into works of literature, and that each reading – even of the most linear, non-ergodic, text – produces a new experience and thus a new work.

---

[27] This correspondence is pointed out by Van Vuuren, '*Passacaglia* van J.S. Bach', 505.

CHAPTER 12

Formal Innovation and Affect in the Contemporary Irish Novel: Kevin Barry, Mike McCormack, and Eimear McBride

Formal Innovation and Affect

The relation between formal innovation in works of literature and readers' affective responses has not been the subject of wide discussion. Modernism, as Julie Taylor notes in her introduction to the collection *Modernism and Affect*, has often been characterised as 'cold, hard and cerebral' in contrast to the Victorian penchant for sentiment that it was challenging (2). Laura Frost, therefore, is being uncontroversial when she refers to the 'daunting, onerous, and demanding reading practices' required to wrest pleasure from modernist texts, and asserts that 'modernism's signature formal rhetorics, including irony, fragmentation, indirection, and allusiveness, are a parallel means of promoting a particularly knotty, arduous reading effect' (*The Problem with Pleasure*, 3). Many modernist writers themselves emphasised their control of emotion, T. S. Eliot only being the most prominent. Moreover, the influential attack on the so-called 'affective fallacy' by W. K. Wimsatt and Monroe Beardsley meant that the practitioners of New Criticism, who found in modernist texts the ideal material for their analyses, were wary of talking about emotional response ('The Affective Fallacy'). (Emotional response was important for I. A. Richards, but this aspect of his approach to literary works was seldom followed up.) And it's commonly assumed that the reader faced with sentences that require unusual effort, language that fails to conform to its own norms, and narratives that defy generic expectations is too busy carrying out the necessary intellectual deciphering to experience an emotional reaction to the text. By contrast with famously unsentimental modernist writing, the argument goes, the realist techniques developed by Victorian novelists (and their counterparts in other linguistic traditions), and carried into the twentieth and twenty-first centuries by numerous novelists, are what can provide readers with finely-drawn characters whose narrated experiences arouse strong empathetic responses.

Among philosophers concerned with literature and affect, few treat questions of form at any length, though one exception is Jenefer Robinson, who, in *Deeper than Reason*, argues that literary form acts as a 'coping device', allowing the reader to deal with painful emotion in a way that produces pleasure.[1] (There are echoes here of Wordsworth's account of metre in the Preface to *Lyrical Ballads*.) The closest Robinson comes to an analysis of innovative formal devices is in a brief mention of Robert Coover's short story 'The Babysitter', of which she writes:

> [F]orm is so foregrounded that almost our every response is controlled and managed by the master manipulator who relates the story. Our ordinary emotional processes have very little chance of getting going before they are nipped in the bud by assertive reminders that the (implied) author is firmly in command and that readers are responding to an artfully constructed story that celebrates not life but the supremacy of form and structure. The story is more like a hall of mirrors than a slice of life. Postmodern stories of this sort may still appeal to our emotions in a sense – they can be funny or disturbing – but the emotions evoked are managed to such a high degree that we are mainly aware as we read of the cognitive pleasures of intellectualizing and distancing than of the rewards of deep emotional engagement with the characters or situations described. (228)

I doubt if every reader finds the sex and violence in Coover's story as evacuated of emotional impact by wayward form as Robinson does, but it's not unreasonable to assume that conspicuous formal devices invite an intellectual engagement that masks or dulls any potential affective response. Paige Reynolds expresses a similar view of the effect of the formal innovations of Eimear McBride's *A Girl Is a Half-formed Thing* (to which we shall return): 'McBride's use of modernism offers a prophylactic from intense absorption, keeping us at bay with its difficulty, its obfuscations, its knowing invocations of literary tradition'.[2]

The question I am posing, then, is this: is it possible to use innovative formal devices inherited from modernist writing in the service of, rather than as a distraction from, literary works' emotional power?

[1] Robinson's chapter 7 is titled 'Formal Devices as Coping Mechanisms' (195–228).
[2] Reynolds, 'Trauma, Intimacy, and Modernist Form'. In 'Bird Girls', Reynolds advances a similar argument, but only as a *possible* effect of modernist stylistic innovation, going on to say that '[i]n this novel, form fails to protect the careful reader' (189).

Affect in Theory

In order to explore this question, something needs to be said about the amorphous body of 'affect theory'. I say 'amorphous' because no single, coherent theoretical argument has emerged from the flurry of writing over the past twenty-five years to which this label has been attached.[3] Since my interest in this chapter is in the way writers use the resources of language to evoke emotional responses in readers, I don't wish to theorise about the psychology of affect or to erect yet another scheme attempting to distinguish among the related but slippery terms emotion, affect, and feeling.[4] (I will use all three terms more-or-less interchangeably.) One major branch of affect studies seems to me to offer very little to my own project: the theory of affects as pre-cognitive and pre-linguistic – and even pre-subjective – derived from Deleuze and Guattari, and from their readings of Spinoza and Bergson.[5] The common-sense view that emotion is both physiological and mental, with a constantly operative relay between the two, seems to me the most useful: if I freeze with fright at the sudden appearance of a figure in my bedroom the physiological is primary, but when I read a scary passage in *The Mysteries of Udolpho* it's my mind that communicates fear – or something like fear – to my body.

In discussing affect in a literary context, one fundamental distinction – an obvious one, yet one not always observed in these discussions – is that between the *representation* and the *eliciting* of emotion: the former involves the emotions experienced by the characters in the fictional world and, sometimes, by the narrator of the fiction; the latter the emotions experienced by the reader. Although the reader's feelings are often an empathetic echo of the character's or the narrator's, it's equally possible for the two emotional registers to be very different. Think of all those moments when a character is heading, in blissful ignorance, into a trap of which the reader has been made aware: when the events are related by a neutral narrator the experience of fearful apprehension is the reader's alone, a feeling actually heightened by the absence of fear on the part of the character.

---

[3] Gregg and Seigworth usefully spell out in their introduction to *The Affect Theory Reader* the 'multiple trajectories' of their theme (12).

[4] I have discussed these terms, and analysed one kind of emotional response to fictional writing, in chapter 9 of *The Work of Literature*.

[5] See, for instance, Massumi, *Parables for the Virtual*, and Abel, *Violent Affect*. For concise critiques of this branch of affect theory, see Ruth Leys, 'The Turn to Affect' and 'Trauma and the Turn to Affect'. Leys usefully traces the history of affect studies in *The Ascent of Affect*.

We also hear occasionally about the *expression* of emotion, with the implication that the task of the writer is to feel strongly, and then encode those feelings in language so that the reader experiences them in turn. This may be a true account of how some literary works get written, but it's certainly not a generalisable one. A more likely scenario is that when the writer becomes the reader of their own work during the process of composition, they experience feelings in the same way as their future readers will do – though the feelings aroused by the fictional representations in works of art aren't identical to the feelings aroused by events in our lives. The sorrow we may feel at Cordelia's death is related to, but not the same as, the sorrow we would feel at the loss of a daughter.

My interest, then, is in the use of literary techniques both to represent and to elicit emotion. As I've been suggesting throughout this book, the work of literature is not an object to be interpreted but an event experienced by a reader – and an important part of that experience is the complex of feelings it arouses. However, the terms we have at our disposal to describe such feelings are extremely limited; it's part of the power of literature that it can affect our bodies and minds in ways that exceed our descriptive powers. In discussing some exemplary passages of formally innovative fiction I hope to show the strength but also the elusiveness of the affective power they possess.

The Debt to Joyce

In 2013, a literary prize was established by Goldsmiths, University of London, 'to celebrate the qualities of creative daring associated with the University and to reward fiction that breaks the mould or extends the possibilities of the novel form'.[6] Three of the first four were Irish: Eimear McBride in 2013, for *A Girl Is a Half-formed Thing*; Kevin Barry in 2015, for *Beatlebone*; and Mike McCormack in 2016 for *Solar Bones*. These authors have all made clear the importance to them of the earlier achievements of Irish modernism. McCormack expresses it clearly:

> In Ireland, our pinnacle, our Mount Rushmore, is the Father, Son and Holy Ghost: James Joyce, Flann O'Brien and Samuel Beckett. And it feels like we're digesting their legacy. I don't know if it's something about being able to see them clearly now, but people are no longer afraid to name-check the three masters. My generation were a bit wary of picking up the challenge those old fellows had laid down for us. Now I see it not as a challenge, but

---

[6] https://www.gold.ac.uk/goldsmiths-prize/about/.

a license. Beckett and Joyce and Flann are giving me the quest: go forth and experiment.[7]

Barry has commented, 'I love the radical streak – Beckett and Joyce and Flann O'Brien were happy to go nuts on the page and be inventive',[8] and when he was asked whether he included 'Beckettian and Joycean moments' in *Beatlebone* deliberately, he replied: 'Very often they'll come in without your quite knowing it. Irish writing has this wonderful reputation, and so much of it is built on the work of three writers: Beckett and Joyce and Flann O'Brien in the first half of the 20th century'.[9] And McBride's anecdote about her initial inspiration for *A Girl Is a Half-formed Thing* is well-known but worth repeating:

> Joyce really set my universe on its end. Reading *Ulysses* changed everything I thought about language, and everything I understood about what a book could do. I was on a train on the way to a boring temp job when I was about 25; I got on at Tottenham, north London, and opened the first page of *Ulysses*. When I got off at Liverpool Street in central London, I don't think it is an exaggeration to say the entire course of my life had changed. ('My Hero, James Joyce')[10]

These three writers have accepted the challenge laid down by their modernist predecessors and have shown that it's possible to create highly successful fiction that, though it may be unimaginable without the earlier example of the Irish modernists, breaks open new ground in the writing of fiction.[11] All three of the novels I've mentioned have been described in reviews as 'moving'; my question is whether this quality is achieved by means of or in spite of their formal and linguistic innovations.

---

[7] McCormack, interview with Stephanie Boland, *New Statesman*. See the Introduction for comments on the challenge for the Irish writer after Joyce.

[8] Barry, interview with Anita Sethi, *The Guardian*.

[9] Barry, interview with Julia Brodsky, *Irish America*.

[10] The other major influence McBride acknowledges is the playwright Sarah Kane (see White, '"It was like lightning"').

[11] Ruth Gilligan quotes a comment by McBride made in a lecture about the oft-made comparison of her work with Joyce's: 'I think it can be obstructive as well, that people then only look at the ways in which it's like Joyce, or consider that it's kind of sub-Joyce because it's not doing what he's doing, rather than really realising that it's doing something different' ('Eimear McBride's Ireland', 789). Gilligan is quoting from McBride's 'Revolutions in Literature', a lecture given at the LSE Literary Festival on 23 February, 2017.

Kevin Barry

Kevin Barry was known as the author of two accomplished collections of short stories and a frankly weird novel, *City of Bohane*, depicting gang warfare in a dystopian future, when, in 2015, *Beatlebone* appeared. Its formal peculiarities are many, including stretches of minimalist dialogue scattered over the page without even Joyce's initial dash to indicate speech; unannounced shifts of time and space; sections set out as playtexts; a six-page monologue with no punctuation other than question marks and dashes; and a twenty-eight-page section detailing the author's own adventures in researching for the book (an account that may also be fictional, of course) together with some of the fruits of those researches. The background described in that section concerns John Lennon's purchase in 1967 of a small island in Clew Bay on the west coast of Ireland, his visits to it in that same year and in the following year, and the alternative communities who lived on islands in the bay in the 1970s. The main narrative of the novel imagines a third visit by Lennon, now aged thirty-seven, in 1978, in the hope of rekindling his apparently extinguished creative energies. (Lennon fans will know that the period 1975–80 was a fallow one in his musical career, a period during which his life seems to have revolved around Yoko Ono and their young son.)

Two types of writing dominate the novel: a narrative of Lennon's actions, thoughts, and feelings, slipping easily into free indirect discourse from time to time and maintaining the character's perspective on the world, and dialogues between him and Cornelius O'Grady, his irrepressibly mordant driver, boatman, and guide to the strange world of Clew Bay. These dialogues are for the most part brilliant comedy, though they often have a tinge of melancholy; they clearly owe a great deal to Flann O'Brien, and particularly to the conversational preposterousness of Sergeant Pluck in *The Third Policeman*. When the narrative focus is on John – he is called by his first name throughout these passages – the tone varies considerably, but one of the achievements of the novel is to convey, through all its variations in style, the array of conflicting emotions that has driven the stalled artist to this apparently crazy expedition. (Late in the novel, John is asked 'what class of feelings' he is having, and his reply is 'Very fucking complicated ones' (258).) The stylistic diversions play their part in keeping a sense of imaginative creativity alive during a period of despondency, and the reader's response is likely to be a mixture of empathetic recognition of the condition of creative blockage and amused contemplation of the absurdity of the events and conversations.

It's not possible to select a 'representative' passage, since there are so many different styles in the novel, but let me take one that illustrates both the waywardness of the narrative and the affective complexity it induces at a turning point in the story. John has fetched up, thanks to Cornelius, in the Amethyst Hotel on Achill Island, to the north of the bay, which is occupied by a community devoted to a version of primal scream therapy (a practice that Lennon and Ono had themselves engaged in for a while). After a section titled 'The Rants' and modelled on the playtext form of Joyce's 'Circe' episode, the style reverts to a close-up portrayal of John's inner world as he escapes from the hotel in the early morning and finds a cave on the shore to hide in. He is there all day and all night, and reaches some kind of accommodation with his situation and his past, memories of which have been haunting him and threatening to drown him in sentimental recollection. The agent of this accommodation is a seal, which appears in the cave during the night and starts a conversation:

> There is a hard splash as the water splits, and the great sleek head shows, and the dapper spindles of the moustache, and the long fat body works its muscles onto the rocks.
>
> It sidles up to the cave's entry – hello? – and pokes a sober look inside.
>
> The sad doleful eyes; the night caller; the seal.
>
> There is a moment of sweet calm as their eyes lock on each other's.
>
> Alright? he says.
>
> Alright, John, the seal says. (181–2)

If the reader has retained their suspension of disbelief to any degree during the unlikely events that precede this moment, the last shreds are surely now blown away; Barry has availed himself of the Joycean mode I call pararealism, discussed in Chapter 4. The deadpan presentation of an absurd, impossible event is, first of all, comic, but it's also oddly moving as a kind of wish fulfilment at this point in John's creative life, a dream of communication that anyone will recognise who has been looked at by a seal's 'sad doleful eyes'.

One way of understanding the seal's intervention is that it's the emergence of another part of the self, an interpretation strengthened when we learn that the animal has a Liverpool accent. But the seal is less prone to sentimentality than John, who has been reciting to himself the numbers of the Liverpool buses and recalling the 'rainsome air and the steam of a caff'. The creature admonishes him:

> Reality, John, tends not to hang around. A lonely bloody suburb in 1955 – it's gone – and the rattle of the train for Central under your bony arse – it's gone – and the smell of the sweat and the red raw of the acne and a tumble in the Formby dunes – it's gone – and her with a kisser on that tastes of salt and Bovril . . .

> He hadn't remembered the Bovril tang – a strange seal this.

> . . . and all of it, John? It's all got the same weight as a bloody dream.

> So what's left that's real?

> This, the seal says. Where you're sat just now.

> The clouds drift to hide the moon; the cave darkens. A pool of silence is allowed to open. (185)

This is an example in which the reader is invited to share the affective experience of the character to some degree, though John's response to the talking seal is a good deal more matter-of-fact than the reader's is likely to be. The message that the seal brings would be trite if spelled out in conventional terms, but the novelty of the situation and the vividness with which memories are presented even while their reality is being denied make the passage, for this reader at least, one that works in subtle ways on the emotions. The feelings aroused by knowledge of the pastness of the past at the same time as a registering of its lasting power are both negative and positive – what we might call, if it weren't a cliché, bittersweet emotions. The very specificity of the visual, tactile, audible, olfactory, and gustatory memories evoked by the seal testify to that power, though the oddity of the seal's superior memory contributes to the strangeness of the scene – just what part of John's consciousness or unconscious does the seal speak from? And while it's true that there is something Hollywoodish about the clouds drifting over the moon at just the right moment, the darkness and the silence are necessary to signal that the seal's hard truth is sinking in. A short while after this encounter, and clearly in consequence of it, John is seized with the idea of a new album.

Mike McCormack

While Barry's novel swings, Joyce-like, from style to style, the other two novels I'm looking at, *Solar Bones* and *A Girl Is a Half-formed Thing*, remain stylistically consistent from beginning to end. Mike McCormack, like Barry, had published two collections of short stories before the appearance of the novel we're looking at: *Getting It in the Head* (1996) contains some early examples of his stylistic inventiveness and liking for bizarre narratives; *Forensic Songs* (2012) is stylistically more conventional, but still dark. In between, McCormack published two novels, *Crowe's Requiem* (1998) and *Notes from a Coma* (2005). The former rather awkwardly mixes magic realism with a tale of a lonely heart, but latter achieves a much more controlled juxtaposition between, at the top of each page, a series of voices telling the story of a Romanian orphan's unusual life in Ireland, and at the bottom a running commentary on the events of the narrative from an unidentifiable voice or voices, sometimes clinically exact, sometimes lyrical; an example, that is, of a non-linear novel as discussed in Chapter 11.

The Goldsmiths Prize-winning novel is different again; as the reviewers liked to observe with due awe, it consists of a single sentence running across its 223 pages (or, in the 2017 Canongate edition, 265 pages). For this work, McCormack has devised a style that looks forbidding on the page but is in fact highly readable – we realise quite quickly that we don't need the stop and start of sentence endings and beginnings as conjunctions will do quite as well.[12] Unlike the 'Penelope' episode of *Ulysses*, which this style superficially resembles, we don't have to mentally insert the full stops that make the language comprehensible. McCormack has made reading progress easier by inserting paragraph breaks on every page, sometimes several, sometimes just one or two; apart from any local effects achieved by these breaks, they enable the reading eye to remain aware of its place on the page. A solid page of prose such as occurs occasionally in *Beatlebone* and *A Girl Is a Half-formed Thing* – and of course in Molly Bloom's monologue – is, for purely physiological reasons, more of a challenge. Sometimes a paragraph break in McCormack's text contributes to the articulation of the sense or the evocation of emotion; sometimes it coincides with a syntactic break or a change of speaker; sometimes it occurs in the middle of a grammatical unit. McCormack can thus avail himself, as we shall see, of some of the resources of free verse.

The novel is a long series of reminiscences and meditations by an Irish engineer, Marcus Conway, while he stands and sits in the kitchen of his house outside Louisburgh, County Mayo, on 2nd November, All Souls Day, 2009. There is no conventional narrative, but there are gripping accounts of

[12] Another recent Irish novel that looks forbidding on the page but is relatively easy to read is Patrick McCabe's *Poguemahone* (2022), which, as I have indicated, is set out in short lines like a modernist poem (or perhaps like a parody of a modernist poet such as Don Marquis' Archy or *Private Eye*'s E. J. Thribb).

significant episodes of Marcus's life as a father and an engineer, and harrowing descriptions of his wife's suffering from cryptosporidiosis, a virus that lodges in the digestive tract and is derived from human waste – an illness contracted, along with many other victims, as a result of civic incompetence. (This is only one of the signs of a disintegrating world that these recollections chart.) And it's intensely moving – at least one reviewer confessed being reduced to tears near the end of the book.

However, it's not easy to give names to the emotions that are likely to be aroused during the reading of *Solar Bones*. Past experiences involving powerful feelings are related, but they are now looked back on from a present in which Marcus is no longer a passionate participant in the urgent affairs of life. Although some of the book articulates strong condemnation of the corrupt political practices and shoddy engineering that for Marcus have darkened the world in which he has lived, the anger is mediated by the distance implied in this retrospective gaze. The evenness of the run-on sentence contributes to this sense of muted emotion: no utterance is allowed to fully complete itself before the language is busy moving on to the next one, and the breaks on the page ask to be crossed over by the voice because of the grammatical continuity. There are therefore few moments of climactic culmination, such as powerful feeling seems to demand: climaxes, instead of arresting the narrative, become part of its onward current.

Let me look at one moment of strong emotion, recalled by Marcus as he thinks back to the artistic career of his daughter Agnes. He and his wife have attended the opening of Agnes's show in Galway, for which she has covered the walls of the gallery with texts taken from newspaper reports of criminal court cases written out in a red substance, which Marcus gradually realises is his daughter's own blood. His response is not what we might expect:

> Agnes's blood was now our common element, the medium in which we stood and breathed so that even as she was witness-in-chief, spreading out the indictment which, however broad and extravagant it may be on rhetorical flourish, however geographically and temporally far-flung it might be, the whole thing ultimately dovetailed down to a specific source and point which was, as I saw it
>
> me
>
> nothing and no one else but
>
> me
>
> plain as day up there on the walls and in the sweep of each word and line, I was the force beneath, driving it in waves up to the ceiling and it was clear to me through that uncanny voice which now sounded in my heart, a voice all the clearer for being so choked and distant, telling me that
>
> I did this

I was responsible for this
whatever it was
definitely something bad and not to my credit because only real guilt
could account for that mewling sense of fright which took hold of me there
in the middle of that room, something of it returning to me now
sitting here at this table
that same cramping flash within me which twisted some part of me . . .

(46–7)

For a moment, the relative calm with which Marcus surveys his past is broken as he relives the feeling of guilt his daughter's artwork produced in
him and re-experiences something of the physical pain that hit him at that
moment. But what are the reader's feelings? I can only speak for myself, of
course, not having undertaken a survey of reader responses. I find I share
something of the unease experienced by the viewers in the gallery at the
thought of pints of Agnes's blood being collected and used as ink, but
the prose doesn't attempt to elicit a visceral response to the artwork itself;
the focus is all on Marcus's extraordinary reaction, as he takes his daughter's
creation to be a reflection of some horror in her own life and consequently
as an indictment of his own treatment of her as a father. The breaks in
the sentence underline this focus on personal responsibility: the isolated
'me', twice, and the separate lines for 'I did this' and 'I was responsible for
this' – all the more effective in the context of the continuities of the prose.
I as reader can't feel any of Marcus's powerful emotion, but rather feel something like compassion for this man so unsure of his own relationship with
his daughter in the past and now so tortured by the memory – even though
the subsequent meeting with his wife and daughter puts his fears to rest.

McCormack could have written this passage, and the book, in conventional sentences, and the result would certainly have communicated complex emotions to the reader to some degree. But it's McCormack's handling
of English syntax that imparts a unique affective quality to the writing: he
takes advantage of the many ways in which an utterance can be prolonged,
sometimes bending the rules though seldom leaving the reader uncertain as
to meaning, in order to capture the incessant onrush of thought and emotion peculiar to the situation in which Marcus finds himself (an unusual
situation only revealed at the end of the novel).[13] In the quoted passage
we begin with something like a main clause with subject and predicate:
'Agnes's blood was now our common element'; this is followed by a noun

---

[13] Neil Murphy demonstrates the connection between Marcus's situation and the
innovative form of the novel in 'The Novel as Heartbeat', 66–7.

in apposition to 'blood' – 'the medium' – itself followed by a relative clause, 'in which we stood and breathed'. Then there is a conjunction ('so that') leading to a new main clause ('the whole thing ultimately dovetailed down to a specific source and point'), but separated from that clause by an adverbial clause ('even as she was witness-in-chief') qualified by an adjectival phrase ('which, spreading out the indictment') which is in turn modified by two adverbial clauses ('however broad and extravagant it might be on rhetorical flourish'; 'however geographically and temporally far-flung it might be') that *also* seem to lead to 'the whole thing' and thence to the climactic 'me'. And 'me' is only a momentary stopping point; it's immediately further specified and elaborated on as the language rolls forward. If the reader felt it necessary to parse every phrase, the intellectual effort would certainly inhibit the affective response; however, the slightly indeterminate nature of the grammatical relationships allows for unimpeded reading and the evocation of a sequence of shifting emotions that invite an equally delicate affective play on the reader's part.

Eimear McBride

If reviewers reported themselves moved, and occasionally brought to tears, by *Beatlebone* and *Solar Bones*, the emotional responses recorded in accounts of Eimear McBride's *A Girl Is a Half-formed Thing* were of a different quality: 'wrenching', 'emotionally overwhelming', 'raw and devastating', 'visceral', are some of the terms used by reviewers. 'It explodes into your chest', wrote one early reviewer. Announcing the winner of the inaugural Goldsmiths Prize, Tim Parnell said of the work: 'If ever a novel gave the lie to the notion that formal inventiveness necessarily precludes feeling, it is this one'.[14] Yet of the three novels, this is the one that takes most liberties with the English language and the conventions of the novel. At the opposite extreme from McCormack's continuous sentence, McBride's prose is truncated, sliced, spliced, shredded; sentences are either chopped into fragments or run together.[15] The story the novel tells is of a sister's love for a brother as the one sustaining element in a life wrecked on the shoals of male sexual appetites, starting with sex at the age of thirteen at the urging of a forty-one-year-old uncle, and thereafter, and in consequence, with boys at her school and later with men, so many men, mostly anonymous and uncaring. When

---

[14] Cited in Collard, *About a Girl*, 152.

[15] A forebear among Irish writers is Dorothy Nelson, whose exploration of the dark side of family life in *In Night's City* (1982) and *Tar and Feathers* (1987) also stretches and deforms language in the expression of pain, albeit not so drastically.

the brother – there are no names in the novel – dies after a recurrence of
the brain tumour that had first been operated on when he was a baby, the
girl's self-destructive sexual encounters reach a new pitch and the desire to
live abandons her.

Writing that invites an emotional response from the reader occurs on
almost every page, and once more this response is a complex combination
of feelings that resists simple labelling. We feel sympathy for the exploited
girl, anger at those who mistreat her, dismay at her self-destructiveness, and
horror at some of the things that happen to her. But it's not the events of
the narrative alone that elicit the comments I've quoted, I believe, painful
though they are, but the language in which these events are related.

The most viscerally affecting passages in the novel deal with sex, none
of it of a pleasurable nature. (In her second novel, *The Lesser Bohemians*,
McBride uses a related technique to describe much more positively experienced sex.)[16] The passage I am going to quote is by no means one of the
most graphic. Devastated by her brother's death, the girl leaves the house at
night for the place where she expects to find a man who earlier had violent
sex with her; he is there, and the coitus that follows is more brutal than any
of the earlier encounters – something that is reflected in the way the very
words themselves are damaged and eruptions of upper-case letters occur in
unexpected places. The text becomes literally unreadable (though McBride
makes a good attempt in her audio performance of the book), our struggle
with the words, one might say, becomes part of our physiological response
to the episode – emotion experienced in the gut as much as the brain.

When the girl is home again, her uncle finds her in the bathroom and
insists on sex, which she tries unsuccessfully to resist. This passage follows,
a sequence of thoughts in which she continues to address her dead brother
as 'you':

> i go i off to the room where i lie and lie down on my face. Think of this. Did
> i give him all he asked for then? Mouth tasting of sick. Eye back in my head.
> A burning stomach. A body wet from the rain. It did tonight I remember.
> I recall. Wet and freezing. No it. Did it? I. Give it to him if he wanted it. I
> don't. I think he did. Fuck the. I'm the girl. Did that is that love to me. I'm.
> Spite and spit and sick. That's me that was. Is now. What me? In the layers
> of make-up? In the smear on his shirt? In the cold pocket between my legs?
> Where do I live? Where am. Someone he can see and cut into. Good to be.

---

[16] For an astute commentary on *The Lesser Bohemians* and on the importance of bodily affect in McBride's modernist style, see Battersby, *Troubling Late Modernism*,
chapter 6.

Butter and knife. No. What he takes. What he takes is the what there is of me. Now you've. I thought was nothing left. Now you've. How he knows it. He knows it is there for the beating the stealing the. I. Some place around that. No. I am there. Now you've. I. What's it like in the silence when. You. I. Where. I. Hello. Hello. Is he are you there? Sssssss. There? I'm only here in my bones and flesh. Now you've gone away. (198)

As noted earlier, Paige Reynolds has argued that the fragmented style of *A Girl is a Half-formed Thing* acts to reduce our emotional involvement in the narrative. Here is a fuller extract from her argument, which deserves careful consideration: Reynolds does not deny the work's powerful emotional impact, but doesn't see the modernist techniques as contributing to it:

> The shocking and lurid details accompanying the disturbing sexual encounters recounted throughout *A Girl Is a Half-Formed Thing* confirm that McBride is not seeking in this novel to perform modernist impersonality. However, by adeptly adopting and adapting so many elements of modernist form, she does offer a buffer for her readers. McBride's use of modernism offers a prophylactic from intense absorption, keeping us at bay with its difficulty, its obfuscations, its knowing invocations of literary tradition. Strikingly, this tactic is in dialogue with her endeavor through graphic portrayals of all varieties of transgressive sex (among other unsettling moments in the protagonist's life) to pull us into the narrative. . . . The armature of modernist intertextuality provides readers protection from identifying too closely with the protagonist's abnegation. It thwarts our readerly empathy, engaging our intellects even as our emotions are pulled into the suffering of this young woman. By interjecting these overtly modernist formal maneuvers, McBride provides the reader, though not her character, the protections afforded by the literary, and by language. ('Trauma, Intimacy, and Modernist Form')

My own sense is that passages like the one I've quoted – and I could have quoted from just about any page – show the opposite (and the responses of other readers suggest I'm not alone): that the linguistic abnormalities result in an unusually *direct* communication of affect. Even more than is the case in *Solar Bones*, the rules of the English language are transgressed, and an attempt to pin down each word as a participant in a grammatical sequence would lead to an intellectualisation likely to empty the writing of affective power. However, such pinning-down is not an appropriate way to read McBride's prose: one has to take the language as it comes, allowing the meaning – often the shreds of meaning – to emerge. (I observed in Chapter 5 that one of the lessons of *Finnegans Wake* is that it's not necessary to understand everything on a first reading to enjoy a work.)

There isn't space to look at the passage in detail, but the point may be made if we rewrite part of it in conventional sentences:

I go off to the room where I lie face-down and think of what happened. Did I give him all he asked for, then? My mouth tastes of sick. My eyes feel as though they have been forced back into my head, and I have a burning stomach and a body wet from the rain. It did rain tonight, I remember. I can recall being wet and freezing. No, it didn't rain, did it? I always gave my body to him if he wanted it. I don't know why, though I think he did. He wanted to fuck the girl that I am. I'm the girl he always wanted. He did that to me – is that love? I'm not sure.

The rewritten passage seems to me much less powerful than the original in its capacity to arouse emotion. It creates the impression of a reflective speaker, standing back slightly to observe her actions, feelings, and thoughts, even though it's in the present tense. It also narrows down meaning considerably: for instance, I've guessed that 'No it. Did it?' refers to the rain, but this is only one possibility; it's more likely that there is some inexpressible impulse relating to the sex act. I have no way of expanding the 'I' that follows – is it the beginning of a thought that gets cut off? A verbless reference to the self in its helplessness and hurt? ('I' appears often in the text in isolation like this, including instances later in this paragraph.) These ambiguities might be considered a weakness, but they seem to me to be an effective part of the writing's texture, suggesting a maelstrom of thoughts that reach verbal form only in splinters: that is to say, there is no complete verbal utterance that these fragments are part of; rather, they are isolated words thrown up by the inchoate mental processes. 'You. I. Where. I.' can't be completed; they are pain-ridden gestures of love, loss, and who knows what else. The effect is of a more direct access to the character's inner life than conventional prose is capable of. At one point, there is only a sound: 'Sssss'. At other times, syntax gives way under the stress of emotion, for instance in: 'What he takes is the what there is of me', which nevertheless makes perfect sense, especially when followed by 'I thought was nothing left', or 'Is he are you there?', where attention to the uncle gives way to the focus on the brother.

This is not a passage likely to elicit emotions that echo those of the narrator, except perhaps for a reader who has experienced something like the girl's situation and feelings, but it's very hard to give a precise account of what one's affective response is. Compassion, again, is part of it, and anger at what has been done to the girl, and a chill at the words she chooses to refer to her vagina – 'the cold pocket between my legs' – and at her simile for sex with her uncle – 'Butter and knife'. And there is also something more positive, though also poignant, in the way she continues to address her brother through the miasma of suffering and self-laceration.[17]

McBride's fractured language invites an emotional response on every page of *A Girl Is a Half-formed Thing*. But as *The Lesser Bohemians* proves, it's not a matter of linguistic fragmentation automatically producing negative affect: such language may also be used to convey and celebrate the excitement of fulfilling sexual experiences. After all, intense physical passion at its most life-enhancing can be just as destructive of the conventional structures of grammar. It's McBride's successful fusing of formal innovation and the evocation of a life lived at the mercy of destructive impulses from both without and within that makes the affective consequences of the novel so close to being unbearable.

Form and Affect

To read any of the three novels I've been discussing is to be emotionally engaged from start to finish, which means both to be attentive to the emotions experienced by the three main characters and to respond affectively to their feelings, experiences, thought-processes, and revelations, as these are fashioned by the text. And an important aspect of that fashioning is the chosen technique in each case: Barry's shifting styles and spaced-out dialogues, McCormack's unbroken verbal sequence and visual breaks, McBride's fragments of language dislocated syntax – all are part and parcel of the emotions invoked.

Of course, there are many other writers who are publishing formally and generically innovative work today, not all of whom are committed to eliciting from their readers powerful and complex affective responses. In Chapter 14, I discuss Tom McCarthy's novels, in which many of the major characters are portrayed as lacking in affect, and where the reader's enjoyment of the fiction doesn't require any emotional involvement with them. This is not to judge either type of writing as better; just to note the difference. What these contrasting examples show is that there is no necessary connection between formal innovation and affective resonance: form, like every other aspect of literary writing, can be exploited to elicit powerful emotions or to keep affect from playing a significant part in the reader's responses. While the pleasures offered by much of *Ulysses* and *Finnegans Wake* are

---

[17] Annie Ryan's stage version of the novel, brilliantly performed in 2016 by Aoife Duffin, consists of only about one-sixth of the original, and is as emotionally draining, for performer and for audience, as anything I have seen in the theatre.

intellectual, both works have passages with a strong affective charge; ALP's final monologue in the latter book, for instance, is one of literature's most moving representations of ageing, loss, and acceptance woven together to produce a complex tissue of feelings. Whether a literary work adheres to the formal conventions of the realist tradition or challenges those conventions through linguistic and generic innovation does not, in itself, lead to predict-able affective responses: the appeal that each work makes to the intellect and the emotions is singular, and that singularity is built from a variety of different materials that, in the final analysis, exceed any critical determina-tions such as 'modernist' or 'realist'.

CHAPTER 13

Form, Politics, and Postcolonial Fiction: Kamila Shamsie's *Home Fire*

Literature, Politics, and Postcolonial Studies

One of the most vexed questions in the debates about literary form is its relation to politics. For many critics, to take a strong interest in form is to turn one's back on the overriding goal of contributing to the betterment of society; if literature is to serve political goals, such critics believe, content must be at the forefront of the critical process, since it's there that the writer's engagement with the concrete political issues of the day is to be found. And it's characteristic of recent literary theorists who do argue for the importance of an engagement with formal questions that they feel obliged to make a direct connection between these questions and political effectiveness.[1]

As I suggested in the Introduction, any consideration of the contribution literature may make to political causes needs to take account of one simple fact: only through the experience of readers engaging with literary works can this contribution occur, and then only if that experience effects a significant and lasting change in the reading consciousness. Such a change can happen only if the encounter with the work is also an encounter with a previously unacknowledged way of seeing the world or of experiencing feelings about it. Examining a literary work for the political sympathies it betrays, the political events it charts, or the material conditions it exposes as if it were a static object whose properties are to be investigated may be

---

[1] See my brief discussion in the Introduction of Caroline Levine's *Forms*, Tom Eyers' *Speculative Formalism*, and Joseph North's *Literary Criticism* as examples of arguments of this type, although the proposals they put forward are quite different (2–3). North, who emphasizes the educative potential of literary works on actual readers, comes closest to my own thinking about this issue.

a valuable exercise in literary criticism but cannot in itself demonstrate the work's effectiveness in this domain; a political analysis needs to be undertaken with an awareness that only as an event experienced by readers can a work have any purchase on the outside world – and only if readers are different after that event from what they were before it.[2] If the experience of a work leaves the reader unaffected, they will not act in the world. A further requirement for political change, of course, is either that a large number of readers are moved to act in the service of some kind of popular movement – a requirement rarely met by the literary works most highly regarded by the critical establishment – or, even less likely, that a small number of highly influential figures, inspired by a book they have read, proceed to bring about a transformation in their environment. And much as those of us who have dedicated our lives to the study and teaching of literature would like to believe otherwise, the power of literary works to effect political transformation is tiny compared to the other discourses that circulate in society. The publication of *Oliver Twist* and *Uncle Tom's Cabin* may have had a beneficial effect on social and political reality, but if so, they are exceptions.

The ethico-political value and importance of literary works, therefore, is primarily a matter of individual experience. When critics describe the way in which a novel interrogates power structures or a play upends sexual conventions they are describing the way these works operate for them, not their effect on those structures or conventions as they are to be found in the wider world. And it's probably the case that most readers of works that have strong political implications are already sympathetic to the positions being endorsed; the result of reading may be less a change of political heart than a refinement in understanding or an intensification of feeling. Critical approaches that operate on the basis of what has been called 'symptomatic' reading – tracing the occluded ideological biases of the writer, for instance – are not involved in making claims about the political effectiveness of the work being read, although their authors are often implicitly making claims about the political effectiveness of their own criticism. Since literary criticism is even less potent in the socio-political sphere than literature, such

---

[2] For discussions of literature understood as an event, see Attridge, *Singularity*, 79–89, *The Work of Literature*, 24–38, and 'The Event of the Literary Work', in Mukim and Attridge, eds, *Literature and Event*, 229–42. The other essays in *Literature and Event* offer valuable engagements with the topic. A further problem for readings that instrumentalise literary works in the service of political aims is that the changes wrought by artworks cannot be predicted in advance with any certainty, since the experience of art is an experience of the unforeseen and unforeseeable.

claims are hard to give much credence to. However, there is a realm in which both literary works and their interpretation are more likely to have a lasting impact on a significant number of people, and that is the classroom: anecdotes about the impact of a particular teacher's discussion of a work of literature abound. Once again, it's the students' experiences that have the potential to produce change.

One area of the literary landscape in which the question of politics is central is postcolonial studies. This field of academic enquiry came into existence in part out of critics' growing awareness of the cultural dimension of colonial history and the terrible cost of that history to the colonised peoples. The postcolonial writer, as I am using the term, is one whose work emerges from the conditions of colonial domination and its aftermath, whether to record the damage done, celebrate resistance, or explore possibilities of a better future.[3] Hence the critical enterprise of postcolonial studies cannot avoid paying attention to the political dimensions of such work. (The recent rise of 'World Literature' as a field of study marks a retreat from this explicit concern with politics.)[4] At the same time, the question of the formal features of postcolonial works has received short shrift. Anthologies of postcolonial criticism typically, and understandably, emphasise content, and more often than not, political content.[5] As Robert Young puts it, in his inaugural editorial for the postcolonial journal *Interventions*,

[3] A broader definition would encompass all writers based in the former colonies of the European powers whether or not they are concerned with the damaging effects of colonialism, but for the purposes of this chapter my interest is in the narrower understanding of the field. Writing by members of settler colonial populations constitutes a marginal category; Catton's *The Luminaries*, for instance, discussed in Chapter 10, is not in any straightforward sense a postcolonial novel, and writing by white South Africans, treated in Chapters 8 and 11, are as much European as postcolonial. Irish writing is also in an ambiguous position; in putting together a collection of essays on Joyce and postcolonialism, Marjorie Howes and I appropriated a lexical item in *Finnegans Wake* to signal this ambiguity: 'semicolonial' (Attridge and Howes, eds, *Semicolonial Joyce*).

[4] A different approach to global literary culture is that based on world-systems theory as developed by Immanuel Wallerstein, an approach which is explicitly political in its examination of the reflection in literature of the inequalities produced by global capitalism. See, for example, Warwick Research Collective, *Combined and Uneven Development*. The increasing awareness of the effects of globalisation and migrancy has also produced some important studies that challenge the traditional boundaries of postcolonial studies; see, for example, Clingman, *The Grammar of Identity*.

[5] Examples are Williams and Chrisman, eds, *Colonial Discourse and Post-colonial Theory*, and Ashcroft, Griffiths, and Tiffin, eds, *The Post-colonial Studies Reader*.

Writing is now valued as much for its depiction of representative minority experience as for its aesthetic qualities. Postcolonial writing has decisively articulated itself through history and historical rewriting, reforming and retrieving an historical sensibility through the creative processes of contemporary writing. This suggests that in its own way, despite an appropriation of forms of thinking associated with poststructuralist and postmodernist anti-foundationalism, in practice postcolonial studies can be strongly foundationalist, grounded in an epistemology which gives primacy to an authentic historical reality. ('Editorial', 7)

One of the few postcolonial critics to address the question of formal properties directly, Deepika Bahri, refers to 'the remarkable lack of a sufficiently developed critical framework for addressing "the aesthetic dimension" (in Herbert Marcuse's words) of postcolonial literature' (*Native Intelligence*, 1), and laments, 'The care of the aesthetic in readings of postcolonial literature has for too long been the love that dare not speak its name' (13). Criticism of Francophone postcolonial literature is no different: in the Preface to *Postcolonial Poetics: Genre and Form* (in the 'Francophone Postcolonial Series'), a rare example of a volume of essays devoted to formal questions in postcolonial studies, Dominique Combe observes that 'apart from a few essays, most Francophone postcolonial critics deal with historical, ideological and political issues' (viii).

It's obvious that documentary novels that provide vivid and compelling representations of the harmful effects of colonisation and its problematic aftermath upon individuals can be thought of as weapons in the struggle against the dominant powers, especially if they are widely enough read to have an impact on public perceptions and policy. (The same is true, or perhaps truer, of accurate and graphic reporting.) Yet what distinguishes literary discourse from other, often very closely related, discourses is form; even novels that masquerade as factual accounts (Defoe's *Robinson Crusoe*, for example), when read as literature, invite attention to the formal choices made by the author in a way that doesn't happen in the case of reading purely for information – and, as Nicholas Harrison points out, 'even if it appears to offer "information" of one sort or another, the literary text cannot itself ever indicate reliably which "information" within it is truthful or "representative"' ('Who Needs an Idea of the Literary?', 13).

But it's important not to exaggerate the direct impact of the formal features of postcolonial. Although it has been argued that formal innovation and experiment in postcolonial writing is politically effective in its undermining of dominant discourses, it's as well to pay attention to Eli Park Sorensen's warning against what he calls a '"tacit", allegorising leap', referring to the 'uncritical *assumption* that a set of politically subversive concepts corresponds to formal disruption, meta-fictive strategies and labyrinths of narrative structures' (*Postcolonial Studies and the Literary*, 10). (Sorensen draws on the young Lukács to defend, from a formal perspective, postcolonial fiction that employs the techniques of realism.) A stronger argument, to my mind, is that such modernist devices have an ethical force in staging an encounter with otherness,[6] but the experience of the reader in negotiating those devices still has to be taken into account. One study that approaches postcolonial literature from the viewpoint I'm advocating is Elleke Boehmer's *Postcolonial Poetics*. Boehmer explains that her focus is 'on the text as *something that is read*, and on the heuristic power of literature *as literature*':

> This focus entails reflecting more closely on the status of the literary in a field in which literature has tended to be read illustratively or symptomatically, as an instantiation of paradigms drawn from a range of extra-literary studies – such as cultural studies, diaspora studies, anthropology. These approaches have consistently tended to take for granted the features of the literary object that distinguish it as different from other kinds of object. (3)

The formal features employed in postcolonial novels are as varied as those to be found any large body of fiction. There are superbly detailed representations of the lives of imagined characters fully in the tradition of nineteenth-century realism: among a large number of examples one could cite, rather arbitrarily, Amitav Ghosh's *The Glass Palace*, Naguib Mafouz's *Cairo Trilogy*, Rohinton Mistry's *A Fine Balance*, Tsitsi Dangarembga's *Nervous Conditions*, Neel Mukherjee's *The Lives of Others*, and Ngũgĩ wa Thiong'o's *Petals of Blood*. Some make use of the longstanding convention of telling a story through documents such as journals and letters, like Ahdaf Soueif's *The Map of Love* or Joseph O'Connor's *Redemption Falls*. By contrast, other postcolonial novels challenge the norms of verisimilitude by means of linguistic playfulness, improbable events, or ventures into the unconscious or the supernatural; again, there are numerous examples, including Salman Rushdie's *Midnight's Children*, G. V. Desani's *All about H. Hatterr*, Yvonne Vera's *The Stone Virgins*, Dambudzo Marechera's *Black Sunlight*, Ben Okri's *The Famished Road*, and Bessie Head's *A Question of Power*. Zakes Mda's *The Map of Redness* and Zoë Wicomb's *David's Story* (discussed in Chapter 9) combine a leap across history with a free-ranging imagination of the past. Many of these formally inventive works draw on local oral traditions,

---

[6] See Attridge, *J. M. Coetzee and the Ethics of Reading*, chapter 1, 'Modernist Form and the Ethics of Otherness'.

though in academic circles they tend to receive labels such as 'postmodern' and 'magic realist'.

Debates about which of these tendencies is most central to postcolonial fiction, or to the academic enterprise of postcolonial studies, can never be resolved;[7] approached from the point of view of the reader's experience, both finely-detailed realism depicting the reality of colonial and postcolonial lives and verbal or generic games exposing the repressiveness of governing discourses and demonstrating the fragmentary, hybridised, ungrounded postcolonial condition can produce a disturbance of settled ideas and lead to action. (As I have already noted, to the extent that these works operate *as literature*, their effect on readers, as an experience of new ways of thinking and feeling, is not mechanical and predictable; however, taking pleasure in and being moved by a literary work can reinforce a response to its more documentary features.)

While realist postcolonial novels sometimes draw on Joyce's development of stylistic resources – such as interior monologue – to represent the inner lives of characters, it's obviously the second tendency that is more clearly indebted to Joyce in its linguistic play, disruptions of linear sequence, and other challenges to realist conventions. Rarer in postcolonial writing is another inheritance from Joyce, the one discussed in Chapter 10: the use of an external model that determines the unfolding narrative, so that the events that occur, while exhibiting verisimilitude in themselves, can at the same time be seen to conform to a larger scheme of which the characters are unaware. In the case of *Ulysses*, of course, this 'inorganic form', as I have termed it, is made up of the plot and major characters of the *Odyssey*. In the novel I wish to turn to, Kamila Shamsie's *Home Fire*, the governing framework is Sophocles' *Antigone*.[8] The question that poses itself is whether this dimension of the novel contributes to its impact on

---

[7] Earlier accounts of postcolonial fiction tended to favour more formally and discursively inventive writing, but a strong counter-current soon emerged. Examples of the latter include Ganguly, *States of Exception*; Gikandi, 'Theory after Postcolonial Theory'; Lazarus, *The Postcolonial Unconscious*; and Parry, 'The Institutionalization of Postcolonial Studies'. David Attwell, in *Rewriting Modernity*, has challenged the idea, most influentially put forward by Lewis Nkosi, that black South African writing failed to draw on the innovations of modernism; see Nkosi, 'Postmodernism and Black Writing', and 'Fiction by Black South Africans'.

[8] Shamsie has commented on the importance of *Ulysses* to her: 'The granddaddy of all classical retellings, and simply one of the greatest novels ever written. Joyce closely followed the structure of The Odyssey, but rather than writing about a great adventurer who travels the world for 10 years, Joyce gives us a salesman making his way around Dublin across 24 hours' ('Kamila Shamsie's 6 favorite books').

the reader, and thus can be understood as potentially having effects in the world that can be termed political.[9]

Kamila Shamsie's *Home Fire* and Sophocles' *Antigone*

Many postcolonial novels take as their starting point a classic western text.[10] *The Tempest* has been revisited many times, and Conrad's *Heart of Darkness* is another favourite, as is Defoe's *Robinson Crusoe*: all these works invite a recasting in which the relationships between coloniser and colonised (or as yet uncolonised) are scrutinised.[11] Caryl Phillips's *The Lost Child* revisits *Wuthering Heights* and his *The Nature of Blood* incorporates a retelling of *Othello*. Tracking the doings of a single character in a single day, Amit Chaudhuri's *Odysseus Abroad* engages with Homer, as the title suggests, but more importantly with *Ulysses*. If we turn to poetry, Derek Walcott's *Omeros* is another obvious heir of *Ulysses*, being based, like Joyce's work, on the *Odyssey*.

A less substantial presence in postcolonial fiction is Sophocles's *Antigone*, no doubt because its plot doesn't lend itself to a consideration of colonial relations, although it has frequently been rewritten by metropolitan authors and its influence down the centuries has been scrutinised in many studies.[12] It has had a new life as a play by postcolonial authors, though, both in Fémi Òsófisan's *Tègònni* and in Edward Brathwaite's *Odale's Choice*; it also features as a play within a play in Athol Fugard, John Kani, and Winston Ntshona's *The Island*.[13] As Boehmer puts it,

[9] Harrison addresses the issue of the political effectiveness of postcolonial fiction by means of a consideration of the impact of Conrad's *Heart of Darkness* on European imperialism in Africa, and concludes that not only is any quantification of its impact impossible but that the nature of literature as such means that 'historical and contingent factors' are more important factors than literary qualities (*Postcolonial Criticism*, 50–61).

[10] See Ashcroft, Griffiths, and Tiffin, *The Empire Writes Back*, 189–94 and *passim*; Boehmer, *Colonial and Postcolonial Literature*, 199–206; Marx, 'Postcolonial Fiction'; and Mukherjee, *What Is a Classic?*

[11] See Brydon, 'Re-writing The Tempest'. Innes gives a useful account of several postcolonial revisitings of *Heart of Darkness* (and Conrad's *The Shadow Line*) in 'The Postcolonial Novel'. Coetzee's *Foe* is only the most famous of the numerous rewritings of *Robinson Crusoe*.

[12] Examples include Butler, *Antigone's Claim*; Chanter, *Whose Antigone?*; Honig, *Antigone, Interrupted*; Steiner, *Antigones*; Žižek, *Antigone*.

[13] Lawn interestingly reads Carl Nixon's 2010 novel *Settler's Creek* as an anti-Antigone work, in which there is a clash between Pākehā and Māori value systems concerning the burial of a corpse, and the kinship-based tenets of the indigenous community are given more weight than those of the settler society ('The anti-*Antigone*').

For the once-colonized to interpret Homer or Shakespeare or Dante *on their own terms* meant staking a claim to European tradition from beyond its conventional boundaries. Take-over or appropriation was in its way a bold refusal of cultural dependency. It signified that the powerful paradigms represented by Europe's canonical texts were now mobilized in defence of what had once been seen as secondary, unorthodox, deviant, primitive. (*Colonial and Postcolonial Literature*, 205)

In none of these rewritings, however, is there an attempt to derive a formal scaffolding from the precursor text as well as using it as a thematic resource. *Home Fire* does just that: this contemporary version of the *Antigone* plot is structured as five sections corresponding to five characters derived from the original. In Sophocles's play these characters are Ismene and Antigone, daughters (and sisters) of the ill-fated Oedipus, their brother Polyneices (who is dead before the play begins), Antigone's betrothed Haemon, and Haemon's father Creon, the ruler of the city-state of Thebes and the uncle of Antigone and Ismene. In *Home Fire* three of these characters become the members of a Pakistani family living in London: the sisters Isma and Aneeka Pasha and their brother Parvaiz (who is Aneeka's twin). Creon is rewritten as a British Conservative politician who becomes Home Secretary, Karamat Lone,[14] and Haemon as his son Eamonn, who comes to be Aneeka's lover. The prophet Tiresias in the play has an equivalent in Lone's wife Terry. And where Sophocles writes of the political tensions in Thebes arising from the conflict between the rival rulers Eteocles and Polyneices, the sons of Oedipus, a conflict that results in the death of both of them, Shamsie writes of the political pressures in the UK caused by the rise of ISIS and the appeal of jihad to some of its citizens.[15]

The five sections of *Home Fire* are named after these five characters, tracing the events of the plot in sequence (with some retrospective passages), and each section reflects the point of view of the character after whom it is

[14] In 2018, on the appointment of Sajid Javid as Home Secretary, Shamsie wrote that when the idea of 'a Tory with a Muslim background holding one of the great offices of state' first occurred to her, she rejected it as ridiculous, and that she still could not conceive of a Pakistani-British prime minister ('True story'). In 2019 Javid announced that he was revoking the citizenship of Shamima Begum, who, at fifteen, had travelled to Syria intending to join ISIS. See Rutkowska, 'The Political Novel'.

[15] The name of the militant Islamic movement is not mentioned by the younger characters. The media reports call it 'ISIS' (Islamic State in Iraq and Syria), Karamat refers to it as 'Islamic State', and Farooq terms it 'the Caliphate'. When Parvaiz is inducted, he is told he is now a member of 'al-Dawa – The State', and it's by this name that it's referred to in connection with his activities.

named.[16] Only the short chapter headed 'Aneeka' deviates from this pattern, interspersing the character's actions and thoughts (relayed in a variety of styles) with news reports, tweets, and a poem. The first section, 'Isma', relates the older sister's journey from London to Amherst to join a PhD programme, where she encounters Eamonn. She grows increasingly attached to him, though the relationship is complicated by her awareness of his father's public dismissal of her own father's imprisonment at Bagram and subsequent death en route to Guantánamo. In the second section, 'Eamonn', the young man, now back in London, begins an intense relationship with Aneeka, having met her while delivering a package from Isma to a neighbour. Aneeka insists on their affair remaining secret, and when Eamonn learns that her twin has left the country to join ISIS his first impulse is to suspect her motives and reject her. He changes his mind, however, and instead goes to his father to plead Parvaiz's case. We turn to Parvaiz himself in the third section, where we learn of his recruitment in London by Farooq, an ISIS fighter, his journey to the ISIS headquarters in the Syrian city of Raqqa, his training and subsequent attachment to the media wing, and then, in the narrative present, his movements in Istanbul as he embarks on an attempt to return to Britain. The section ends with Parvaiz about to enter the British Consulate, thinking of home. There is a temporal jump to the next section, 'Aneeka', which begins with the character's grief on learning that her twin is dead, murdered as a traitor to the cause by Farooq before he could go into the Consulate. The media excerpts in this section (doing duty for the Greek chorus)[17] reflect the right-wing outcry as the story of Aneeka and Parvaiz becomes public, while the narrative tells of Aneeka's journey to Karachi to await the arrival of Parvaiz's body, Lone as Home Secretary having refused permission for it to be taken to the UK for burial. 'Karamat', the final section, deals with Lone's attempts to take control of the developing situation, which he is watching unravel on television: Aneeka exposing Parvaiz's body in a public park in Karachi and Eamonn on his way to join her. Lone's

[16] Most of the novel employs standard third-person narration, not free indirect discourse, as many commentaries claim. Free indirect discourse is used sparingly throughout.

[17] In an interview, Shamsie recounts how the idea of the media as the equivalent of the Greek chorus came to her. She comments, 'The way the chorus functions in *Antigone* is that they are quite fickle; they change character, and sometimes they're commentating on something, sometimes they put forward a certain point of view; their sympathies are changing. And the more I thought about that, the more I thought: it's social media; it's the news' (Shamsie, interview with Tolan, *Contemporary Women's Writing* 131).

decision to intervene to save them, provoked by his wife's words, comes, like Creon's response to Tiresias's warning, too late. 'Two men in beige shalwar kameezes' – ISIS fighters? emissaries of the British government? – strap a suicide vest onto Eamonn's body, and the subsequent detonation kills the pair as they embrace.

The narrative is a compelling one, exploring several issues of contemporary importance; it would have been a timely, powerful, absorbing novel had it been written in a straightforward realist manner without any reference to *Antigone*. From the relatively light-hearted opening section the story moves to the passionate affair between Aneeka and Eamonn, then to the much darker accounts of Parvaiz's radicalisation and induction into ISIS, Aneeka's determination to rescue his body, and the final tragedy in Karachi. The potent forces inducing a young man like Parvaiz to join a militant fundamentalist movement are convincingly depicted: subject to the daily reminders of the suspicion in which Muslims in Britain are held, learning of his father's almost mythic status as a jihadist, made aware of the horrors of the 'war on terror' such as those recorded in the prison at Bagram air base, and seduced by images of the coming Caliphate as a land of plenty and peace, he has many incentives to leave his stultifying life in London for what is presented as work in media for a noble cause. The reality of Parvaiz's life as a member of the ISIS media unit is chillingly described, above all the making of a video of a beheading for public consumption, and – the event that crystallises his awareness of the terrible mistake he has made – the suffering of a woman under a collapsed wall who cannot be helped by the men present because she has removed her veil and her face is exposed. Also explored, in the figure of Karamat Lone, are the compromises and self-deceits necessary for a Muslim to rise up the political ladder in a party that has failed to eradicate Islamophobia, and the sacrifices required of the wife of an ambitious politician.

One 'political' reading of the novel would be to focus on its realistic representation of these events and situations: Shamsie gives us a vivid picture of the destructive negativity of Islamic extremism and the compromised position of the Muslim politician in the United Kingdom, within the broader context of Britain's troubled historical relation to Islam. In so doing she could be said to endorse and promote a more benign world view and a fuller understanding of Islam. Does such a reading demonstrate the political power of literature? The problem with this claim is that a factual account of these issues would be even more compelling: it would be free to use literary techniques while having the advantage of being a direct report on reality. It might be argued that a novel, by inviting sympathetic identification with characters, can achieve an intensity excluded from factual reportage, but many journalistic accounts succeed in evoking just such a response in their descriptions of actual people caught up in the events they are reporting on. It's true that literature attracts readers who don't read factual accounts, and to this extent the novel may serve a useful purpose; but it's highly likely that the large majority of the readers of works such as *Home Fire* are already aware of the facts on which it draws and share its concerns. Indeed, the novel assumes that readers are familiar with some of the atrocities it refers to; the torture of prisoners at Bagram, for instance, plays an important part in the grooming of Parvaiz though the images are left undescribed. If there is a case to be made for the distinctive contribution works of literature can make to the readers' political awareness, it must be by paying attention to what is distinctive about literary experience. And a cardinal feature of that experience is a response to the operation of form. We shall return to this point.

If we move from politics, narrowly understood, to the broader domain of ethics, we find in the novel weighty ethical questions that, although they are inherited from Sophocles's play, require no awareness of the novel's precursor text to have an impact. The love Antigone/Aneeka feels for her brother prompts a defiance of the laws and power of the state and leads ultimately to her death; set against this self-destructive devotion is the pragmatic outlook of Ismene/Isma, slow to side with her sister and willing to negotiate with the powers that be. On the other side of the power struggle, Creon/Karamat is torn between, on one hand, upholding the laws of the state and containing its simmering tensions and, on the other, behaving compassionately towards a woman who is acting out of principle and is his son's beloved. Haemon/Eamonn is also faced with a difficult choice: to obey a father or to cleave to a loved woman, even though the latter means certain death.

The issue around which these ethical quandaries swirl is itself a complex one: does a corpse demand the same respect as a living being? Although Polyneices/Parvaiz is dead, the symbolic importance of the body is not lost on the ruler: in Thebes, to leave a corpse unburied is to dishonour it, and when there is a possibility of civil unrest in the name of the dead man, such dishonouring is a prudent political choice; in London, the decision to forbid the return of the body is a signal that to become an Islamic fundamentalist is to forfeit all rights in one's native country. To Antigone/Aneeka, however, the corpse of the loved brother is as deserving of honour as the living man was. In Ancient Greece, this belief means sprinkling some earth on the body and pouring the appropriate libations over it; in the contemporary world, it means honouring the dead man's wish to return to his home. Both works are tragedies, depicting a world in which the compromisers and timeservers survive and the principled and passionate are destroyed.

There are, of course, many differences between the two plots. Karamat's wife does not kill herself as Creon's does, for instance, and while Creon openly articulates his remorse (at first because of the warning given him by Teiresias and then because of the deaths of his son and wife), Karamat's humbling after the death of his son, and the likely loss of his wife, is only implied. Unlike the relationship between Aneeka and Eamonn, that between Antigone and Haemon is not secret and there is no possible operation of ulterior motives. There's no flirtation between Ismene and Haemon as there is between Isma and Eamonn; Isma is the older, not the younger, sister (a change also introduced by Jean Anouilh in his version of the play); nor is there a background of incest and fratricide to mark the younger generation as anomalous and troubled.

Notwithstanding the inevitable differences, the parallels with the earlier work are brilliantly managed. One example is the two political situations confronting the individual in power. The political circumstances Creon faces are the result of the conflict depicted in Aeschylus's *Seven Against Thebes*: in that play Polyneices allies himself with a foreign enemy, the Argives, in order to attack the city ruled by his brother Eteocles. He is not simply a traitor, however; Eteocles has reneged on the agreement whereby the brothers were to rule the state in turn. Creon, in honouring Eteocles by granting his body a proper burial and refusing it to Polyneices, is making a strong political statement: however justified the grievances of the leader of the opposing force, the state requires stability above all else. The position of the British government vis-à-vis ISIS is very different, but there is a similar blanket condemnation of anyone attracted to the movement's programme. To take another example, Antigone's stand in Thebes receives a direct echo in Aneeka's short speech over her brother's body in Karachi:

'In the stories of wicked tyrants men and women are punished with exile, bodies are kept from their families – their heads impaled on spikes, their corpses thrown into unmarked graves. All these things happen according to the law, but not according to justice. I am here to ask for justice. I appeal to the Prime Minister: let me take my brother home' (225).

And even the Greek device of the messenger reporting on violent acts that are not portrayed on stage is mirrored in the television broadcast by means of which the tragic events are relayed to viewers and to the reader.

The ripples that Sophocles's play has produced down the centuries since its composition and first performance have, as I've noted, often been charted, and multiple adaptations and rewritings have been undertaken. Among these reimaginings of the play, *Home Fire* is one of the richest and most powerful. But if, as I've suggested, the reader unaware of the relationship between the two works could still respond to its vivid and engrossing narrative, what does that relationship contribute to the reader's experience? One answer would be in terms of perspective: the political and ethical issues surrounding Islamic fundamentalism today are given added weight by being shown to be versions of some of the oldest concerns in human history. Aneeka does not know that she is re-enacting Antigone's stance (as with all rewritings, we have to a imagine a world in which the original text does not exist), but our knowledge of the connection deepens and enriches her action.

Inorganic Form in *Home Fire*

The further question that remains to be considered is what, if anything, is added by the strict formal organisation of the work into five sections (reminiscent of the five acts of the modern play) named after, and employing the perspective of, the five central characters? What Shamsie has imposed upon herself is a set of rules of the sort examined in Chapter 10: not only shall the plot follow the outline of *Antigone*, but that plot shall be presented in a strict formal arrangement based on the five leading characters. The model here is, of course, *Ulysses*. Joyce based the plot of his novel on a precursor, the *Odyssey*, giving each chapter a title taken from an episode of the early epic, often singling out a named character – Telemachus, Nestor, Calypso, the Cyclops, Nausicaa, Circe, Eumaeus, Penelope. And he gave to each episode a set of features – scene, hour, organ, colour, symbol, art, and technic – that influence its formal properties.[18] By announcing herself as an heir of Joyce, Shamsie claims for her novel a central place in contemporary fiction, inviting the reader to judge the work by the most daunting yardstick.

As in the case of *Ulysses* – and Catton's *The Luminaries*, discussed in Chapter 10 – the formal scaffolding of *Home Fire* can't be said to affect the reader's engagement with the characters and events of the represented world: without it, we would still respond to the unfolding events and the final tragedy. Critical accounts often ignore this formal scaffolding to focus on the content of the novel.[19] What the strict form does accomplish is to impress the reader by the skill with which the potentially

[18] See Chapters 2 and 10 for discussions of the schemata of *Ulysses*.

[19] Examples include Burns, in *Postcolonialism after World Literature*, and Claire Chambers, 'Sound and Fury'. Chambers focuses revealingly on the sounds and silences of the novel.

amorphous jumble of doings and sayings, places and characters, feelings and thoughts, has been controlled: it is, that is to say, a matter of *craft*, a topic discussed in the Introduction. As with Donal Ryan's *The Spinning Heart*, also touched on in Chapter 10, the narrative is handed like a baton from character to character, each shift broadening the canvas on which the story is being told. There is inevitably something arbitrary about the procedure – every section could have been told from the point of view of at least one other character – but arbitrariness is a feature of what I have called inorganic form, the operation of formal constraints over and above what is necessary to further the realistic narrative. Another example of a novel that engages brilliantly with the politics of coloniality and its aftermath is Damon Galgut's *The Promise*, which traces some of the changes, and failed opportunities, in South Africa over the period of its shift from a racist state to a democracy, and does so by means of a tight formal structure: four sections, each named after a different member of the Swart family, each presenting the funeral of that person, and each evoking a different era in the country's turbulent transformation.

Foregrounded formal structures of this kind keep the author's controlling hand in view, a fault only in the eyes of those who expect novels to appear to be self-generating. (Unlike the unobtrusive narrator of *Home Fire*, Galgut's narrator indulges in flamboyant gestures, adding to the sense of an authorial presence.) The danger with a fixed form is that it can have a detrimental effect on the content it is being used to present. In *Home Fire* the reader comes to know and like Isma in the opening section, and her almost complete disappearance thereafter may be felt as a loss.[20] It's also possible to find the absence of the younger generation's perspectives in the final, 'Karamat', section regrettable. (On the other hand, confining the second section to Eamonn's point of view and postponing the section that reveals Aneeka's thoughts allows the question of the latter's real feelings towards him to remain unanswered – until it is answered, implicitly, at the very end of the novel.) The need to match Aneeka's stance over her brother's corpse with Antigone's results in a scene that moves beyond the realism of the rest of the novel – the Greek heroine's libations become blocks of ice piled on the body in a tableau that is hard to imagine, and the dust storm that momentarily blots both Antigone and Aneeka from sight is more appropriate in the retelling of a Greek myth than in a contemporary fiction. If anything, the slight sense of strain in the final pages testifies to the importance of the novel's formal construction, encouraging readers to remain aware of

---

[20] Natalie Haynes, reviewing the novel in *The Guardian*, comments that 'it is difficult not to pine for her in the later stages of the novel'.

the fictional, authored status of what they are reading while responding to the terrible scene it represents.[21]

This achievement of a high level of craft, especially in a novel dealing with such intense emotions and extreme political actions, contributes importantly to the reader's pleasure – at least if the reader is open to the possibilities of formal artistry. Both the mapping of the narrative onto one of the most famous of literary works and the skilful organisation of points of view contribute to this enjoyment as the novel unrolls. And heightened pleasure leads to greater impact and memorability: where a formally uninteresting novel dealing with this topic might fade quite quickly from the mind, *Home Fire* is more likely to retain its place in the reader's mental world. Thus, any change in the reader's ethical and political attitudes produced by the content is likely to be more lasting – though, as I've suggested, this is a long way from claiming political significance for the novel in the wider world.[22]

There is another way in which a novel like this can be thought of as ethically important and thus possessed of political significance. I've argued in a number of places that literary works, understood as literature and not some other genre, don't lend themselves to political instrumentalisation. The effects they have on the reader, the changes they bring about, can't be predicted or channelled in particular directions. However, the ethical importance of literature – and of art more generally – stems from the rewards available to those who approach works with a readiness to see the world, and themselves, in a new light and to experience unfamiliar modes of feeling and thinking. This openness to the new and the other that literature invites and recompenses is itself a fundamental ethical quality, and must be the basis for any political programme that goes beyond the self-serving and the mercenary. *Home Fire*, like many other postcolonial novels, responds to a responsible reading that relishes its formal inventiveness and its willingness to enter untrodden territory, and thus rewards an unprejudiced and open-minded approach to literature.

21 Rehana Ahmed justifies the shift in the novel's final two sections as a deliberate distancing device, the 'self-conscious theatricality' and 'melodrama' of the final 'act' serving to prevent an 'anthropological' reading of the Muslim woman ('Towards an Ethics of Reading Muslims').

22 It could be argued that the formal craft on display in *Home Fire* is a method of controlling the diverse and fissiparous materials of the novel, just as T. S. Eliot famously saw *Ulysses* as 'a way of controlling, of ordering, of giving a shape and a significance to the immense panorama of futility and anarchy which is contemporary history' ('*Ulysses*, Order, and Myth'). Eliot's view of contemporary history was not Joyce's, however, and the reader's experience of neither novel is likely to be one of chaos rendered orderly.

CHAPTER 14

Joycean Innovation Today:
Tom McCarthy's Fiction

Modernism and Close Reading

Tom McCarthy's fiction is a gift to academic critics. His five novels, *Men in Space, Remainder, C, Satin Island,* and *The Making of Incarnation,*[1] abound in allusions, more or less overt, to other works of literature, to the visual arts and music, and to the theories of Continental – mostly French – philosophers. They engage with a number of the issues that we literary critics and theorists like to talk about, such as the impossibility of authenticity, the aftermath of trauma, the omnipresence of signification, the ubiquity of communication networks, and the corporate capture of progressive thought. They are structured by means of complex relays of repetition and cross-reference. And they further challenge the norms of the conventional novel by presenting characters lacking depth and plots in which narrative tension and personal development are not paramount.[2] In all these ways, they provide a seductive invitation to today's professional critics to deploy the latest instruments of academic interpretation, including allusion

---

[1] *Men in Space* (2007); *Remainder* (2006); *C* (2010); *Satin Island* (2015); *The Making of Incarnation* (2021). I list *Men in Space* first because, as McCarthy has explained in a number of interviews, it was his first novel, turned down by publishers until the success of *Remainder* made it a commercially more attractive option. He did, however, revise and shorten it before publication.

[2] Pieter Vermeulen observes that McCarthy's fictions 'attempt to do without the elements that are often assumed to make up a novel: readerly empathy, plot and character, social vision, and psychological depth' (*Contemporary Literature*, 23). This is an exaggeration – there is almost too much plot in *Men in Space*; there is plenty of social vision in *Satin Island*; there are credible characters in all the novels – but one can understand the impetus behind the comment.

tracking, influence detection, theoretical extrapolation, cultural analysis, and cryptographic decoding, and they allow us to enlist McCarthy as a heroic partisan under the flag of fiction that, keeping alive the radicalism of the modernists of the early twentieth century, resists the mainstream of 'humanist' or 'lyrical' or 'liberal' realism.[3]

McCarthy, moreover, unlike those writers who shy away from commenting on their own work, has no hesitation in talking about his novels, and has given numerous interviews in which he suggests interpretations, identifies allusions, adduces influences, and explains his assault on the ubiquitous 'middlebrow' novel and the publishers who solicit and promote it.[4] His collection of essays, *Typewriters, Bombs, Jellyfish*, entertainingly sets out some of the founding principles of his fiction: the first essay, for instance, titled 'Get Real', skewers unexamined views of 'realism' and the 'real'.[5] McCarthy has also written an e-book in which he expounds his view of the writer as a transmitter rather than an originator of verbal material, a study of Hergé's *Tintin* that uncovers many of his favourite thematic webs in the amazing adventures of that young hero, and a piece on anthropology and writing in *The Guardian* that sets out some of the underpinning of *Satin Island*.[6] 'Calling All Agents', an essay in a collection of documents from the International Necronautical Society – a 'semi-fake' organisation of which he is the General Secretary[7] – explores the major sources of *C*.[8]

All this has provided the material for a number of valuable essays on McCarthy's fiction, demonstrating its importance and timeliness, examining

[3] Zadie Smith's contrasting of McCarthy's *Remainder* with Joseph O'Neill's *Netherland* in 'Two Paths for the Novel', published in the *New York Review of Books* in 2008, did much to establish this contrast. See also Mark McGurl's modification of Smith's argument after the publication of *Satin Island* in 'The Novel's Forking Path'.

[4] A few online examples: interview in *Believer Magazine*; interview with Christopher Bollen, *Interview Magazine*; interview with James Corby and Ivan Callus, *Countertext*; interview with Andrew Gallix, *3 A.M. Magazine*; interview with Lee Rourke, *The Guardian*; interview with Mark Thwaite, *ReadySteadyBook*; interview with Dan Wagstaff, *Raincoast Books*.

[5] 'Get Real: Or What Jellyfish Have to Tell Us about Literature' in McCarthy, *Typewriters, Bombs, Jellyfish*, 183–202.

[6] *Transmission and the Individual Remix; Tintin and the Secret of Literature*; 'The death of writing'.

[7] See http://www.necronauts.org/.

[8] Though McCarthy asserts that '[a] writer, once the work is written (if not long before), becomes just another reader of the work – not necessarily a good one, and certainly not a reliable one' ('Foreword', 1), it would be hard to deny the effective authority his comments carry in practice.

its place in contemporary culture, and relating it to current theoretical work. There will doubtless be many more excellent critical studies of along these lines; this is a vein that is far from having been fully mined.[9] In this chapter, however, I want to do something a little different: I want to ask, continuing a central thread of this book, what it's like to *read* McCarthy's fiction, what are its peculiar pleasures, and whether the critical instruments associated with the tradition of 'close reading' are of any use in describing and explaining these responses. In doing so, one question will be in the back of my mind: in what sense can McCarthy be said to be continuing the project of Joycean modernism and the rewards and demands it offers its readers?[10]

I want to acknowledge immediately that what the essay reflects is my own response to these novels, a response that, for all I know, is idiosyncratic rather than widely shared. However, the reading subject that I am – what I've called elsewhere my idioculture – is constituted by assumptions, predilections, pieces of knowledge, and habits of thought and feeling that I have absorbed in a host of cultural and interpersonal experiences (including, of course, my reading of McCarthy's non-fiction writing and many of the authors he cites as well as critical studies of his work). It's likely, then, that I share a great deal of what I bring to McCarthy's fiction with many other readers, and that my responses will be more than merely subjective. As in all criticism which proceeds from a singular response, though, the test of its worth lies in the dialogue, or polylogue, it initiates with other readers.[11]

To justify this privileging of the singular response, I appeal to the notion, mentioned in the Introduction, of the literary work as an *event*, taking place in the reading process and living on in memorial revisitings of that process. Critical accounts that treat the work as an object existing independently of

[9] Among the most interesting essays to have appeared thus far are Nieland, 'Dirty Media'; Miller, 'Intentional Fallacies'; Quarrie, 'Sinking, Shrinking, Satin Island', and Serpell, '"Synchronicity": Metareading Tom McCarthy's *Remainder*', chapter 6 of *Seven Modes of Uncertainty*. *Tom McCarthy*, ed. Dennis Duncan, is a valuable collection of essays.

[10] McCarthy's novels – so far – do not exploit the resources of inorganic form discussed in Chapter 10 nor do they belong to the canon of ergodic works discussed in Chapter 11. They do, however, stage a paradox that has been well described by Jordan, quoting from *C*: 'McCarthy articulates the double bind of the accident that is both "genuinely unplanned" and simultaneously "hatched by the network"' (*Late Modernism*, 215). What arrives as an unpredictable surprise is seen, in retrospect, as the function of a web of connections not unlike that which governs the characters of *The Luminaries*.

[11] For a critical study premised on the value of this kind of dialogue, see Attridge and Staten, *The Craft of Poetry*.

acts of reading, though they can provide valuable information about a text as cultural entity, moral example, philological object, autobiographical revelation, or historical trace, tend to miss what is peculiarly literary about it, and often fail to do justice to what Wordsworth called the 'grand elementary principle of pleasure' that must animate all artistic endeavour and motivate all our engagements with works of art as art. Although the literary event takes place, in the first instance, in an individual reading, in its multiple repetitions it becomes not only something that happens to a single idioculture but one that happens to the broader culture within which it is situated. (To quote McCarthy himself: 'One of the real structural understandings of great literature, from Greek tragedy to Beckett and Faulkner, is that it's an *event*' (*Believer* interview).) I start, therefore, with the fact that I've enjoyed reading and re-reading McCarthy's novels – including the fact that my pleasure in them has, at many points, arisen from their humour, a property that not all critical accounts acknowledge. This is not, then, a search for the 'meaning' of the works, except in so far as this word may be understood as a verb referring to the continuous play of semantic traces.[12]

As I've already suggested, one of the pleasures in reading a McCarthy novel is identifying the allusions and making sense of them in the context of the work. To give some quick examples, the name 'Anton Markov' in *Men in Space* may trigger a memory that the 'Markov chain' has something to do with a random series, an allusion that fits nicely with the sequence of events in the novel; the building selected for re-enactment in *Remainder* is called Madlyn Mansions, recalling Proust's madeleine and underscoring the importance of recovered memory in the story; in *C*, a novel in which insects play a major part, it's pleasing that the deaf children recite from Golding's translation of Ovid's *Metamorphoses*; and there's an appropriateness in the way the vaguely described 'Koob-Sassen project' in *Satin Island* shares a name with Saskia and Hilary Koob-Sassen, sociologist and artist mother and son with an interest in globalisation and urban environments.[13] The ambitious science-fiction film being made in *Incarnation* is a close re-creation of Wagner's (and to some extent Gottfried von Strassburg's) *Tristan and Isolde*, a mirroring of which none of those involved in it seem to be aware.

Recognising these allusions, of which there are a multitude, is fun, and having Google at hand allows the reader to venture into the far reaches

[12] Jenny Turner, in an insightful review of *C*, recognises that 'easy hermeneuticising' isn't the point ('Seeing Things Flat', 7).
[13] Tom McCarthy and Hilary Koob-Sassen held a 'conversation' at the Institute for Contemporary Arts in London in 2015 (https://archive.ica.art/whats-on/lsff-errorists-present-ascendant-accumulation-realism).

of allusive territory. I didn't know, until I looked him up, that Alexander Graham Bell, exactly like Serge Carrefax, the hero (antihero?) of *C*, had a deaf mother and a father who ran a school for the deaf at which he practised his own method of speech teaching. Google is also invaluable in authenticating many of the specific historical references, especially in *C*, which makes extensive use of the actual history of early twentieth-century communications technology, First World War bombing techniques, and Egyptian archaeology.[14] *Incarnation* makes one ashamed of having been unaware of the extraordinary career of Lillian Gilbreth, to whom we owe many of the practical features of our homes today. To someone who knows Prague well, the plethora of specific locations in *Men in Space* will summon up a map of the city, and Google Earth is always available to help the rest of us.

The effect of these repeated invitations to investigate the textual surface for allusions and echoes is a puncturing of the illusion that the words are reflections of ongoing events independent of the literary work, and they remind the reader that they are engaging with a carefully-chosen, often overdetermined, sequence of words and sentences. The early chapters of this book explore some of the methods by which Joyce enriched the reading experience by such means, and McCarthy is only too happy to acknowledge his debt to his modernist precursors: 'Modernism is a legacy we have whether we want it or not. It's like Darwin: you can either go beyond it and think through its implications, or you can ignore it, and if you do that you're a Creationist' ('The death of writing'). Asked by another interviewer if he feels 'a particular affinity with the Modernist "project"', he answers:

> My god yes. That's where we're at – or at least the legacy we have to deal with. Modernism (which in reality isn't a single project but rather a whole wave of interlinked events – wave upon wave, a giant tsunami) is as seminal an event as the Renaissance was, and the shock-waves of something that big take centuries to play themselves out. In the 'geological' time of the arts, *Finnegans Wake* happened a few seconds ago: we've hardly even realised that it's happened, let alone set up a coordinated response. (Interview with Wagstaff)

[14] Google also allows one to catch inaccuracies: for example, the ace German pilot Fritz Kempf's motto, *Kennscht mi noch?*, which haunts Serge in *C*, was painted on his Fokker triplane, not on an Albatros biplane. Furthermore, Martin Eve points out that there is no record of Kempf downing an RE8 such as the one in which Serge flies (*Literature against Criticism*, 67–8). But it's not clear what one should do with such nit-picking discoveries; perhaps they are simply reminders that we're reading fiction, not history. (Eve makes the fruitful suggestion that it's part of the novel's 'quasi-facticity', different only in degree from all historical fiction in both inviting and frustrating a search in the archive.)

The experience of reading a McCarthy novel, then, may well include a certain welcoming of distraction, as the fictional world one is temporarily inhabiting is put on hold while one chases up, mentally or with the aid of research tools, a proper name that seems to hold out some additional significance, or a scene that echoes something one has read before. Jenny Turner describes her way of engaging with the novel as follows:

> As will, I think, be obvious, I had a whale of a time with this book, propped on my laptop, Wikipedia open in one window and in another, the *OED*. It was like being a guest at the dream-party of an extremely well-read host: things read a long time ago and more or less forgotten, things never read that I always meant to, things I certainly will read now, having seen how McCarthy can make them work. ('Seeing Things Flat', 8)

Close reading, as developed by Richards and Leavis, Wimsatt and Brooks, is not well equipped to deal with this diversion from the imaginative involvement with the represented world; indeed, Leavis's strictures on Joyce make it clear that he would have hated McCarthy's fiction. Reviewing some of the advance publications of sections of *Finnegans Wake*, Leavis asserts that '[a] certain vicious bent manifested itself very disturbingly in *Ulysses*, in the inorganic elaborations and pedantries', and these he finds taken further in the 'self-stultifying', 'offensively spurious' later work, with its 'deliberate, calculating contrivance' and 'mechanical manipulation'. He adds, '[T]he kind of attention demanded by each one of the closely packed "effects" is incompatible with an inclusive, coordinating apprehension'('Joyce and "The Revolution of the Word"'). McCarthy's fiction is equally designed to block the unified, organic, absorption of the text that Leavis, and at least one version of the practice of close reading, demands.[15] This, we may feel, is one of McCarthy's significant achievements.

And yet: to sew the fabric of your fictional text with a host of clever spangles is not necessarily to write a great novel. Deciphering McCarthy's sly allusions and coded references, uncovering the fakes and masks, tracing the networks and grids, are certainly part of what is entertaining, and often funny, in the experience of reading his fiction, and if one shares at least some of his impatience with the ubiquity of novels written as if modernism hadn't happened there is the added pleasure of seeing the legacy

---

[15] American New Criticism was more fully allied to the innovations of modernism, whose difficult texts demanded a new degree of close textual attention; however, the Romantic notion of organic form remained a powerful element in their analyses.

of Joyce and Kafka given fresh life. There is an ethico-political dimension to this assault on the conventional novel, too, undermining as it does the governing idea of the autonomous, freely-choosing subject; as McCarthy puts it in one of his interviews, the common notion of the novel is that it is 'the rational expression of a self-sufficient subject — as though we weren't constantly made and unmade within language, desire, history, symbolic networks and so on' (Interview with Gallix). But for all his meticulous use of sources and his crafting of cross-references, McCarthy frequently points to something else in the creation of his novels, something he labels, more than once, an 'intuitive' dimension (Interviews by Gallix and *The Believer*). And he says, with who knows how much of his tongue in his cheek, 'But it's not like I set out to write an anti-humanist manifesto. All I set out to do is make good art. It's really simple' (Interview with Rourke). I will spend the rest of this chapter considering short passages from his novels, asking why I find the writing affectively as well as intellectually rewarding, and whether this approach to literature has any ethical implications.[16]

Five Ways of Dying

A subject that tends to demand a pulling out of all the emotional stops is death. Dying, approaches to death, and death itself feature in all McCarthy's novels, and these topics often come up in his interviews and his non-fiction writing. Blanchot's 'Literature and the Right to Death' and Cocteau's *L'Orphée* are among his constant references, and the name of the Necronautical Society speaks for itself.

Men in Space

All three main characters in *Men in Space* die, and in two cases – the aforementioned Anton Markov and the Englishman Nick Boardaman – we are privy, through the use of Joycean interior monologue, to the moments before death.[17] (This statement is not strictly true, since these two deaths

---

[16] I began this project by re-reading the four novels that had been published by 2016 and keeping a diary, part of which appeared as 'Reading Tom McCarthy's Novels'.

[17] The third death, that of the artist Ivan Maňásek, is only reported, his last words being a name he has been trying to remember – a name associated with a particularly idyllic period of his life – that puzzles his hearers but not the astute reader. Another resonant death is that of a relatively minor character, Joost van Straten, who is known largely through letters, the last of which is written from Tallinn just before he walks out on the ice to find the 'horizonless horizon' (216).

are not actually registered in the text; what *is* registered is the sense of impending death.) These sequences are among the most immediately affecting in the book, and reveal that ingenious play with intertextual references and thematic interconnections need not render the text desiccated or distanced: the language attains a vividness and emotional power that in some ways is quite traditional.[18] There is space to look at only the first of these pre-death passages.

Towards the end of the novel, Anton, who provides one of the central consciousnesses of the novel, is picked up near the Prague Summer Palace by a group of fellow Bulgarians, members of a criminal group introduced at the very start of the work. Hoping to get his wife's children out of Bulgaria where they are stranded, he has become involved in this group's activities; now, thanks to their contacts in the secret service, they have discovered that he came close to betraying them when in prison. He, however, is not aware of their dark purposes and is puzzled by their frosty mien, so unlike the camaraderie evident in the novel's opening pages. Even on a first reading, it's clear that this journey will not end well: although the interior monologue provides only Anton's perceptions, the signs of an impending catastrophe are unmistakeable. Throughout these gripping pages (243–54), Anton's free associations – including thoughts of his wife and her children – contrast chillingly with his colleagues' awkward attempts to disguise their nefarious designs behind a casual demeanour.

They reach a high plain – 'Must be the highest point around Prague: top of the white mountain' (249), thinks Anton – and get out of the car. The intensity of Anton's experience as they walk on signals his awareness at some level that this is no ordinary expedition (he's been told, unconvincingly, that they are to clinch a deal) and at the same time contributes to the reader's involvement. Here is part of the passage:

> The hidden sun's making a patch of cloud grow brighter – a sphere that seems to buzz or hum: what's making that . . . It's an aeroplane, circling above the plain: must be held in a queue, waiting to land, in which case why's it smaller than the raven it's just passed beneath? Is this some kind of optical illusion only Kepler or Toitov would understand? It's turning now, outlined against some trees that rise behind a wall on the plain's far side. What on . . . Now he sees them, standing on the grass: two kids holding a radio controller with a pointy aerial, guiding their model's twists and loops. (249–50)

---

[18] The capacity for a poetic evocativeness in McCarthy's prose is brilliantly brought out in the short film made by Johan Grimonprez, 'from *Satin Island*', in which the author reads a passage from the novel over a series of haunting images.

The passage, like so many in the novel, is full of reminders of the painting at the heart of the story, in which a floating saintly figure seems to be disappearing into a golden elliptical halo; these reminders include the bright patch of cloud, the circling aeroplane, and the illusory perspective. Kepler is in Anton's mind because he has recently seen the astronomer's statue, which reminded him of his Sofia physics teacher, Toitov; but it's also clearly relevant that Kepler's major contribution to cosmology was his deduction that planetary orbits are ellipses, like the one in the painting, and not circles. Radio communications, too, have coursed through the text, as have buzzings or hummings. The sense of impending catastrophe is augmented by the bird Anton notices: ravens are symbols of death in many mythologies, and in Wagner's *Götterdämmerung* they fly overhead just before Siegfried is murdered by those he took to be his allies. But leaving all these allusions aside, the passage is also powerful as descriptive writing suggestive of Anton's physical sensations and mental responses: the sound of the buzzing model plane, the confusion about its height, the sight of the children completely wrapped up in their own activities – in their very unconnectedness with what is happening to him they speak of the ordinary life he is about to lose.

The group walks on towards a star-shaped hunting lodge with red-and-white striped shutters, whose name, Hvĕzda, Anton realises, means 'star': another allusion to cosmography. But the novel's almost obsessive concern for accurate topographical detail is also evident here: Google Earth enables one to home in on this hunting lodge and see both its situation at the end of a long avenue in a wooded plain and its striped shutters.[19] Anton, in this high place, a man in space, is about to be sucked into the elliptical vortex of non-being. Nevertheless, the text remains resolutely, as well as literally, down-to-earth as Anton kneels on the ground, and at no point does he consciously reflect on what might be about to happen. A chain of ominous but indistinct events is coming to a climax: a strange bumping in the boot of the car as they drove (we know there is a spade in there, but Anton doesn't), one of the group's going back for 'the thing in the car' and his reappearance in the distance carrying something that looks like a surveyor's pole, and then what feels like a twig prodding Anton in the back. Then, in the final words of the section:

Anton, still kneeling, turns round. Behind Janachkov, who's holding some kind of black thing, a calculator on which he's working out figures,

[19] Anton observes that '[t]he walls jut in and out to form a kind of pentagon': in fact, the building is hexagonal, but from ground level it would be difficult to see this – and 'pentagon' carries more significant associations. (In fact, Anton has just reflected that Prague Castle, which they have been passing, is bigger than the Pentagon (245).)

exchange rates – or perhaps a toy, some kind of toy like kids were playing with somewhere, his and Helena's kids or the ones she's got already or perhaps himself when he was small, Anton can see the star's face, winking one of its eyes at him, then winking another, red and white eyes on a white face, closing. (254)

Re-reading this passage, I find I am as uncertain as Anton is about the 'black thing' being operated by one of the others – he associates it with the deal they are supposed to be clinching, and then with the children he had planned to have and the ones he was hoping to retrieve from Bulgaria – but we know that it spells his death.

Remainder

Deaths punctuate the end of *Remainder*, too. The nameless narrator has been awarded eight-and-a-half million pounds after an accident involving an unnamed object falling onto him from the sky, and he uses the money to stage re-enactments of three different events that possessed a profound meaningfulness for him when they occurred. He then organises his most ambitious event, the robbing of a bank in which all the non-actors at the scene will be unaware that the crime is not a real one. McCarthy's prose in this novel is very different from the writing in *Men in Space*: now reflecting only one consciousness instead of several, it's hard-edged and economical, more Ballard than Joyce. Here is the moment that precipitates the final disaster, when the narrator carries one of the bags of money to the door behind 'Robber Four' and 'Robber Five':

> I glided across the floor with it towards the door. Four and Five glided in front of me. Two was still standing static, moving his gun from one corner of the bank towards the other and then back again, slow and regular as a lawn-sprinkler. I raised my bag slightly as it and I cleared the airlock's stump, then lowered it again and let it glide above the carpet like a crop-spraying aircraft gliding over fields of wheat. I let my eyes follow the carpet's surface as we glided, let them run along its perfectly reproduced gold on red, its turns and cut-backs, the way these repeated themselves regularly for several yards then quickened, shortening as the carpet crinkled in the rise up to the kink on which Five, gliding two feet in front of me, was about to re-enact his half-trip. My eyes moved forward to his foot and lingered there, watching it anticipate the kink; I saw the foot surge forwards, its toes pointing downwards, backwards, turning over like a ballet dancer's toes . . .
> But there was no kink in this carpet. (268–9)

In this case the power of the writing stems from the *absence* of affect; at a moment of high excitement, the climax of the narrator's experiments, shocking happenings are described as if they were everyday events. The similes are inappropriately remote from the action: a lawn-sprinkler, a crop-spraying aircraft, a ballet-dancer. (The crop-spraying aircraft will have ominous associations if the reader is reminded of Hitchcock's *North by Northwest*.) Although events are unfolding at great speed, the narrator has the time and mental calmness to examine the pattern on the carpet (whose 'perfect reproduction' alludes, inevitably, to his re-enactment attempts), and to watch the movements of Robber Five's foot as if it were in slow motion. The narrator's desire to overcome the drag of matter that has been a constant motif in the book seems fulfilled in the way he and the other re-enactors are repeatedly said to 'glide', but in the end it's matter that defeats him – or, rather, more complicatedly, the non-presence of expected matter.[20] Robber Four, his foot not striking the kink his rehearsals had led him to expect, topples into Two, who involuntarily pulls his gun's trigger, killing Four. The narrator, far from being dismayed at this turn of events, however, is delighted; the thin line between re-enactment and reality has been abolished in the most absolute way possible.

The reader's engagement with this prose, I want to suggest, is that of appalled involvement. Earlier examples of the narrator's heartlessness – for example, his acceptance that large numbers of cats must die in order to satisfy his desire to replicate a particular moment (or imagined moment) in his past – have a kind of black humour about them, and by this point we have become engrossed in his mad project of creating an impossible experience of authenticity. But the bank heist puts an end to any amusement: the cold sentences bespeak a mind to be marvelled at rather than empathised with.

C

In *C*, McCarthy's writing is different again: its model is the nineteenth-century realist novel, with a young hero, Serge Carrefax, whom we first meet

---

[20] Partington and Slote, in their contributions to Duncan's collection of essays on McCarthy, both draw attention to the role of matter in *Remainder* ('Dummy Chambers and Ur-Houses' and 'The Recidual Remainder'). McGurl, in 'The Novel's Forking Path', points out that the nausea-inducing materiality of the chestnut tree roots in Sartre's *La Nausée* is an antecedent of this motif, one which is continued in the narrator's (and McCarthy's) fascination with oil spills in *Satin Ireland* and the centrality of bodies in varied material environments in *The Making of Incarnation*.

as a child and then follow through a succession of adventures involving a mysterious illness, wartime experience, the unmasking of a fake medium, and incidents in Egyptian tombs (Tintin's adventures are not far away), until he meets his untimely death from an insect bite. The third section of *C*, 'Chute', which relates Serge's experiences as an observer in a First World War reconnaissance biplane, includes a number of passages that work superbly as vividly described responses seen from the hero's perspective. What is missing, and what makes the novel a challenge to the realist tradition even when it seems most conventional, is any insight into Serge's feelings; it's no accident that his Air Force role is that of observer, as he is strangely uninvolved in the scenes he witnesses.

In the following passage, Serge and the pilot, Gibbs, are flying over a battlefield strewn with parts of machines and men. Once again, it's matter that takes centre-stage:

> Gibbs flies above them for a while, then pulls the plane up and takes them back for a peep above the smoke. No sooner have they cleared it than Serge hears a rhythmic tapping: it's as though a mechanic were standing beside the machine rapping on the fuselage to get their attention. The taps make the canvas on the plane's back section tauten and jump; little holes appear in a straight line along it. They look like a row of popper-buttons springing open, starting at the tail and advancing towards his cabin, which they then move across as well, pocking its floor. A mass of shadow runs behind them, bringing with it a loud sound he doesn't recognise. As the sound climaxes and falls off, Serge looks up and sees, coming from where the sun should be, a wave of brightly-coloured metal hurtling downwards. It sinks beneath them; he swivels his head to follow it, and watches the mass resolve itself into the shape of an Albatros. It's turning below them, getting ready to come back; then it's climbing behind them, just out of range, amassing altitude so it can dive again. Colours radiate from its underbelly – the central part of which, the lower wing, has words painted across it. He can't make the words out, but he can see some of the letters: there's a *K*, an *m*, a *c* . . . (172)

Although death could well be imminent, there's no sense here that Serge is experiencing extreme tension or fear; on the contrary, the raking of their aeroplane by bullets summons up the most innocuous of similes, the rapping of a mechanic to get attention and the springing open of popper-buttons. The ostensible reason for his detachment is that he is high on diacetylmorphine, or heroin, used as a painkiller at this time. I have found no evidence that drug-taking was common among First World War flyers, but as a narrative device it works brilliantly to transform what would be Biggles-like airborne thrills into Serge's affectless observations – or, to be more precise, to replace excitement and terror by curiosity and puzzlement. The effect is akin to what Victor Shklovsky termed *ostranenie*, or defamilia-risation, using the example of Natasha Rostova's first visit to the opera in *War and Peace*, although in this case the experience of having one's aircraft riddled with bullets is hardly a familiar one in the first place. If there is tension in the passage, it's produced by the reader's awareness of what is really happening: the 'mass of shadow', the 'wave of brightly-coloured metal hurtling downwards', is not an aesthetically pleasing object but a potentially lethal enemy aircraft whose pilot, a human enemy whose existence is never acknowledged by Serge, is intent on destroying him.

The culmination of the paragraph is even more out of place than the earlier similes: Serge becomes fascinated with the lettering on the German plane, and, as he does throughout his life in numerous different situations, attempts to decode the symbols he can see. They turn out to be the words *Kennscht mi noch?*, a sentence in a German dialect that Serge translates as 'Do you still recognise me?' A little research reveals that the German flying ace Fritz Kempf had these words painted on the middle wing of his triplane; he is not mentioned in the text, however. [21] Instead, it's the enemy aircraft that is given agency as it dives and climbs, and that provides one more puzzle for Serge to solve.

Satin Island

With *Satin Island* McCarthy turns his back on the Victorian novel, the genre with which *C* had made such play. The text is given in numbered paragraphs, and the novel proceeds not so much by way of plot, of which there is little, but as a sequence of mini-essays or descriptive pieces. The narrator, who invites us, Ishmael-like, to call him 'U', is an anthropologist deploying his expertise in the service of a large corporation. Like McCarthy's only other first-person narrator, the reconstructor in *Remainder*, he seems to lack normal affective and ethical responses, not because he is in search of authenticity but because he is fascinated by the inauthentic world of which he knows he is part. (Staten Island, which figures in a dream of U's, appears to stand for some kind of transcendence, but it's one that is ultimately rejected.)

A number of narrative strands are repeatedly picked up and dropped[22] – including U's recording of stories of failed parachutes (men in space again!), his physical relationship with a woman named Madison (reminding us of

[21] Some of the results of research are mentioned in footnote 14 of this chapter.
[22] One of the many single-star reviews on Amazon calls it, with greater aptness than the writer knew, a 'bazaar' novel.

a certain Avenue), and his curiosity about, and imagined speech in praise of, oil spills. Among these strands is the story of his friend Petr's cancerous goitre and the various unsuccessful attempts to treat it, ending with Petr's death and funeral. The following paragraph occurs about three-quarters of the way through the novel:

12.17 Petr died two days later. I learnt of his death by text. His wife, whom most of his friends didn't really know (they'd been estranged for several years), must, as his official next of kin, have been handed his mobile phone, and sent the announcement out to everybody in the contacts file – taxi firms and takeaway restaurants and all. Petr passed away peacefully 11.25 a.m. today, it read. My first thoughts on receiving it – the thoughts you're meant to think in such a situation (*How sad; At least he's at rest; I'll miss him; And so forth*) – seemed so crass that I didn't even bother to think them. Instead, I thought about the message itself, its provenance. It had, as I said, come from Petr's estranged wife; but my phone, of course like those of all the other people who would have received it, listed the sender as Petr. The network provider, logging every last transaction, would have marked the sender down as Petr too; if anybody cared to look it up in years to come, the record would affirm the same thing. To almost all intents and purposes, the sender *was* Petr. His existence, at that moment, was impressing itself on me, and on hundreds of others, with as much force as – if not more than – at any other time. All we need to do to guarantee indefinite existence for ourselves is to keep our network contracts running, and make sure a missive goes out every now and then. We could have factories of Chinese workers do it; pre-pay five or ten years by bequest-subscription; give them a bunch of messages to send out in rotation or on shuffle; or default to generic or random ones; I don't know. It would work, though. Key to immortality: text messaging. (137)

U's tone, diction, and patterns of thought, like those of the narrator of *Remainder*, are distinctive and sustained with impressive consistency throughout the novel. U is very different from the narrator of *Remainder*, however; he is intelligent, articulate, well-read, well-travelled, and well-informed about global issues. In this passage, his not entirely convincing belief in his own sophistication emerges when he thinks the commonplace thoughts on hearing of a friend's death only to say that he has not thought them. That he devotes his mental energy not to mourning Petr but to speculating on the implications of the text message he has received is typical of his lack of the expected emotions; that those speculations have the veneer of rationality but end up as far-fetched is in keeping with his other flights of fancy; that the tone is never entirely serious is part of his veneer of ironic detachment. The joke about 'Chinese factory workers' is in bad taste, but so

are many of the products of his mental activity. His rejection of the platitudes of grief – whose platitudinousness need not, of course, imply lack of
genuine feeling – is on a par with his dismissal of bourgeois values. The
language is unbuttoned, almost conversational ('taxi firms and takeaway
restaurants and all'; 'I didn't even bother'; 'I don't know'). The unpoetic,
instrumental relation of the narrator to the English language is conveyed
by the slight woodenness of the style in sequences like 'with as much force
as – if not more than – at any other time' and 'It had, as I said'. And the reduc-
tion of the idea of an existence after death – once manifested in bequests to
chantry priests to say requiem masses – to regular SMS messages is resonant
with the entire book's representation of contemporary culture's evacuation
of the spiritual and emotional in favour of the textual and mediatised.

Although this prose is stylistically far from the conventional prose of
realistic fiction, its purpose is not untraditional: it marks a step in the plot,
it further enriches the portrayal of the central character, it adds to the picture of the context in which he exists, and it provides entertainment for the
reader. What defeats expectations derived from traditional novels is that
the plot is minimal, the central character lacks psychological and affective
depth, the context is one of signs and messages rather than substantive and
permanent entities, and the entertainment is tainted by a certain queasi-
ness. It's writing that may be truer to the world we live in than the colourful,
affect-heavy fictions it's seeking to displace.[23]

The Making of Incarnation

The Making of Incarnation is a rare example of a Joycean novel that takes
the 'Ithaca' episode as its model rather than the 'Penelope' episode, which
lies behind so many recent novels with a modernist heritage, from Ann
Quin's *Berg* to Eimear McBride's *A Girl is a Half-formed Thing* and Will Self's
Umbrella trilogy. The title refers to the imagined science-fiction film aspects
of whose production we witness, but also to the ever-present theme of the
material body and its movement in space. There is little sense of a narrator whose feelings we might intuit, and although we gain insights into the
personal histories of several characters, psychological exploration is usually
made subordinate to external description. Technical language abounds, and

---

[23] There is one section of the novel which stands out as a mini-narrative of a more
traditional sort: Madison's account of her experiences during the protests at the
2001 G8 summit in Genoa, which takes up all of chapter 13. Her story of bizarre
abuse makes a direct affective impact on the reader in a manner eschewed by
most of the novel; as one might expect, it seems to mean very little to U.

the reader may well experience feelings of irritation at having to work so hard – especially on a first reading – at tracking characters and following plot developments through the web of unfamiliar vocabulary. As I've mentioned, there are, as with all McCarthy's novels, pleasures of recognition, both internally as the threads of the narrative are dropped and picked up, and externally, as allusions are registered.

With an approach even more hard-edged than in McCarthy's previous works, the novel's handling of the subject of death is, as one would expect, shorn of any of the conventional stylistic trappings that go with the topic. Such narrative drive as the novel possesses is created by the search, on the part of a number of agents, for the mysterious Box 808, one of a series constructed by the aforementioned Lillian Gilbreth as part of her study of the movements of the human body. Mark Phocan, on the trail of the missing box, makes his way to Riga (with a stopover in Bergen to watch acrobats at work) to visit Raivis Vanins, a retired Soviet physicist, whose pathbreaking discovery the box is said to concretise. He meets Vanins, though he fails to get the information he is seeking. Having made the acquaintance of the old man's granddaughter, he goes on an outing with her. When they return to the house, she runs ahead of him into the aviary situated in the grounds. We then have a description of the scene witnessed by Phocan:

> She's kneeling on the ground inside their little bower; he's floating above her like a saint or cosmonaut – or, rather, since the rope running between him and the beam, quite visible, belies the illusion of weightlessness, a Bergen acrobat, if you subtracted all the energy and motion.

Few accounts of the discovery of a hanged body could be less charged with emotion: any powerful affective response on Phocan's part is trumped by his obsession with bodily movement and his memory of the recent visit to Bergen. There is even an allusion to *Men in Space* for the reader to pick up. And yet in its avoidance of direct emotion the passage is all the more powerful: it requires the reader to do the work of transforming the oblique language into the horror of a suicide.

The discovery of Box 808 that ensues is, with typical McCarthian refusal of conventional climax, made only by the reader when one of the bird boxes in the aviary is described by the neutral narrative voice. And the explanation for the mysterious letters 'TT' that had accompanied Vanins's excited announcement to Gilbreth that he had made a discovery that 'changes everything' – the discovery encapsulated in Box 808 – is provided even more indirectly. In a chapter entitled 'The Molecularity of

Glass', we learn of Phocan's departure from the scene of Vanins's suicide followed by ten pages devoted to a single window in the professor's study. This is the beginning of the description:

> It's a wood-framed window with four panes. The panes, as Phocan noticed two days ago, seem imperfectly matched to one another. And with reason: they're not just of different ages but of different constitutions too. Three of them (from garden side: bottom left, top left, top right) are made of float glass – soda-lime-silica-constituted, bath-mixed, tin-bath-poured, roller-lifted, lehr-cooled and strainlessly annealed, machine-cut rectangles display-ing a regularity, indeed sharpness, of light propagation with refraction kept right down at <1.5 per cent and scattering, reflection and such manner of distortions similarly minimised. The fourth, though (bottom right), has been cut from different quartz-cloth: cylinder-blown sheet glass, trench-swung, stand-cooled, heat-scored, flattened and hand-measured – tailored, as it were, to order, to the frame's dimensions. (305)

As with the 'Ithaca' episode, there's somewhat perverse enjoyment to be had in the text's refusal to abide by the novelistic convention that physical detail will be kept to a reasonable minimum and will serve the interests of the plot; we're invited instead to relish the language of glass-making for its own sake just as we might relish the language of landscape description or the evoca-tion of birdsong. But there's little in the content that evokes emotion: it's just a window with four panes. We are beyond matters of life and death: no-one is looking at this window, which is pure matter – as we've seen, always a cen-tral concern of McCarthy's. If this writing is an example of what Peter Boxall has so illuminatingly discussed as the 'prosthetic imagination',[24] its concern with the human/nonhuman interface is registered only in the manufactur-ing process that produces window glass.

However, as with Joyce's 'Ithaca', the possibility that our feelings will be engaged is always there. The description of the window gives way to an extraordinary discussion of ancient pottery as a potential recording device, the clay capturing the sounds in the air during the moulding process. This is followed by the speculation that, given the liquid nature of glass, the one unreplaced windowpane might have recorded nearby events, including the breakthrough moment when Vanins, watching his wife through the window, understood her game of swingball – or 'tether tennis' (TT) – as a 'kinetic symphony' (314). (It was from this observation that Vanins

---

[24] Boxall, *The Prosthetic Imagination*. Tom McCarthy is not among the novelists discussed by Boxall.

gained the insight into the motions of the human body in time that he communicated so enthusiastically to Gilbreth.) These pages are a fantasy of permanence and survival in the face of disappearance and loss that, although highly technical, produce an aura of sadness – including sadness at the fact that this is only a fantasy: most of the past is lost to us forever.

It would be wrong to say that the emotions evoked by the content in *The Making of Incarnation* are negligible. The junior lawyer Monica Dean's research into Gilbreth's work develops into an exciting quest, especially when she's blocked by shadowy forces; Phocan, too, has to deal with elusive opponents in pursuing his lifelong fascination with the recording of physical motion. Some readers might be fascinated by experiments in hydraulic chambers, wind tunnels, and other high-tech laboratory environments, while the account of drone warfare would be chilling for any reader. But above all, McCarthy's achievement, to an even greater degree than in his earlier novels, is having built on the example of Joyce's 'Ithaca' to produce a work that invites the reader to relish – in what must count as an affective response – the power of language to operate independently of, though never entirely separable from, human needs and emotions.

Ethics and Pleasure

Here, then, are five passages that engage, in one way or another, with that most hallowed of literary topics, death. (None of them, of course, can be used as watertight evidence for the nature of the entire novel; I present them only as specimens whose representativeness remains to be judged by those who know the works.) The reader who expects the topic of death to provide an experience of deep emotional involvement – fear of the unknown, horror at the end of everything, grief at the loss of a human existence – will be disappointed; McCarthy is clearly suspicious of literature that goes for the affective jugular. Only the first of these examples invites an affective response to death of a relatively traditional sort: we feel and fear the impending close of Anton's life even though, or perhaps especially because, he remains unaware of it. What we do experience in all of them – and, for some readers at least, experience with great pleasure – is the game being played with generic expectations, the undermining of the clichés around 'great art', the revelation of the discursive construction of venerated ideals and principles. This is McCarthy's debt to modernism, or rather to that strand of modernism that achieved lasting art by purging the literary work of its attachment to the values championed by Leavis and often reflected in the tradition of close reading: the conception of individual human being as organic, continuous, and forever striving towards wholeness, and the conception of society as an intimately interrelated cluster of such beings. The passages above make little attempt to represent characters and communities in this light, but they do typify many of the considerable qualities of these works. The subtlety of the writing, the consistency of each novel's stylistic and generic world, and the freshness with which the elements of fiction are handled, to name a few of these qualities, make for pleasurable and satisfying reading when approached in the right spirit of openness.

It is true that we often feel unsure about how to take the words and behaviour of McCarthy's characters, and ethical questions will not go away. Where is the moral centre of *Men in Space*? Is Serge's lack of affective engagement an ethical weakness? How far can we excuse the selfish and finally deadly actions of the narrator of *Remainder*? Does *Satin Island* buy into the depthlessness of global corporate culture too readily? Is technology a friend or an enemy in *Incarnation*? What passes for the 'ethics of literature' in many places – especially, it seems, among certain philosophers who see in literary works lessons for living – can gain little purchase on these novels: they present no paradigmatic characters who can teach us what is evil and what is good, no wrestlings with ethical choices that mirror our own conflicts, no delicately drawn human relationships that serve as models for our treatment of others. Yes, the blithely committed mass murder at the end of *Remainder* is a moral crime of huge extent; yes, Sophie's suicide in *C* is an extremely regrettable index of male sexual power; yes, the 'Company' in *Satin Island* is a vast waste of human talent and energy; yes, the murder by drone in *Incarnation* is appalling. But we already knew about the evils of murder, enforced sex, corporate capitalism, and drone warfare; the novels aren't making any kind of contribution to philosophical discourse about the ethics of such matters, though they may induce readerly discomfort or satisfaction with the way they stage moral issues and in this way effect changes in individuals.

Where, then, does the ethical lie in our reading of these novels? I've argued elsewhere that it's in the reader's engagement with the literary work as an event that the question of ethics arises. Modernist writing like Joyce's makes more evident what is true of all literature: it requires an active reader, creatively engaging with the inventiveness of the work.[25] And, as I suggested in the previous chapter, this involves a kind of responsibility: an openness to the work's challenges to ingrained habits and familiar knowledge, and a willingness to be changed by the experience of reading. Sometimes reading McCarthy's fiction can be frustrating: the complex web

---

[25] For a valuable discussion of 'high modernism' in these terms, see Mahaffey, *Modernist Literature*.

of characters and places in *Men in Space*, the increasingly unsympathetic narrator of *Remainder*, the at times mystifying allusions in *C*; the plotlessness of *Satin Island*; the remorseless technical language of *Incarnation* – these and many other features of the novels, as the reviews on Amazon testify, can be a barrier to enjoyment. But they can also encourage an ethical recalibration: not of what it is to lead a good life but of what it means to live in a world permeated by words and other signifying systems, where the ability to employ and respond to those systems with skill, judgement, passion, self-reflectiveness, and humour is an important part of what it is to be human, and where an acceptance that there is no final answer, no inner core, no absolute authenticity, and no ultimate transcendence is not an admission of imperfection or cause of grief but part of the joy of living. I have found that re-reading these novels not only increases my admiration for them and for McCarthy as a writer but reveals more and more of their particular kinds of richness. If the attention to form encouraged by the tradition of 'close reading' means a way of engaging with the text as an event experienced by an open-minded reader rather than a certain kind of academic and pedagogic exercise, it's what these novels require in order to reveal their full complexity – intellectual, affective, and ethical – and to do this in greatly pleasurable ways.

WORKS CITED

Aarseth, Espen J. *Cybertext: Perspectives on Ergodic Literature*. Baltimore: Johns Hopkins University Press, 1997.

Abbott, H. Porter. *The Fiction of Samuel Beckett: Form and Effect*. Berkeley: University of California Press, 1973.

Abel, Marco. *Violent Affect: Literature, Cinema and Critique after Representation*. Lincoln: University of Nebraska Press, 2008.

Adorno, Theodor. 'Notes on Beckett'. *Journal of Beckett Studies* 19.2 (2010): 157–78.

Ahmed, Rehana. 'Towards an Ethics of Reading Muslims: Encountering Difference in Kamila Shamsie's *Home Fire*'. *Textual Practice* 35 (2021): 1145–61.

Alexandrova, Boriana. *Joyce, Multilingualism, and the Ethics of Reading*. Cham: Palgrave, 2020.

Anker, Elizabeth S. 'Postcritical Reading, the Lyric, and Ali Smith's *How to Be Both*'. *Diacritics* 45.4 (2017): 16–42.

Anker, Elizabeth S., and Rita Felski, eds, *Critique and Postcritique*. Durham: Duke University Press, 2017.

Anon. 'The shocking number of books the average South African author sells'. *BusinessTech*, 23 August 2016. https://businesstech.co.za/news/trending/134230/the-shocking-number-of-books-the-average-south-african-author-sells/

Apter, Emily. *Against World Literature: On the Politics of Untranslatability*. London: Verso, 2013.

—. *The Translation Zone: A New Comparative Literature*. Princeton: Princeton University Press, 2006.

Armstrong, Paul. 'In Defense of Reading: Or, Why Reading Still Matters in a Contextualist Age'. *New Literary History* 42 (2011): 87–113.

Ashcroft, Bill, Gareth Griffiths, and Helen Tiffin, eds. *The Empire Writes Back: Theory and Practice in Post-colonial Literatures*. London: Routledge, 1989.

—, eds. *The Post-Colonial Studies Reader*. 2nd edn. Abingdon: Routledge, 2006.

Aston, Elaine. *Caryl Churchill*. London: Northcote House, 1997.

Attridge, Derek. 'Contemporary Afrikaans Fiction in the World: The Englishing of Marlene van Niekerk'. *Journal of Commonwealth Studies* 49 (2014): 395–409.

—. 'Context, Idioculture, Invention'. *New Literary History* 42 (2011): 681–99.

—. *The Experience of Poetry: From Homer's Listeners to Shakespeare's Readers*. Oxford: Oxford University Press, 2019.

—. *J. M. Coetzee and the Ethics of Reading: Literature in the Event*. Chicago: University of Chicago Press, 2004.

—. *Joyce Effects: On Language, Theory, and History*. Cambridge: Cambridge University Press, 2000.

—. 'Joycean Form, Emotion, and Contemporary Modernism: Ellmann's *Ducks, Newburyport'*. *Journal of Modern Literature*, forthcoming.

—. *Moving Words: Forms of English Poetry*. Oxford: Oxford University Press, 2013.

—. *Peculiar Language: Literature as Difference from the Renaissance to James Joyce*. Ithaca: Cornell University Press, 1988; 2nd edn, London: Routledge, 2004.

—. '"A Pinch of Salt and a Dash of Lemon": Ingrid Winterbach's Troubles'. In Andrew van der Vlies, Louise Viljoen, and S. J. Naudé, eds, *Ingrid Winterbach: Writing and Vision*. Forthcoming.

—. 'Reading Joyce'. In Derek Attridge, ed., *The Cambridge Companion to James Joyce*, 2nd edition. Cambridge: Cambridge University Press, 2004. 1–27.

—. 'Reading Tom McCarthy's Novels: A Diary'. *Études britanniques contemporaines*, 50 (2016). http://ebc.revues.org/3015.

—. Review of James Joyce's *Finnegans Wake* read by Patrick Healy. *James Joyce Quarterly* 32 (1994): 130–2.

—. *The Rhythms of English Poetry*. London: Longman, 1982.

—. 'Singularity'. In John Frow, ed., *The Oxford Encyclopedia of Literary Theory*. Oxford: Oxford University Press, 2022.

—. 'Singularity'. In Sean Pryor, ed., *The Cambridge Companion to the Poem*. Cambridge: Cambridge University Press. Forthcoming.

—. *The Singularity of Literature* (2004). 2nd edn. Abingdon: Routledge, 2017.

—. 'Untranslatability and the Challenge of World Literature: A South African Example'. In Benjamin Robinson and Francesco Giusti, eds, *The Work of World Literature*. Berlin: ICI Berlin Press, 2021. 25–56.

—. 'What Do We Mean by Experimental Art?' *Angles: French Perspectives on the Anglophone World*, Special Issue on Experimental Art, ed. Anne-Laure Fortin-Tournès (December 2017). https://journals.openedition.org/angles/962.

—. *The Work of Literature*. Oxford: Oxford University Press, 2015.

Attridge, Derek, and Anne Fogarty, '"Eveline" at Home: Reflections on Language and Context'. In Vicki Mahaffey, ed., *Collaborative 'Dubliners': Joyce in Dialogue*. Syracuse: Syracuse University Press, 2012. 89–107.

Attridge, Derek, and Henry Staten. *The Craft of Poetry: Dialogues on Minimal Interpretation*. London: Routledge, 2015.

Attridge, Derek, and Marjorie Howes, eds, *Semicolonial Joyce*. Cambridge: Cambridge University Press, 2000.

Attwell, David. *Rewriting Modernity: Studies in Black South African Literary History*. Pietermaritzburg: KwaZulu-Natal University Press, 2005.

Attwell, David, and Derek Attridge, eds. *The Cambridge History of South African Literature*. Cambridge: Cambridge University Press, 2012.

Badiou, Alain. *Beckett: L'increvable désir*. Paris: Hachette, 1995.

—. *On Beckett*. Ed. Nina Power and Alberto Toscano. Manchester: Clinamen, 2003.

Baetens, Jan. 'Oulipo and Proceduralism'. In Joe Bray, Alison Gibbons, and Brian McHale, eds, *The Routledge Companion to Experimental Literature*. Abingdon: Routledge, 2012. 115–28.

Bahri, Deepika. *Native Intelligence: Aesthetics, Politics, and Postcolonial Literature*. Minneapolis: University of Minnesota Press, 2003.

Baker, Nicholson. *The Mezzanine*. London: Granta, 1986.

Bakhtin, Mikhail. *Problems of Dostoevsky's Poetics* (1929/1963). Trans. Caryl Emerson. Minneapolis: University of Minnesota Press, 1984.

Banks, Iain. *Feersum Endjinn*. London: Orbit Books, 1994.

Banville, John. 'Survivors of Joyce'. In Augustine Martin, ed., *James Joyce: The Artist and the Labyrinth*. London: Ryan Publishing, 1990. 73–81.

Barnhisel, Greg. *Cold War Modernists*. New York: Columbia University Press, 2015.

Barry, Kevin. *Beatlebone*. Edinburgh: Canongate, 2015.

—. Interview with Anita Sethi. *The Guardian*, 8 November 2015. https://www.theguardian.com/books/2015/nov/08/kevin-barry-interview-beatlebone-john-lennon-city-of-bohane.

—. Interview with Julia Brodsky. 'Long and Winding Road: An Interview with Kevin Barry'. *Irish America*, April/May 2016. http://irishamerica.com/2016/03/long-and-winding-road-an-interview-with-kevin-barry/.

Battersby, Doug. *Troubling Late Modernism: Ethics, Feeling, and the Novel Form*. Oxford: Oxford University Press, 2022.

Beasley, Rebecca. *Russomania: Russian Culture and the Creation of British Modernism, 1881–1922*. Oxford: Oxford University Press, 2020.

Beckett, Samuel. *The Unnamable* (1958). Ed. Steven Connor. London: Faber & Faber, 2010.

—. *Watt* (1953). London: John Calder, 1976.

Begam, Richard. *Samuel Beckett and the End of Modernity*. Stanford: Stanford University Press, 1996.

Beinart, William, and Colin Bundy. *Hidden Struggles in Rural South Africa: Politics and Popular Movements in the Transkei and Eastern Cape*. London: James Curry, 1987.

Benjamin, Walter. 'The Task of the Translator' (1955). In *Illuminations*. Ed. Hannah Arendt, trans. Harry Zohn. London: Collins, 1973. 69–82.

Benstock, Shari. 'At the Margin of Discourse: Footnotes in the Fictional Text'. *PMLA* 98 (1983): 204–25.

Bersani, Leo. *The Culture of Redemption*. Cambridge: Harvard University Press, 1990.

Best, Stephen, and Sharon Marcus. 'Surface Reading: An Introduction'. *Representations* 108 (2009): 1–21.

Billington, Michael. '"The Skriker" review – Maxine Peake in a Midsummer Night's vision of climate catastrophe', *The Guardian* 5 July 2015. https://www.theguardian.com/stage/2015/jul/05/the-skriker-review-maxine-peake-in-a-midsummer-nights-vision-of-climate-catastrophe.

Bixby, Patrick. 'In the Wake of Joyce: Beckett, O'Brien, and the Late Modernist Novel'. In Gregory Castle, ed., *A History of the Modernist Novel*. Cambridge: Cambridge University Press, 2015. 464–82.

Boehmer, Elleke. *Bloodlines*. Cape Town: David Philip, 2000.

—. *Colonial and Postcolonial Literature*. Oxford: Oxford University Press, 1995.

—. *Postcolonial Poetics: 21st-Century Critical Readings*. London: Palgrave Macmillan, 2018.

Bök, Christian. *Eunoia*. Toronto: CoachHouse Press, 2001.

Botha, Martin P. 'The Representation of Gays and Lesbians in South African Cinema'. *Kinema* Fall, 2013. http://www.kinema.uwaterloo.ca/article.php?id=129&feature.

Boulter, Jonathan. *Beckett: A Guide for the Perplexed*. London: Continuum, 2008.

Boxall, Peter. *The Prosthetic Imagination: A History of the Novel as Artificial Life*. Cambridge: Cambridge University Press, 2020.

Britz, Etienne. 'Marlene van Niekerk, *Memorandum: 'n verhaal met skilderye*: 'n handleiding vir *Insig* se boekklub' (2007). Online. No longer available.

—. '*Nooit meer slapen* deur Willem Frederik Hermans is in Afrikaanse vertaling 'n groot leesavontuur'. *LitNet* 6 February, 2019. https://www.

litnet.co.za/nooit-meer-slapen-deur-willem-frederik-hermans-is-in-afrikaanse-vertaling-n-groot-leesavontuur/.

Brooks, Douglas. 'Symbolic Numbers in Fielding's *Joseph Andrews'*. In Alastair Fowler, ed., *Silent Poetry: Essays in Numerological Analysis*. London: Routledge & Kegan Paul, 1970. 234–60.

Brotchie, Alastair, and Harry Mathews, eds. *Oulipo Compendium*, rev. edn. London: Atlas Press, 2005.

Brydon, Diana. 'Re-writing *The Tempest'*. *World Literature Written in English* 23 (1984): 75–88.

Burger, Willie. 'So-hede wat die tong uit die mond jaag agter benoeming aan, elke keer weer, tot in ewigheid: Marlene van Niekerk oor haar skryfwerk'. *Journal of Literary Studies/Tydskrif vir Literaturwetenskap* 2 (2009): 152–6.

Butler, Judith. *Antigone's Claim: Kinship between Life and Death*. New York: Columbia University Press, 2000.

Burns, Alan, and Charles Sugnet, eds. *The Imagination on Trial: British and American Writers Discuss Their Working Methods*. London: Allison and Busby, 1981.

Burns, Lorna. *Postcolonialism after World Literature: Relation, Equality, Dissent*. London: Bloomsbury Academic, 2019.

Carpentier, Martha C., ed. *Joycean Legacies*. Basingstoke: Palgrave Macmillan, 2015.

Carter, Angela. *Shaking a Leg: Journalism and Writings*, ed. Jenny Uglow. London: Chatto & Windus, 1997.

Casanova, Pascale. *The World Republic of Letters*. Trans. M. B. DeBevoise. Cambridge: Harvard University Press, 2004.

Cassin, Barbara, ed. *Dictionary of Untranslatables: A Philosophical Lexicon*. Trans. and ed. Emily Apter, Jacques Lezra, and Michael Wood. Princeton: Princeton University Press, 2014.

—. *Vocabulaire européen des philosophies: Dictionnaire des intraduisibles*, Paris: Seuil, 2004.

Castle, Gregory, ed. A *History of the Modernist Novel*. Cambridge: Cambridge University Press, 2015.

Catton, Eleanor. 'Eleanor Catton on how she wrote *The Luminaries'*. *The Guardian*, 11 April 2014; https://www.theguardian.com/books/2014/apr/11/eleanor-catton-luminaries-how-she-wrote-booker-prize.

—. *The Luminaries*. London: Granta, 2013.

—. *The Luminaries*. Audiobook. Read by Mark Meadows. Audible, 2013.

Chambers, Claire. 'Sound and Fury: Kamila Shamsie's *Home Fire'*. *The Massachusetts Review*, 59.2 (Summer 2018): 202–19.

Chanter, Tina. *Whose Antigone?: The Tragic Marginalization of Slavery*. Albany: SUNY Press, 2011.

Churchill, Caryl. *The Skriker*. New York: Theatre Communications Group, 1994.

Clingman, Stephen. *The Grammar of Identity: Transnational Fiction and the Nature of the Boundary*. New York: Oxford University Press, 2009.

Coe, Jonathan. *Like a Fiery Elephant: The Story of B. S. Johnson*. London: Picador, 2004.

Coetzee, J. M. 'Homage'. *The Threepenny Review*, 53 (1993): 5–7.

—. 'Samuel Beckett's "Lessness": An Exercise in Decomposition'. *Computers and the Humanities* 7 (1973): 195–8.

—. *Slow Man*. London: Secker & Warburg, 2005.

Coleridge, Samuel Taylor. *Sybilline Leaves: A Collection of Poems*. London: Rest Fenner, 1817.

Collard, David. *About a Girl: A Reader's Guide to Eimear McBride's 'A Girl Is a Half-formed Thing'*. London: CB Editions, 2016.

Collingwood, R. G. *The Principles of Art*. Oxford: Clarendon Press, 1938.

Combe, Dominique. 'Preface'. In Patrick Crowley and Jane Hiddleston, eds, *Postcolonial Poetics: Genre and Form*. Liverpool: Liverpool University Press, 2011. vii–xii.

Connor, Steven. *Beckett, Modernism and the Material Imagination*. Cambridge: Cambridge University Press, 2014.

—. '"Jigajiga . . . Yummyyum . . . Pfuiiiiiii . . . bbbbblllllblblblblobschb!": "Circe"'s Ventriloquy.' In Andrew Gibson, ed., *Reading Joyce's 'Circe'*. European Joyce Studies 3. Amsterdam: Rodopi, 1994. 93–142.

—. 'Modernism after Postmodernism'. In Vincent Sherry, ed., *The Cambridge History of Modernism*. Cambridge: Cambridge University Press, 2016. 820–34.

—. *Samuel Beckett: Repetition, Theory and Text*. Oxford: Blackwell, 1988.

Conway, David. '30 Years of Drowning by Numbers: A Q&A with Peter Greenaway'. *Exeposé*. https://exepose.com/2018/10/05/30-years-of-drowning-by-numbers-a-qa-with-peter-greenaway/.

Corcoran, Neil. *After Yeats and Joyce: Reading Modern Irish Literature*. Oxford: Oxford University Press, 1997.

Cuddy-Keane, Melba. 'Modernist Soundscapes and the Intelligent Ear: An Approach to Narrative through Auditory Perception'. In James Phelan and Peter J. Rabinowitz, eds, *A Companion to Narrative Theory*. Malden: Blackwell, 2005. 382–98.

—. 'Virginia Woolf, Sound Technologies, and the New Aurality'. In P. Caughie, ed., *Virginia Woolf in the Age of Mechanical Reproduction: Music, Cinema, Photography, and Popular Culture*. New York: Garland, 2000. 69–96.

Culler, Jonathan. *Theory of the Lyric*. Cambridge: Harvard University Press, 2017.

Danius, Sara. *The Senses of Modernism: Technology, Perception, and Aesthetics*. Ithaca: Cornell University Press, 2002.

Dass, Minesh. 'A Place in which to Cry: The Place for Race and a Home for Shame in Zoë Wicomb's *Playing in the Light*'. *Current Writing* 23 (2011): 137–46.

Davis, Kathleen. *Deconstruction and Translation*. Manchester: St Jerome, 2001.

De Kock, Leon. '"A change of tongue": Questions of Translation'. In Attwell and Attridge, eds, *The Cambridge History of South African Literature*, 739–56.

—. 'Cracking the Code: Translation and Transgression in *Triomf*'. *Journal of Literary Studies*, 25.3 (2009): 16–38.

—. 'Translating *Triomf*: The Shifting Limits of Ownership in Literary Translation or: Never Translate Anyone but a Dead Author'. *Journal of Literary Studies* 19 (2003): 345–59.

Deleuze, Gilles. 'The Exhausted'. In Daniel W. Smith and Michael A. Greco, eds., *Essays Critical and Clinical*. Minneapolis: University of Minnesota Press, 1997. 152–74.

Deming, Robert H. *James Joyce: The Critical Heritage*. 2 vols. London: Routledge & Kegan Paul, 1970.

Dennis, Amanda. 'Radical Indecision: Aporia as Metamorphosis in *The Unnamable*'. *Journal of Beckett Studies* 24 (2015): 180–97.

Dent, R. W. *Colloquial Language in 'Ulysses': A Reference Tool*. Newark: University of Delaware Press, 1994.

Denton, William. 'Fictional Footnotes and Indexes', https://www.miskatonic.org/footnotes.html.

Derrida, Jacques. *Acts of Literature*. Ed. Derek Attridge. New York: Routledge, 1992.

—. 'Force of Law: The "Mystical Foundation of Authority"'. In Gil Anidjar, ed., *Acts of Religion*. New York: Routledge, 2002. 228–98.

—. *The Gift of Death*. Trans. David Wills. Chicago: University of Chicago Press, 1995.

—. 'Living on / Borderlines' (1979). Trans. James Hulbert. In Harold Bloom et al., *Deconstruction and Criticism*, 2nd edn. London: Continuum, 2004. 62–142.

—. *Monolingualism of the Other, or, the Prosthesis of Origin*. Trans. Patrick Mensah. Stanford: Stanford University Press, 1998.

—. 'Ulysses Gramophone: Hear Say Yes in Joyce'. In Derrida, *Acts of Literature*, 256–309.

—. 'What Is a "Relevant" Translation?' *Critical Inquiry* 27 (2001): 174–200.

Devarenne, Nicole. '"In Hell You Hear Only Your Mother Tongue": Afrikaner Nationalist Ideology, Linguistic Subversion, and Cultural Renewal in Marlene van Niekerk's *Triomf*, *Research in African Literatures*, 37.4 (Winter, 2006): 105–20.

Diamond, Elin. 'Caryl Churchill: Feeling Global'. In Mary Luckhurst, ed., *A Companion to Modern British and Irish Drama 1880–2005*. Malden: Blackwell, 2006. 476–87.

Doyle, Roddy. *Paddy Clarke Ha Ha Ha*. London: Secker and Warburg, 1993.

Driver, Dorothy. 'Afterword'. In Zoë Wicomb, *David's Story*. New York: The Feminist Press. 215–71.

—. 'Zoe Wicomb's Translocal: Troubling the Politics of Location', in Easton and Attridge, eds, *Zoë Wicomb & the Translocal*, 7–33.

Duncan, Dennis. '"Joyce, un pornographe": *Ulysses*, *A Portrait of the Artist as a Young Man*, and the Sally Mara Novels of Raymond Queneau'. *James Joyce Quarterly* 52 (2015): 351–68.

Duncan, Dennis, ed. *Tom McCarthy: Critical Essays*. Canterbury: Gylphi, 2016.

Duncan, Joseph E. 'The Modality of the Audible in Joyce's *Ulysses*'. *PMLA* 72 (1957): 286–95.

Easton, Kai, and Derek Attridge, eds. *Zoë Wicomb & the Translocal: Scotland & South Africa*. Abingdon: Routledge, 2017.

Effinger, Elizabeth. 'Beckett's Posthuman: The Ontopology of *The Unnamable*'. *Samuel Beckett Today/Aujourd'hui*, 23 (2011): 369–81.

Eliot, T. S. '*Ulysses*, Order, and Myth'. *The Dial* 75.5 (November 1923): 480–3.

Ellmann, Maud. 'Joyce's Noises'. *Modernism/Modernity* 16 (2009): 383–90.

Eve, Martin. *Literature against Criticism: University English and Contemporary English in Conflict*. Cambridge: Open Book Publishers, 2016.

Eyers, Tom. *Speculative Formalism: Literature, Theory, and the Critical Present*. Evanston: Northwestern University Press, 2017.

'Falkirk Iron Co', *Grace's Guide to British Industrial History*, http://www.gracesguide.co.uk/Falkirk_Iron_Co.

Felski, Rita. *The Limits of Critique*. Chicago: University of Chicago Press, 2015.

Ferrer, Daniel. 'Circe, Regret, and Repression'. In Derek Attridge and Daniel Ferrer, eds, *Post-structuralist Joyce: Essays from the French*. Cambridge: Cambridge University Press, 1984. 127–44.

—. 'Echo or Narcissus'. In Morris Beja et al., eds, *James Joyce: The Centennial Symposium*. Urbana: University of Illinois Press, 1986. 70–5.

Fitch, Brian T. *Beckett and Babel: An Investigation into the Status of the Bilingual Work*. Toronto: University of Toronto Press, 1988.

Frattarola, Angela. *Modernist Soundscapes: Auditory Technology and the Novel*. Gainesville: University Press of Florida, 2018.

Frost, Laura. *The Problem with Pleasure: Modernism and Its Discontents*. New York: Columbia University Press, 2015.

Ganguly, Keya. *States of Exception: Everyday Life and Postcolonial Identity*. Minneapolis: University of Minnesota Press, 2001.

Gąsiorek, Andrzej. *A History of Modernist Literature*. Chichester: Wiley Black-well, 2015.

Gibbons, Alison. *Multimodality, Cognition, and Experimental Literature*. New York: Routledge, 2012.

Gibbons, Luke. '"Have You No Homes to Go to?": Joyce and the Politics of Paralysis'. In Attridge and Howes, eds, *Semicolonial Joyce*, 150–71.

Gibson, Andrew. *Beckett and Badiou: The Pathos of Intermittency*. Oxford: Oxford University Press, 2006.

Giffel, Kaelie. 'Historical Violence and Modernist Forms in Zoë Wicomb's *David's Story*'. *Twentieth-Century Literature* 64 (2018): 53–78.

Gifford, Don, with Robert J. Seidman. *'Ulysses' Annotated: Notes for James Joyce's 'Ulysses'*. Revised and expanded edn. Berkeley: University of California Press, 1988.

Gikandi, Simon. 'Theory after Postcolonial Theory: Rethinking the Work of Mimesis'. In Jane Elliott and Derek Attridge, eds., *Theory after 'Theory'*. Abingdon: Routledge, 2011. 163–78.

Gilbert, Sandra, and Susan Gubar. 'Sexual Linguistics'. Chapter 5 of *No Man's Land: The Place of the Woman Writer in the Twentieth Century*, vol. 1, The War of the Words. New Haven: Yale University Press, 1988.

Gilligan, Ruth. 'Eimear McBride's Ireland: A Case for Periodisation and the Dangers of Marketing Modernism'. *English Studies* 99 (2018): 775–92.

Goldstone, Andrew. *Fictions of Autonomy: Modernism from Wilde to De Man*. New York: Oxford University Press, 2013.

Green, Michael. 'The Experimental Line in Fiction'. In Attwell and Attridge, eds, *The Cambridge History of South African Literature*, 779–99.

Gregg, Melissa, and Gregory J. Seigworth, eds. *The Affect Theory Reader*. Durham: Duke University Press, 2010.

Grimonprez, Johan. *'from Satin Island'*. Film. https://www.youtube.com/watch?v=jr7i6lB84Hc.

Gurnah, Abdulrazak. 'The Urge to Nowhere: Wicomb and Cosmopolitanism', in Easton and Attridge, eds, *Zoë Wicomb & the Translocal*, 34–48.

Gustafson, Alrik. *Six Scandinavian Novelists*. Minneapolis: University of Minnesota Press, 1966.

Guy, Adam. *The 'Nouveau Roman' and Writing in Britain after Modernism*. Oxford: Oxford University Press, 2019.

Guyer, Paul. *A History of Modern Aesthetics*. 3 vols. Cambridge: Cambridge University Press, 2014.

Hale, Dorothy J. *The Novel and the New Ethics*. Stanford: Stanford University Press, 2020.

Halliday, Sam. *Sonic Modernity: Representing Sound in Literature, Culture and the Arts*. Edinburgh: Edinburgh University Press, 2013.

Harbison, Sherrill. 'Introduction'. In Sigrid Undset, *The Cross*, vol. 3 of *Kristin Lavransdatter*. Harmondsworth: Penguin: 2000. vii–xviii.

Harding, Jason, and John Nash, eds. *Modernism and Non-Translation*. Oxford: Oxford University Press, 2019.

Harrison, Nicholas. *Postcolonial Criticism*. Cambridge: Polity, 2003.

—. 'Who Needs an Idea of the Literary?' *Paragraph* 28.2 (2005): 1–17.

Hayman, David. *'Ulysses': The Mechanics of Meaning*, revised edition. Madison: University of Wisconsin Press, 1982.

Hayman, David, and Elliott Anderson, eds. *In the Wake of the 'Wake'*. Madison: University of Wisconsin Press, 1978.

Haynes, Natalie. Review of Shamsie, *Home Fire*. *The Guardian*, 10 August 2017. https://www.theguardian.com/books/2017/aug/10/home-fire-kamila-shamsie-review.

Hermans, Willem Frederik. *Beyond Sleep*. Trans. Ina Rilke. London: Harvill Secker, 2006.

—. *Nooit meer slapen*. Amsterdam: De Bezige Bij, 2013.

Hill, Leslie. *Beckett's Fiction: In Different Words*. Cambridge: Cambridge University Press, 1990.

Hoban, Russell. *Riddley Walker*. Expanded edition. London: Bloomsbury, 2002.

Hoberman, Ruth. 'The Nightmare of History in George Orwell's *A Clergyman's Daughter*'. In Carpentier, ed. *Joycean Legacies*, 92–111.

Hollander, John. *Vision and Resonance: Two Senses of Poetic Form*. Second edn. New Haven: Yale University Press, 1985.

Honig, Bonnie. *Antigone, Interrupted*. Cambridge: Cambridge University Press, 2013.

House, Juliane. *A Model for Translation Quality Assessment*. Tübingen: Narr, 1977.

Innes, C. L. 'The Postcolonial Novel: History and Memory'. In Robert L. Caserio and Clement Hawes, eds, *The Cambridge History of the English Novel*. Cambridge: Cambridge University Press, 2012. 823–39.

Jacobs, J. U. 'Playing in the Dark/ Playing in the Light: Coloured Identity in the Novels of Zoë Wicomb'. *Current Writing* 20 (2008): 1–15.

James, David. 'Afterword: The Poetics of Perpetuation'. In Reynolds, ed., *Modernist Afterlives*, 175–82.

—. 'Introduction'. In James, ed., *Modernism and Close Reading*, 1–16.

—. *Modernist Futures: Innovation and Inheritance in the Contemporary Novel*. Cambridge: Cambridge University Press, 2012.

James, David, ed. *Modernism and Close Reading*. Oxford: Oxford University Press, 2020.

James, David, and Urmila Sheshagiri. 'Metamodernism: Narratives of Continuity and Revolution'. *PMLA* 129 (2014): 87–100.

Jameson, Fredric. *A Singular Modernity: Essay on the Ontology of the Present*. London: Verso, 2002.

Johnson, B. S. 'Holes, Syllabics and the Succussations of the Intercostal and Abdominal Muscles'. In Jonathan Coe, Philip Tew and Julia Jordan, eds, *Well Done God!: Selected Prose and Drama of B. S. Johnson*. London: Picador, 2013. 386–97.

Jordan, Julia. 'Late Modernism and the Avant-Garde'. In David James, ed., *The Cambridge Companion to British Fiction since 1945*. Cambridge: Cambridge University Press, 2015. 145–59.

—. *Late Modernism and the Avant-Garde British Novel: Oblique Strategies*. Oxford: Oxford University Press, 2020.

Joyce, James. *Dubliners*. Ed. Hans Walter Gabler with Walter Hettche. New York: Garland, 1993.

—. *Dubliners: An Illustrated Edition with Annotations*. Ed. John Wyse Jackson and Bernard McGinley. London: Sinclair-Stevenson, 1993.

—. *Finnegans Wake*. London: Faber, 1939.

—. *Finnegans Wake*. Read by Patrick Healy. Dublin: Rennicks Auriton Publishing, RAP CD 01, 1992.

—. *Finnegans Wake*. Abridged and dir. Roger Marsh. Read by Jim Norton with Marcella Riordan. Naxos AudioBooks NA516312, 1998.

—. *Finnegans Wake*. Dir. Roger Marsh. Read by Barry McGovern with Marcella Riordan. Naxos AudioBooks NA0503, 2021.

—. *Letters*. Ed. Stuart Gilbert and Richard Ellmann. 3 vols. New York: Viking, 1966.

—. *A Portrait of the Artist as a Young Man*. Ed. Hans Walter Gabler with Walter Hettche. New York: Garland, 1993.

—. *Ulysses*. Ed. Hans Walter Gabler with Wolfhard Steppe and Claus Melchior. London: The Bodley Head, 1986.

—. *Ulysses*. Directed by Roger March, read by Jim Norton and Marcella Riordan. Naxos Audiobooks, 2004.

Kahn, Douglas. *Noise, Water, Meat: History of Voice, Sound, and Aurality in the Arts*. Cambridge: MIT Press, 1999.

Kamuf, Peggy. '"Fiction" and the Experience of the Other'. In *Book of Addresses*. Stanford: Stanford University Press, 2005. 135–53.

Katz, Daniel. *Saying I No More: Subjectivity and Consciousness in the Prose of Samuel Beckett*. Evanston: Northwestern University Press, 1999.

Katz, Jonah. 'Exercises in Wile'. In Esme Winter-Froemel and Verena Thaler, eds, *Cultures and Traditions of Wordplay and Wordplay Research*. Berlin: De Gruyter, 2018. 137–64.

Kemp, Anna. 'Oulipo, Experiment and the Novel'. In Adam Watt, ed., *The Cambridge History of the Novel in French*. Cambridge: Cambridge University Press, 543–60.

Kenner, Hugh. 'Circe'. In Clive Hart and David Hayman, eds, *James Joyce's 'Ulysses': Critical Essays*. Berkeley: University of California Press, 1974. 341–62.

—. *Reader's Guide to Samuel Beckett*. London: Thames and Hudson, 1996.

—. *Ulysses*. London: George Allen & Unwin, 1980.

Kingsnorth, Paul. *The Wake*. London: Unbound, 2014.

Lahrsow, Miriam. *Self-Annotated Literary Works 1300–1900: An Extensive Collection of Titles and Selected Metadata*. https://publikationen.uni-tuebingen.de/xmlui/handle/10900/111993.

Lang, Anouk. 'Modern Fiction/Alternative Modernisms'. In Coral Ann Howells, Paul Sharrad, and Gerry Turcotte, eds, *The Oxford History of the Novel in English: The Novel in Canada, Australia, New Zealand, and the South Pacific since 1950*. Oxford: Oxford University Press, 2017. 190–204.

Latour, Bruno. 'Why Has Critique Run out of Steam? From Matters of Fact to Matters of Concern'. *Critical Inquiry* 30 (2004): 225–48.

Law, Jules David. 'Joyce's "Delicate Siamese" Equation: The Dialectic of Home in *Ulysses*'. *PMLA* 102 (1987): 197–205.

Lawn, Jennifer. 'The Anti-*Antigone*: Pākehā Settler Masculinity, Racialized Kinship, and Contested Paternity in Carl Nixon's *Settlers' Creek*'. *Journal of Postcolonial Writing* 58 (2022): 361–73.

Lawrence, D. H. *Selected Literary Criticism*. Ed. Anthony Beal. London: Heinemann, 1967.

Lawrence, Karen. *The Odyssey of Style in 'Ulysses'*. Princeton: Princeton University Press, 1981.

Lazarus, Neil. *The Postcolonial Unconscious*. Cambridge: Cambridge University Press, 2011.

Leavis, F. R. *The Great Tradition*. New York: Doubleday, 1954.

—. 'Joyce and "The Revolution of the Word"'. *Scrutiny*, 2 (September 1933): 193–200.

Leith, Sam. 'What could be saner? On the final instalment of Will Self's penetrating consciousness trilogy'. *TLS* 31 May 2017. https://www.the-tls.co.uk/articles/private/will-self-consciousness/.

Le Roux, Beth. 'Book Publishing Industry Annual Survey – Broad Trends over Three Years (2008–2010)'. University of Pretoria School of Information Technology, 2011.

Levin, Harry. 'What Was Modernism?'. *The Massachusetts Review* 1 (1960): 609–30.

Levine, Caroline. *Forms: Whole, Rhythm, Hierarchy, Network*. Princeton: Princeton University Press, 2015.

Levine, George, ed. *The Question of Aesthetics*. Oxford: Oxford University Press, 2022.

Levy, Eric P. *Trapped in Thought: A Study of the Beckettian Mentality*. Syracuse: Syracuse University Press, 2007.

Lewis, Philip E. 'The Measure of Translation Effects'. In Joseph F. Graham, ed., *Difference in Translation*. Cornell University Press, 1985. 31–62.

Lewis, Wyndham. *Time and Western Man*, ed. Paul Edwards. Santa Rosa: Black Sparrow Press, 1993.

Leys, Ruth. *The Ascent of Affect: Genealogy and Critique*. Chicago: University of Chicago Press, 2017.

—. 'Trauma and the Turn to Affect'. In Ewald Mengel and Michela Borgeza, eds, *Trauma, Memory, and Narrative in the Contemporary South African Novel*. Amsterdam: Rodopi, 2012. 3–28.

—. 'The Turn to Affect: A Critique'. *Critical Inquiry* 37 (2011), 434–72.

Lipking, Lawrence. 'The Marginal Gloss'. *Critical Inquiry* 4 (1997): 609–55.

Macmillan, Hugh William, and Lucy Valerie Graham. 'The "Great Coloured Question" and the Cosmopolitan: Fiction, History and Politics in *David's Story*'. *Safundi* 12 (2011): 331–48.

Mahaffey, Vicki. *Modernist Literature: Challenging Fictions*. Malden: Wiley-Blackwell, 2006.

Manning, Mary. *Passages from 'Finnegans Wake'*. Cambridge: Harvard University Press, 1957.

Mansell, James G. *The Age of Noise in Britain: Hearing Modernity*. Urbana: University of Illinois Press, 2016.

Marais, Mike. 'Bastards and Bodies in Zoë Wicomb's *David's Story*'. *Journal of Commonwealth Literature* 40 (2005): 21–36.

Marcus, Laura. 'The Legacies of Modernism'. In Morag Shiach, ed., *The Cambridge Companion to the Modernist Novel*. Cambridge: Cambridge University Press, 2007. 82–98.

Marcus, Sharon. *Between Women: Friendship, Desire, and Marriage in Victorian England*. Princeton: Princeton University Press, 2007.

Marx, John. 'Postcolonial Fiction and the Western Literary Canon'. In Neil Lazarus, ed., *The Cambridge Companion to Postcolonial Literary Studies*. Cambridge: Cambridge University Press, 2004. 83–96.

Massumi, Brian. *Parables for the Virtual: Movement, Affect, Sensation*. Durham: Duke University Press, 2002.

Masters, Ben. *Novel Style: Ethics and Excess in English Fiction since the 1960s*. Oxford: Oxford University Press, 2017.

McBride, Eimear. *A Girl Is a Half-formed Thing* (2013). London: Faber & Faber, 2014.

—. *A Girl Is a Half-formed Thing: Adapted for the Stage by Annie Ryan*. London: Faber and Faber, 2015.

—. 'My Hero, James Joyce'. *The Guardian*, 6 June 2014. https://www.the-guardian.com/books/2014/jun/06/my-hero-eimear-mcbride-james-joyce.

McCabe, Patrick. *The Butcher Boy*. London: Picador, 1992.

—. *Poguemahone*. London: Unbound, 2021.

McCann, Fiona. 'Broadening and Narrowing Horizons in Zoë Wicomb's *The One That Got Away*'. *Commonwealth Essays and Studies* 33 (2010): 55–66.

McCarthy, Tom. *C*. London: Jonathan Cape, 2010.

—. 'Calling All Agents'. In Tom McCarthy, Simon Critchley, et al., eds, *The Mattering of Matter: Documents from the Archive of the International Necronautical Society*. London: Sternberg Press. 162–202.

—. 'The death of writing – if James Joyce were alive today he'd be working for Google'. *The Guardian*, 7 March 2015. https://www.theguardian.com/books/2015/mar/07/tom-mccarthy-death-writing-james-joyce-working-google.

—. 'Foreword: On Being the Subject of a Conference or, What Do I Know?'. In Dennis Duncan, ed., *Tom McCarthy*, 1–2.

—. Interview with Andrew Gallix, *3 A.M. Magazine*. http://www.3ammagazine.com/3am/illicit-frequencies-or-all-literature-is-pirated-an-interview-with-tom-mccarthy/.

—. Interview in *Believer Magazine*. http://www.believermag.com/issues/200806/?read=interview_mccarthy.

—. Interview with Christopher Bollen, *Interview Magazine*. http://www.interviewmagazine.com/culture/tom-mccarthy.

—. Interview with Dan Wagstaff, *Raincoast Books*, http://www.raincoast.com/blog/details/in-conversation-with-tom-mccarthy-part-one/.

—. Interview with James Corby and Ivan Callus, *Countertext*. http://www.euppublishing.com/doi/full/10.3366/count.2015.0014.

—. Interview with Lee Rourke, *The Guardian* 18 September 2010. http://www.theguardian.com/books/2010/sep/18/tom-mccarthy-lee-rourke-conversation.

—. Interview with Mark Thwaite, *ReadySteadyBook*. http://www.readysteady-book.com/Blog.aspx?permalink=20070917072530.

—. *The Making of Incarnation*. London: Jonathan Cape, 2021.

—. *Men in Space*. London: Alma Books, 2007.

—. *Remainder*. Revised edn, London: Alma Books, 2006.

—. *Satin Island*. London: Jonathan Cape, 2015.

—. *Tintin and the Secret of Literature*. London: Granta Books, 2006.

—. *Transmission and the Individual Remix*. Vintage Digital, 2012.

—. *Typewriters, Bombs, Jellyfish: Essays*. New York: New York Review of Books, 2017.

McCormack, Mike. Interview with Stephanie Boland. *New Statesman*, 7 November 2016. https://www.newstatesman.com/culture/2016/11/mike-mccormack-british-fiction-dominated-intellectual-conservatism.

—. *Solar Bones*. (2016) Edinburgh: Canongate, 2017.

MacDonald, Claire. 'Editorial: In Viva Voce'. *Performance Research* 8 (2003): 1–4.

McDonald, Rónán. *The Cambridge Introduction to Samuel Beckett*. Cambridge: Cambridge University Press, 2006.

McGurl, Mark. 'The Novel's Forking Path'. *Public Books*, 1 April 2015. https://www.publicbooks.org/the-novels-forking-path/.

Mesthrie, Rajend. *Language in South Africa*. Cambridge: Cambridge University Press, 2002.

Mda, Zakes. *The Heart of Redness*. Cape Town: Oxford University Press, 2000.

Miller, J. Hillis. *Literature as Conduct: Speech Acts in Henry James*. New York: Fordham University Press, 2005.

Miller, Sydney. 'Intentional Fallacies: (Re)Enacting the Accidental in Tom McCarthy's Remainder'. *Contemporary Literature* 56 (2015): 634–59.

Miller, Tyrus. *Late Modernism: Politics, Fiction, and the Arts between the World Wars*. Berkeley: University of California Press, 1999.

Mitchell, Andrew J., and Sam Slote, eds. *Derrida and Joyce: Texts and Contexts*. Albany: SUNY Press, 2013.

Monk, Ian, and Daniel Levin Becker, eds. *All that Is Evident Is Suspect: Readings from the Oulipo 1963–2018*. San Francisco: McSweeny's Publishing, 2018.

Moody, Alys. *The Art of Hunger: Aesthetic Autonomy and the Afterlives of Modernism*. Oxford: Oxford University Press, 2018.

Motte, Warren F., ed. *Oulipo: A Primer of Potential Literature*. Normal: Dalkey Archive Press, 2015.

Mukherjee, Ankhi. *What Is a Classic? Postcolonial Rewriting and Invention of the Canon*. Stanford: Stanford University Press, 2014.

Mukim, Mantra, and Derek Attridge, eds. *Literature and Event: Twenty-First Century Reformulations*. New York: Routledge, 2022.

Murphet, Julian, Helen Groth, and Penelope Hone, eds. *Sounding Modernism: Rhythm and Sonic Mediation in Modern Literature and Film*. Edinburgh: Edinburgh University Press, 2017.

Murphy, Neil. 'The Novel as Heartbeat: The Dead Narrator in Mike McCormack's Solar Bones'. In W. Michelle Wang, Daniel K. Jernigan, and Neil

Murphy, eds, *The Routledge Companion to Literature and Death*. New York: Routledge, 2020. 109–120.

Naudé, S. J. *The Alphabet of Birds*. Sheffield: And Other Stories, 2015.

—. *Alfabet van die voëls*. Cape Town: Umuzi, 2011.

—. *Die derde spoel*. Cape Town: Umuzi, 2017.

—. *The Third Reel*. Cromer: Salt, 2018.

Nieland, Justus. 'Dirty Media: Tom McCarthy and the Afterlife of Modernism'. *Modern Fiction Studies* 58 (2012): 569–99.

Nkosi, Lewis. 'Fiction by Black South Africans'. In Lindy Stiebel and Liz Gunner, eds, *Still Beating the Drum: Critical Perspectives on Lewis Nkosi*. Johannesburg: Wits University Press, 2006. 245–56.

—. 'Postmodernism and Black Writing in South Africa'. In Derek Attridge and Rosemary Jolly, eds, *Writing South Africa: Literature, Apartheid, and Democracy 1970–1995*. Cambridge: Cambridge University Press, 1998. 75–90.

Norris, Margot. *Suspicious Readings of Joyce's 'Dubliners'*. Philadelphia: University of Pennsylvania Press, 2003.

—. *Virgin and Veteran Readings of 'Ulysses'*. New York: Palgrave Macmillan, 2011.

North, Joseph. *Literary Criticism: A Political History*. Cambridge: Harvard University Press, 2017.

North, Michael. 'History's Prehistory: Modernist Studies before the New'. In Douglas Mao, ed., *The New Modernist Studies*. Cambridge: Cambridge University Press, 2021. 25–40.

—. *Reading 1922: A Return to the Scene of the Modern*. New York: Oxford University Press, 1999.

Page, Ruth, ed. *New Perspectives on Narrative and Multimodality*. New York: Routledge, 2010.

Parrinder, Patrick. *James Joyce*. Cambridge: Cambridge University Press, 1984.

Parry, Benita. 'The Institutionalization of Postcolonial Studies'. In Neil Lazarus, ed., *The Cambridge Companion to Postcolonial Literary Studies*. Cambridge: Cambridge University Press, 2004. 66–80.

Parsons, Cóilín. 'Zoë Wicomb's Telescopic Visions: *You Can't Get Lost in Cape Town* and *October*'. In Easton and Attridge, eds, *Zoë Wicomb & the Translocal*, 83–99.

Partington, Gill. 'Dummy Chambers and Ur-Houses: How to Find Your Way Around in *Remainder*'. In Dennis Duncan, ed., *Tom McCarthy*, 47–68.

Pascale, Blaise. *Pensées*. Trans. W. F. Trotter. https://www.gutenberg.org/files/18269/18269-h/18269-h.htm.

Peake, Charles. *James Joyce: The Citizen and the Artist*. London: Edward Arnold, 1977.

Perec, Georges. *La Disparition: Roman*. Paris: Denoël, 1969.

—. *A Void*. Trans. Gilbert Adair. London: Harvill Press, 1994.

Perloff, Marjorie. 'The Oulipo Factor: The Procedural Poetics of Christian Bök and Caroline Bergvall.' *Textual Practice*, 18 (2004): 23–45.

Phillips, Tom, and Bernard Moxham. *'Humument' Images to Accompany James Joyce's 'Ulysses'*. Openings-Closings Press, 2014.

Preston, Alex. 'Fiction to look out for in 2022'. *The Observer* 26 December 2021, https://www.theguardian.com/books/2021/dec/26/fiction-to-look-out-for-in-2022.

Porter, Jeffrey. '"Three quarks for Muster Mark": Quantum Wordplay and Nuclear Discourse in Russell Hoban's *Riddley Walker*'. *Contemporary Literature* 31 (1990): 448–69.

Quarrie, Cynthia. 'Sinking, Shrinking, Satin Island: Tom McCarthy, the British Novel, and the Materiality of Shame'. *Journal of Modern Literature* 41 (2018): 147–64.

Queneau, Raymond, *Exercises de style*. Paris: Gallimard, 1947.

—. *Exercices in Style*. Trans. Barbara Wright. London: Gaberbocchus, 1958.

Rabaté, Jean-Michel, ed. *1922: Literature, Culture, Politics*. Cambridge: Cambridge University Press, 2018.

—. *Think, Pig! Beckett at the Limits of the Human*. New York: Fordham University Press, 2016.

Rabillard, Sheila. 'On Caryl Churchill's Ecological Drama: Right to Poison the Wasps?' In Elaine Aston, ed., *The Cambridge Companion to Caryl Churchill*. Cambridge: Cambridge University Press, 2009. 88–104.

Reinelt, Janelle. 'Caryl Churchill and the Politics of Style'. In Elaine Aston and Janelle Reinelt, eds, *The Cambridge Companion to Modern British Women Playwrights*. Cambridge: Cambridge University Press, 2000. 174–93.

Reinert, Otto. 'Unfashionable *Kristin Lavransdatter*'. *Scandinavian Studies* 71 (1999): 67–80.

Remshardt, Ralf Erik. Review of *The Skriker*, by Caryl Churchill. Royal National Theatre, London, 12 March 1994. *Theatre Journal* 47 (1995): 121–3.

Reynolds, Paige. 'Bird Girls: Modernism and Sexual Ethics in Contemporary Irish Fiction'. In David James, ed., *Modernism and Close Reading*, 173–90.

—. 'Trauma, Intimacy, and Modernist Form'. *Breac*, Sept 11, 2014. https://breac.nd.edu/articles/trauma-intimacy-and-modernist-form/.

Reynolds, Paige, ed. *Modernist Afterlives in Irish Literature and Culture*. London: Anthem, 2016.

Rice, Thomas J. 'His Master's Voice and Joyce'. In R. Brandon Kershner, ed., *Cultural Studies of James Joyce*. European Joyce Studies 15. Amsterdam: Rodopi, 2016. 149–66.

Richter, Virginia. 'Zoë Wicomb's Ghosts: Uncanny Translations in *David's Story* and *The One That Got Away*'. *Safundi* 12 (2011): 373–88.

Robbins, Bruce. *Criticism and Politics: A Polemical Introduction*. Stanford: Stanford University Press, 2022.

Robinson, Jenefer. *Deeper than Reason: Emotion and Its Role in Literature, Music, and Art*. Oxford: Oxford University Press, 2005.

Robolin, Stéphane. 'Properties of Whiteness: (Post)Apartheid Geographies in Zoë Wicomb's *Playing in the Light*'. *Safundi* 12 (2011): 349–72.

Rudrum, David, and Nicholas Stravris, eds. *Supplanting the Postmodern: An Anthology of Writings on Art and Culture of the Early 21st Century*. New York: Bloomsbury, 2015.

Ruiter, Frans, and Wilbert Smulders, eds. *Journal of Dutch Literature*, Special Issue on 'The Ethics of Autonomy: Willem Frederik Hermans', 6 (2015).

Rutkowska, Urszula. 'The Political Novel in Our Still-evolving Reality: Kamila Shamsie's *Home Fire* and the Shamima Begum Case'. *Textual Practice* 36 (2022): 871–88.

Sachs-Hombach, Klaus, and Jan-Noël Thon, eds. 'Multimodal Media.' Special Issue, *Poetics Today* 40.2 (2019).

Saint-Amour, Paul K. 'Late Joyce and His Legacies: Teaching *Finnegans Wake* and Its Aftertale'. *James Joyce Quarterly* 39 (2001): 123–34.

Salisbury, Laura. *Samuel Beckett: Laughing Matters, Comic Timing*. Edinburgh: Edinburgh University Press, 2012.

Samuelson, Meg. 'The Disfigured Body of the Female Guerrilla: (De)Militarization, Sexual Violence, and Redomestication in Zoë Wicomb's *David's Story*'. *Signs* 32 (2007): 833–56.

Sanders, Mark. 2009. 'Mimesis, Memory, *Memorandum*.' *Journal of Literary Studies* 25(3): 106–23.

Scully, Pamela. 'Critical Cosmopolitanism and Translocal Mobility in the Fiction of Zoë Wicomb'. In Easton and Attridge, eds, *Zoë Wicomb & the Translocal*, 120–33.

Sedgwick, Eve Kosofsky. 'Introduction: Queerer than Fiction'. Special issue of *Studies in the Novel* 28:3 (Fall 1996): 277–80.

—. *Novel Gazing: Queer Readings in Fiction*. Durham: Duke University Press, 1997.

—. *Touching Feeling: Affect, Pedagogy, Performativity*. Durham: Duke University Press, 2003.

Serpell, C. Namwali. *Seven Modes of Uncertainty*. Cambridge: Harvard University Press, 2014.

Shamsie, Kamila. *Home Fire*. London: Bloomsbury, 2017.

—. Interview with Fiona Tolan. '"I don't know who I'd be if I wasn't a writer": Kamila Shamsie'. *Contemporary Women's Writing* 13 (2019): 119–33.

—. 'Kamila Shamsie's 6 favorite books inspired by literary classics'. *The Week* 27 August, 2017. https://theweek.com/articles/720246/kamila-shamsies-6-favorite-books-inspired-by-literary-classics.

—. 'True story: Kamila Shamsie on predicting the rise of Sajid Javid', *The Guardian*, 3 May 2018. https://www.theguardian.com/books/books-blog/2018/may/03/true-story-kamila-shamsie-on-predicting-the-rise-of-sajid-javid.

Sheehan, Paul. 'Introduction'. *Journal of Beckett Studies*, Special Issue on 'Post-Archival Beckett: Genre, Process, Value' 26 (2017): 1–9.

—. *Modernism, Narrative and Humanism*. Cambridge: Cambridge University Press, 2002.

Slote, Sam. 'The Recidual Remainder', in Duncan, ed., *Tom McCarthy*, 121–36.

Smith, Ali. *How to Be Both* (2014). London: Penguin, 2015.

Smith, Zadie. 'Two Paths for the Novel'. *New York Review of Books*, 20 November, 2008.

Smurthwaite, John. 'Verbal or Visual? "Penelope" and Contemporary Psychology'. In Richard Brown, ed., *Joyce, 'Penelope', and the Body*. European Joyce Studies 17. Amsterdam: Rodopi, 2006. 75–84.

Sorensen, Eli Park. *Postcolonial Studies and the Literary*. Houndmills: Palgrave Macmillan, 2010.

Sridhar, Anirudh, Mir Ali Hosseini, and Derek Attridge, eds. *The Work of Reading: Literary Criticism in the 21st Century*. Cham: Palgrave Macmillan, 2021.

Staten, Henry. *Techne Theory: A New Language for Art*. London: Bloomsbury, 2019.

Steiner, George. *Antigones: The Antigone Myth in Western Literature, Art and Thought*. Oxford: Oxford University Press, 1986.

Sterne, Jonathan. *The Audible Past: Cultural Origins of Sound Reproduction*. Durham: Duke University Press, 2003.

Stewart, Garrett, *Reading Voices: Literature and the Phonotext*. Berkeley: University of California Press, 1990.

Sultan, Stanley. *Eliot, Joyce and Company*. New York: Oxford University Press, 1987.

Szafraniec, Asja. *Beckett, Derrida and the Event of Literature*. Stanford: Stanford University Press, 2007.

Taylor, Julie, ed. *Modernism and Affect*. Edinburgh: Edinburgh University Press, 2015.

Terry, Philip. *The Penguin Book of Oulipo*. London: Penguin, 2019.

Thompson, Emily. *The Soundscape of Modernity: Architectural Acoustics and the Culture of Listening in America, 1900–1933*. Cambridge: MIT Press, 2002.

Tompkins, Jane P., ed. *Reader-response Criticism: From Formalism to Post-structuralism*. Baltimore: Johns Hopkins University Press, 1980.

Turner, Jenny. 'Seeing Things Flat: Tom McCarthy's *C*'. *London Review of Books* 9 September, 2010, 7–8.

Tysdahl, B. J. *Joyce and Ibsen: A Study in Literary Influence*. Oslo: Norwegian Universities Press, 1968.

Undset, Sigrid. *Kristin Lavransdatter*. Trans. Tiina Nunnally. 3 vols. Harmondsworth: Penguin, 1997–2000.

Van den Akker, Robin, Alison Gibbons, and Timotheus Vermeulen, eds. *Metamodernism: Historicity, Affect, and Depth after Postmodernism*. London: Rowman & Littlefield, 2017.

Van der Vlies, Andrew. 'Zoë Wicomb's South African Essays: Intertextual Ethics, Translative Possibilities, and the Claims of Discursive Variety'. In Zoë Wicomb, *Race, Nation, Translation*. Ed. Andrew van der Vlies. New Haven: Yale University Press, 2018. 3–33.

Van Heerden, Etienne. *30 nagte in Amsterdam*. Cape Town: Tafelberg, 2008.

—. *30 Nights in Amsterdam*. Trans. Michiel Heyns. Johannesburg: Penguin Random House South Africa, 2012.

—. *The Long Silence of Mario Salviati*. Trans. Catherine Knox. London: Hodder and Stoughton, 2002.

Van Niekerk, Marlene. *Agaat*. Cape Town: Tafelberg, 2004

—. *Agaat*. Trans. Michiel Heyns. Cape Town: Tafelberg/Jonathan Ball, 2006.

—. *The Way of the Women*. Trans. Michiel Heyns. London: Little, Brown, 2007.

—. *Agaat*. Trans. Michiel Heyns. Portland: Tin House Books, 2010.

—. Interview with Jan Steyn. *The White Review*, 2016. http://www.thewhitereview.org/feature/interview-with-marlene-van-niekerk/.

—. *Triomf*. Cape Town: Queillerie, 1994.

—. *Triomf*. Trans. Leon de Kock. Cape Town: Queillerie, 1999.

—. *Triomf*. Trans. Leon de Kock. London: Little, Brown, 1999.

Van Niekerk, Marlene, and Adriaan van Zyl. *Memorandum: 'n verhaal met skilderye*. Cape Town: Human & Rousseau, 2006.

—. *Memorandum: A Story with Paintings*. Translated by Michiel Heyns. Cape Town: Human & Rousseau, 2006.

Van Vuuren, Helize. 'Passacaglia van J.S. Bach en *Das Passagen-Werk* van Walter Benjamin – literêre montage as mosaïekwerek in *Memorandum. 'n verhaal met skilderye* (2006)'. *Tydskrif vir Geesteswetenskappe* 54 (2014): 505–23.

Venuti, Lawrence. *The Scandals of Translation: Towards an Ethics of Difference*. London: Routledge, 1998.

—. *Translation Changes Everything: Theory and Practice*. Abingdon: Routledge, 2013.

—. *The Translator's Invisibility: A History of Translation*. 2nd edn. Abingdon: Routledge, 2008.

Vermeulen, Pieter. *Contemporary Literature and the End of the Novel: Creature, Affect, Form*. Basingstoke: Palgrave Macmillan, 2015.

Vichnar, David. 'Wars Waged with/against Joyce: James Joyce and Post-1984 British Fiction'. In Carpentier, ed., *Joycean Legacies*, 150–71.

Vigouroux-Frey, Nicole. 'Pour des mythologies profanées: *The Skriker* (Caryl Churchill, 1994)'. *Etudes Anglaises* 52 (1999): 175–84.

Viljoen, Louise. Review of Etienne Leroux, *Die eerste siklus*. *Tydskrif vir Letterkunde* 50 (2013): 173–5.

Wasser, Audrey. *The Work of Difference*. New York: Fordham University Press, 2016.

Warwick Research Collective. *Combined and Uneven Development: Towards a New Theory of World-Literature*. Liverpool: Liverpool University Press, 2015.

Weller, Shane. 'Beckett as Late Modernist'. In Olga Beloborodova, Dirk Van Hulle and Pim Verhulst, eds, *Beckett and Modernism*. Basingstoke: Palgrave Macmillan, 2018. 36–52.

—. *A Taste for the Negative: Beckett and Nihilism*. London: Legenda, 2005.

White, Nina. '"It was like lightning": The Theatrical Resonances of Sarah Kane in Eimear McBride's *A Girl Is a Half-formed Thing*'. *Irish Studies Review* 26 (2018): 564–77.

Wicomb, Zoë. *David's Story* (2000). New York: The Feminist Press, 2001.

—. Interview. *The Scotsman*. May 27, 2006. http://www.scotsman.com/lifestyle/books/features/under-the-skin-of-lies-1-1119465.

—. Interview with Eva Hunter. In Eva Hunter and Craig Mackenzie, eds, *Between the Lines II*. Grahamstown: National English Literary Museum, 1993. 79–96.

—. Interview with Hein Willemse. *Research in African Literatures* 33.1 (2002): 144–52.

—. Interview with Stephan Meyer and Thomas Olver. 'Zoë Wicomb Interviewed on Writing and Nation'. *Journal of Literary Studies* 18 (2002): 182–98.

—. Interview with Thomas Olver and Stephan Meyer. 'Zoë Wicomb on *David's Story*'. *Current Writing* 16 (2004): 131–42.

—. 'In the Botanic Gardens'. *Landfall: A New Zealand Quarterly* 44 (1990): 484–92.

—. 'My Name is HannaH', in Easton and Attridge, eds, *Zoë Wicomb & the Translocal*, 196–208.

—. 'Nothing Like the Wind'. *Stand* 5.4 (2004): 48–53.

—. *October*. New York: The New Press, 2014.

—. *The One that Got Away*. Roggebaai: Umuzi, 2008.

—. *Playing in the Light*. Roggebaai: Umuzi, 2006.

—. *Race, Nation, Translation*. Ed. Andrew van der Vlies. New Haven: Yale University Press, 2018.

—. 'Setting, Intertextuality and the Resurrection of the Postcolonial Author'. In Van der Vlies, ed., *Race, Nation, Translation*, 229–40.

—. 'Shame and Identity: The Case of the Coloured in South Africa'. In Van der Vlies, ed., *Race, Nation, Translation*, 114–27.

—. *Still Life*. Cape Town: Umuzi. 2020.

—. *You Can't Get Lost in Cape Town* (1987). New York: The Feminist Press, 2000.

—. 'Zoë Wicomb in Conversation with Derek Attridge'. In Easton and Attridge, eds, *Zoë Wicomb & the Translocal*, 209–19.

Wilder, Thornton. *Our Town, The Skin of Our Teeth, The Matchmaker*. Harmondsworth: Penguin, 1962.

Williams, Patrick, and Laura Chrisman, eds. *Colonial Discourse and Postcolonial Theory*. New York: Columbia UP, 1994.

Wilson, Edmund. *Axel's Castle: A Study in the Imaginative Literature of 1870–1930* (1931). Glasgow: Collins–Fontana, 1961.

—. Review of *Ulysses*. *The New Republic*, 5 July 1922. https://newrepublic.com/article/114325/james-joyces-ulysses-reviewed-edmund-wilson.

Wimsatt, W. K., and Monroe Beardsley. 'The Affective Fallacy'. In W. K. Wimsatt, *The Verbal Icon: Studies in the Meaning of Poetry*. Lexington: University of Kentucky Press, 1954. 21–40.

Wright, Ernest Vincent. *Gadsby: A Story of Over 50,000 Words Without Using the Letter 'E'*. Amazon Books on Demand, 2015.

Young, Robert J. C. 'Editorial: Ideologies of the Postcolonial'. *Interventions* 1 (1998): 4–8.

Ziarek, Ewa Płonowska. *The Rhetoric of Failure: Deconstruction of Skepticism, Reinvention of Modernism*. New York: SUNY Press, 1995.

Žižek, Slavoj. *Antigone*. London: Bloomsbury Academic, 2016.

INDEX

Printed in the USA
CPSIA information can be obtained
at www.ICGtesting.com
JSHW051322151123
52143JS00005B/142